The New
Basic Book
of the CAT

The New
Basic Book of
the CAT

WILLIAM H. A. CARR

CHARLES SCRIBNER'S SONS · NEW YORK

Copyright © 1978, 1963 William H. A. Carr

Library of Congress Cataloging in Publication Data

Carr, William H. A.
   The new basic book of the cat.

   Edition of 1963 published under title: The
basic book of the cat.
   Bibliography: p. 242
   Includes index.
   1. Cats. I. Title.
SF442.C35   636.8   77-27266
ISBN 0-684-15549-4

1 3 5 7 9 11 13 15 17 19 V/C 20 18 16 14 12 10 8 6 4 2

PRINTED IN THE UNITED STATES OF AMERICA

TO MY WIFE

Peg McCormick Carr

Contents

Preface

This is a revised and greatly expanded version of a book which I wrote fifteen years ago. Science's knowledge of the cat has grown immensely over the intervening years. For my part, a succession of splendid felines has provided me with a rich lore of additional experiences, happy and sad. It is my hope that the advances of veterinary medicine and of zoology, blended with sound judgment from practical experience, will make this cat book even more useful than its predecessor.

Cats are like greatness—some people are born into cat-loving families, some achieve cats, and some have cats thrust upon them.

It is with a certain pride that I say that I achieved cats. Dogs were a part of my life from childhood, but cats I viewed with distrust and distaste until well into my adult years. Then I began to appreciate, very slowly at first, the admirable qualities of a friend's cat, Theodora. The friend, finding a sucker in his very living room, promptly presented me with one of Theodora's kittens, a tabby whom I named Tammany (because he was tiger-striped and had the morals of that political institution). A few weeks later a big, short-haired blue cat ventured through the window to investigate Tammany and to steal his food. In a day or two the blue had made himself quite at home. I had been adopted as his companion and provider. He was Mr. Gray. Cats have been an important part of my life ever since.

Dogs are still treasured companions of mine, but I cannot conceive of a life without cats now. There is usually a clowder of cats (*clowder* is the proper noun of assembly for a group of cats—a *kendle* is a gathering of kittens) about me as I write. Nutcake, my beloved comrade for nineteen years, often insisted on perching on my head while I wrote; he died, of kidney disease aggravated by diabetes, during the writing of this book. Bibi lies on the desk, keeping a watchful eye on the movements of the typewriter while I work. Charlie—a huge, imperturbably dignified female—reclines beside me in my chair.

The affinity of writers for cats is something that has never been satisfactorily explained, to the best of my knowledge. Certainly a writer should have a special appreciation for esthetics, and few things in life are as esthetically pleasing as the graceful cat. But perhaps part of the reason for this attitude of writers lies in the skepticism which a writer ought to practice. More than other people, a writer should be inclined to examine prejudices, including his own, coolly. And the only thing that stands between most people and cats is prejudice (on the part of the people).

As every cat owner knows, cats are not sneaky. Indeed, their attempts at stealth during cat games are often hilarious failures. Cats are not treacherous. I've never heard of a cat turning on its owner (although some owners who insist on playing teasing games will get scratched). On the other hand, cats *are* affectionate, sometimes almost suffocatingly so. They are intelligent, clean, and endowed with a sense of humor that enables them to find human foibles endlessly diverting.

They deserve the kind of care that will enable them to live for many long, healthy years as companions to their human families. It is the purpose of this book to make it as easy as possible for the average cat owner to provide that kind of care for his cats.

In the preparation of this book I have been given the generous assistance of a great many people.

Quotations from a number of other published works have been used in this book. For permission to use this material, and for other assistance, I wish to thank Raymond D. Smith, publisher of *Cats Magazine;* Dr. Edwin H. Colbert of the American Museum of Natural History; Dr. Mark Morris and Mark Morris Associates, Inc.; Dr. S. N. Gershoff, of the Department of Nutrition, Harvard School of Public Health; the staff of the National Academy of Sciences—National Research Council; Mrs. Christine Stevens, president of the Animal Welfare Institute; the library staffs of the American Museum of Natural History, in

New York City, and the Academy of Natural Sciences, in Philadelphia; and Arthur Milner and his associates at the Free Library of Philadelphia's Logan Circle headquarters.

I owe a special debt of gratitude to the Cat Fanciers' Federation, and especially to its corresponding secretary, Mrs. Grace M. Clute, for providing me with breed standards, show rules, and other materials, and permitting me to quote extensively from them.

Mary Ann Kelty, Mary Thomas, and Joan Fleming typed the manuscript with a speed and exactitude I wish I could match.

Despite the efforts of all these people, however, this book would never have been completed without the help, advice, and encouragement of my wife, Peg McCormick Carr.

1. THE CAT FAMILY

What is a cat?

To a zoologist, it is any member of the great family called *Felidae.*

Beyond that point, there is very little agreement among scientists. Some divide the family into two groups: the small cats (domestic cats and bobcats, for example) and the big cats (lions and leopards). Others classify the family into three groups: little cats, great cats, and in-between cats (like the mountain lion and the clouded leopard).

Despite this general disagreement, nobody has trouble identifying any member of the family as a cat. As zoologist Dr. Bernard Grzimek has written, "All felids can be readily recognized as 'cats,' whether the animal is an elongated, short-legged jaguarundi or a long-legged cheetah."

Throughout the cat family, males and females resemble each other to a marked degree, although the male is usually somewhat bigger. The sweat glands of cats have generally disappeared, but there are still functioning sweat glands between the toe pads and sole pads, on the lips, the chin, the area around the nipples, and around the anus. All felids bite with the side of the mouth. They have rough, sandpapery tongues which are very useful for licking meat off bones. The members of this animal family walk on their toes and move with extraordinary grace. Although they have a well-developed sense of smell, they rely above all on their hearing, which is very acute. Unlike dogs and many other animals, it appears that they can distinguish colors, for their retinas contain rods and cones, associated with color vision. Their eyes are six times more sensitive to short-wave lengths of light than are human eyes. Behind the retinas, cats have a cell layer (the *tapetum cellulosum lucidum*) which reflects light and makes their eyes shine at night. This layer, together with an ability to dilate or contract the pupils of their eyes, makes it possible for cats to see well in very dim light. On all cats the whiskers are organs of touch, helping them to feel their way when it is too dark for even a cat to see. With only one or two exceptions, the members of the cat family are loners; they prefer not to live in groups. Only the big cats can roar (because their hyoid structure contains cartilage as well as bone), but all cats purr. However, big cats can only purr when they exhale, while small cats can purr while inhaling and exhaling.

"As many as fifty species have been described," zoologist Ivan T. Sanderson has said, "but there is much confusion about them." That confusion extends to the domestic cat. There are several million more cats than dogs in America, but we know very little, relatively speaking, about the cat, in contrast to our enormous store of knowledge about the dog.

Zoologists have many theories but few facts about the domestic cat and its wild cousins. We do not know when or where the cat was domesticated, nor from what wild cats it was bred. We do not know whether it spread throughout the world from a single original site or whether it became a domestic animal at about the same time in several parts of the world. We are not certain how many breeds of domestic cat exist in the world or how many wild animals still prowling the earth belong to the cat family. To compound the confusion, zoologists disagree about the formal designation of the cat; one group argues that it is *Felis domestica,* but a larger group insists that it must be referred to as *Felis catus.*

Even our English word for one who hates cats, *ailurophobe,* is confusing; it was based on the belief that the mouse-killer mentioned in ancient Greek writings was a cat, but we now know that it was some member of the weasel family, probably the marten or polecat.

To augment our ignorance, we do not even know the origin of the word *cat.*

"Ah! Cats are a mysterious kind of folk," as Sir Walter Scott said to Washington Irving.

Despite the unfortunate lack of proved facts, zoologists believe they can make a great many educated guesses about the cat, its origins, and its relatives, and come quite close to the truth. These guesses are based on archeological findings, fossil remains, ancient paintings and writings, studies of mammalian evolutionary patterns, and our knowledge of the genetics of the present forms of the cat.

If the generally accepted theories are correct, the cat can be traced back to *Miacis,* a vicious, weasel-like little carnivore with a long body and short legs that existed on the earth about fifty million years ago. *Miacis* is also considered the ancestor of the dog, the hyena, the raccoon, the bear, the weasel, and the civet, a curious little animal which occurs in several forms today—one of them is the famous snake-killing mongoose—in Africa, Asia, and southern Europe. (The true civet is important to many women; the secretion from its anal glands is, strangely, the best fixative for the most expensive perfumes.) A typical civet is about three feet long with short legs, a long, bushy tail, and a small head. The Germans call it, appropriately, the "half-cat."

It is believed that the first cats evolved about ten million years after *Miacis* made its appearance. This was probably ten or twenty million years before the dog, as we know it, evolved. The transition from *Miacis* to civet to cat was quite abrupt, as evolutionary processes go, despite the millions of years that passed. "The cats . . . suddenly appeared," in the words of Dr. Edwin H. Colbert of the American Museum of Natural History. "One might say that certain civets jumped into the role of the cats with all the evolutionary rapidity of a quick-change artist in a hard-pressed double part."

The cats initially divided into two groups: *Hoplophoneus* and *Dinictis.* The former was notable for its exaggerated upper canine teeth, which were so big that nature had to provide the cat with a flange on the lower jaw to shield those teeth when the mouth was closed. A species of *Hoplophoneus,* which we usually call the saber-toothed tiger (it wasn't truly a tiger at all, but it was a great cat), has been pleasantly designated *Smilodon* by the paleontologists. As large as a lion, the saber-tooth wasn't very fast, but it was a formidable enemy of the huge, slow-moving beasts that shook the earth with their passing in those prehistoric times. *Smilodon* was able to open its jaws very wide, and it could then strike down with its terrible canine teeth, throwing the strength of its powerful neck and the weight of its massive body into the blow. But the time came when the slow-moving beasts which were *Smilodon*'s natural prey began to die out, and the saber-tooth was too clumsy to adapt itself to catching more agile animals. So it, too, became extinct.

This was not the case with *Dinictis,* the ancestor of our modern cats. Fast-moving, lithe, highly adaptable, intelligent, strong, equipped with teeth marvelously designed for stabbing and tearing, *Dinictis* and its descendants were so well suited to the rigors of competitive existence that the latter have remained virtually unchanged, with minor exceptions, to this day. Indeed, every genus found on earth today has been identified in fossils dating back to the Pliocene epoch in Eurasia, and so have several genera now extinct.

The classic description of the cat as it has emerged into modern times is that of Dr. Colbert:

> Of all land-living carnivores, the cats are among the most completely specialized for a life of killing and for eating meat. They are very muscular, alert, supple carnivores, fully equipped for springing upon and destroying animals as large or larger than themselves. They generally hunt by stealth and catch their prey with a long bound or a short rush of great speed. The limbs are heavy and strong, and the feet are provided with sharp, retractile claws that are used for catching and holding their victims. The neck is very heavy to take up the severe shocks imposed by the violent action of the head and the teeth. The teeth are highly specialized for just two functions—stabbing and cutting. The canine teeth are therefore long and strong, and the carnassials are large, perfected shearing blades; the other teeth are reduced or completely suppressed. The smaller cats are adept tree-climbers, but the larger cats spend most of their time upon the ground.

These are the cats as they developed before man walked upon the earth, before the great Pleistocene glaciers covered much of the globe. They have been with us ever since in their varied forms: the great cats, the lesser cats, the domesticated cat. It has been said that "God made the cat in order to give man the pleasure of petting the tiger," and certainly most felinophiles are fascinated by the tiger in domestic cats and, conversely, by the kitten in tigers. So let us now take a look at the incomparable and magnificent animals that comprise the cat family, wild and domestic, as we know it today—animals that command our admiration for their grace, their dignity, and their awesome powers of reasoning.

The science of classifying living creatures is called *taxonomy*. The biologists who practice this curious specialty seldom agree with one another on anything except the importance of pigeon-holes. In classifying cats, they have followed many different systems. Some believe the cats belong to one genus, *Felis*. Others list as many as twenty-eight distinct genera.

All this may be confusing to the taxonomists, but it doesn't trouble the cats, nor should it perplex you. For the purposes of this book, we shall follow those taxonomists who divide the cat into three genera: *Panthera* (the great cats), *Acinonyx* (the cheetah, which is quite different from other cats), and *Felis* (all the rest, including the cat that is, I hope, purring in your lap at this moment).

Since prehistoric times, most of the felines have moved between the Old World and the New, and a number of them have reached the extreme southern tip of South America. Before man began carrying them with him, the cats were distributed in every part of the world except Australia and its satellite islands and Madagascar (now called Malagasy). There are creatures in Australia called "native cats" and "tiger cats," but they are marsupials whose correct name is dasyure. They don't look like cats, and why they were ever called cats is something that perhaps only an Australian could tell you. All over the world, including our own country, people have a way of putting the label "cat" on many creatures other than cats.

The "polecat," for example, is not a cat; it is the ferret, part of the weasel family. (In America the skunk is sometimes called a polecat, too.) Then there is the "bashful cat" of tropical Asia, which is actually a tiny, odd-looking primate called the loris. The "black cat" to which our Northern woodsmen sometimes refer is properly identified as a large species of marten. The "phoby cat" which pops up in the speech of back-country folk in America is the skunk. The "miner's cat," or "ring-tailed cat," is correctly designated the cacomistle, a pretty, furry little member of the raccoon family which makes a pleasant pet and is guaranteed to keep the premises cleared of rats.

Because of its skill at hiding and stalking, its camouflage, and its nocturnal and arboreal habits, the cat, in most of its species, is difficult to find. Hence we really cannot be sure that this quick survey of the world's cats is by any means complete. There are probably species in abundance that are unknown to the scientific world.

The *Panthera* known to us are the lion, the tiger, the leopard, the snow leopard (which is an entirely different species from the leopard), the clouded leopard, and the jaguar.

Despite his traditional title of "King of the Beasts," the lion is, in most respects, less impressive than the tiger. Lions and tigers can and do interbreed; if a male lion and a female tiger mate, the result is called a *liger,* but if the sire is a tiger and the dam a lioness, the cub is a *tiglon.* Nothing, it seems, is simple in the cat world.

Without their skins—a predicament in which they seldom, fortunately, find themselves—lions look identical to tigers. Generally a lion is smaller than its striped cousin. It is also less to be feared, being a disgraceful but rather engaging coward. Many things frighten the lion—flapping laundry, small children, a skunklike little animal called the zorille, and so on.

From many points of view the lion is an attractive beast. It kills only when it is hungry and makes several meals off the carcass. When it isn't hungry, it wouldn't harm a living thing, except perhaps to guard its young or to defend itself against real or fancied danger. Men have stood within a few feet of lions who were feeding, without any menacing actions by the lions. When a lion isn't hungry, antelope and other animals can and do graze near it, knowing that they are safe.

Sometimes a lion will just turn bad, and that's another matter. Usually these are lions that are unable because of age or infirmity to kill desirable game. But a man-eating lion is a formidable creature. The most famous man-eaters were a pair of lions that held up construction of the Uganda Railway in Africa, just before the turn of the century, by devouring twenty-eight Indian laborers in addition to scores of Africans.

A lion can break a man's back with one blow of its paw. In making a kill of its natural prey, the lion crouches low, then springs forward in a dash that has been clocked at forty miles an hour.

Of all the cats, with the possible exception of the domestic cat, only the lion is gregarious. The usual pride of lions consists of five or six members, both males and females; the latter usually kill the game which the males have driven in their direction.

The mating urge of the lion is prodigious. One pair of lions in captivity mated 45 times a day for 8 days. One male has been recorded copulating 157 times in 55 hours. The king of beasts, indeed!

"The known history of the lion," says Dr. Philip J. Darlington, Jr., of Harvard University's Museum of Comparative Zoology, "is . . . one of retreat before man during a period of nearly two thousand years." Within the period of recorded history, lions were to be found in southeast Europe as far north as Rumania and as far west as Italy, throughout all of Africa (except in the West African forests and the interior of the deserts), and in southwestern Asia as far as India's western provinces. The lion has been slowly withdrawing toward the heartland of Africa in modern times. There may be a few lingering survivors in Iraq and Iran, but the only known concentration outside Africa is in the Forest of Gir, Kathiawar, northwestern India, where they are protected. Even in Africa they have been on the retreat. There haven't been any lions in Cape Province, South Africa, for a century. In Algeria and Tunis the lion was last seen in 1891, although it managed to survive until the 1920s in neighboring Morocco. Now it is found in abundance only below the Sahara.

The lion is sometimes shown with the tiger in fanciful movie scenes, but actually the two are seldom if ever found together in the same locale in nature. There are no tigers in Africa and few lions, as has been noted, anywhere else.

The tiger is one of the most fascinating of the big cats, if only for its sometimes surprising habitats. It ranges from the far-below-zero cold of eastern Siberia to the intense heat of the jungles of southern India. The original home of the tiger was in or near the Arctic, zoologists generally believe, and the great Amurian tiger, sometimes called the Siberian snow tiger, is still the biggest of all the cats, attaining a length of more than thirteen feet and a maximum weight in excess of six hundred and fifty pounds. Tigers gradually moved down through east and southeast Asia to India and the islands of Sumatra, Bali, and Java (but not, for some strange reason, Ceylon), and also in a southwestward migration from Siberia by way of central Asia to

Afghanistan, Iran, and southern Russia all the way west to the Caucasus. But the tiger has never forgotten the climate of its origin; in the almost unbearable heat of the Malayan jungle, the tiger will go for a swim to keep cool. Indeed, it loves to swim, as many of the cats do, although it hates to get just a little wet, as from the dew.

Tigers are universally feared as indiscriminate man-eaters, but we have the word of the ultimate expert on that subject, Jim Corbett, that this is a canard. Like the lion, the tiger makes man its prey only when it is unable to obtain its preferred natural food. A tiger, unless molested, will do no harm to man, says Lieutenant Colonel Corbett in his fascinating book, *Man-Eaters of Kumaon,* a recounting of his true experiences as India's foremost exterminator of man-eating tigers and leopards. "I have not seen a case where a tiger has been deliberately cruel or where it has been bloodthirsty to the extent that it has killed, without provocation, more than it has needed to satisfy its hunger or the hunger of its cubs," writes Corbett. And there has been no better salute to an honored foe than Corbett's statement on the tiger's character: "A tiger is a large-hearted gentleman with boundless courage."

Like almost all the big cats (and many of the small cats, too) the tiger is threatened with extinction. Fear of the animal, its slaughter by fur traders, and the encroaching of human settlements all contribute to make this cat an endangered species.

There is a considerable variation in the ground color of the tiger, ranging all the way from the most common bright reddish-orange to eggshell white. The only black-and-white tiger in captivity outside India is a blue-eyed beauty in the Smithsonian Institution's National Zoological Park in Washington, D.C., which was obtained from Rewa, one of the few regions of India where white tigers abound.

The white tigers probably reflect an albino strain in the species. Just the opposite is true of the leopards: albinos are unknown, but a tendency toward melanism—that is, black mutation—is marked. The black leopard is usually referred to popularly as a black "panther," although properly the panther is any great cat that can roar.

Leopards are far deadlier than lions or tigers; they can become man-eaters simply because they acquire a taste for human flesh. Somewhat hysterical and easily frightened, they are night hunters and anything living is their prey, including farm animals, fowl, dogs, and monkeys. Somewhat smaller than the lion and the tiger, the leopard is really more dangerous; it often takes to the trees, adding a new dimension to the menace of the big cats. It is also incredibly intelligent; sometimes a leopard will roll crazily on the ground to excite curiosity in a herd of antelope and lure them close enough to be killed.

The British Isles were once a home to the leopard. Its range extended all the way east to Japan and south throughout all of Asia except for the Himalayan highlands. It was also found on Ceylon and the Indonesian islands. Today it is still found in the Caucasus—which remains a sort of unintentional refuge for many harried forms of fauna—and even in Siberia, as well as throughout east and southeast Asia, the Middle East, and all of Africa.

The snow leopard is also called the *ounce,* a word that comes through Old French and Middle English from the Latin *lynx,* strangely enough. It lives in the thin-aired upper reaches of the Asian mountains from the Himalayas north to Siberia and Sakhalin Island. Its double coat protects it against the intense cold it must endure, and its colors—whitish-gray with yellow rings on the back and plain white on the belly—are not as flamboyant as those of its jungle cousins, and thus not as easily noticed by its prey on the mountainous heights.

The clouded leopard is one of the smallest, rarest, and most beautiful of cats. Its body is only about three feet long, although it has a tail disproportionately long for its body. Its thick, full, soft fur is gray or grayish-yellow, marked with small, square-shaped black forms with dark brown in the center. There are stripes on the face, spots on the legs, and rings on the tail. It has the longest canine teeth of any cat. A nocturnal prowler that sleeps in the day, it can seldom be detected in its natural habitat, which ranges from South China to Sumatra and Borneo, in addition to the island of Formosa.

The only American cat among the *Panthera* is the jaguar, inaccurately but commonly called *"el tigre"* by our Latin-American neighbors. Its range in the past was from the mountains of the southwest United States (principally Arizona and New Mexico) south to the Santa Cruz River in Patagonia, near the southern tip of South America. But some authorities believe that the jaguar now can be found only in the Chaco, a vast region in northern Argentina, Bolivia, and Paraguay. This may be incorrect, however. Jaguars have reportedly been sighted in 1956 near Ruby, Arizona, northwest of Nogales; in 1958 in the Patagonia Mountains east of Nogales; and in 1960 in the Sonora River Valley near the Mexican border.

This spotted cat, the best tree-climber of all the great cats, likes both humid jungle and arid desert. It may occur as an albino or as a black mutation. It enjoys swimming and will pursue its prey into the water or even tackle an alligator in a stream. It is renowned for its ferocity, but some zoologists assert that not a single human killing by a jaguar has been authenticated.

In the genus *Acinonyx* there is only one species, the cheetah, although it is possible that this cat may be found in two or three varieties sufficiently distinct to be called species. The cheetah is the famous hunting cat. The most tractable large cat, it makes an excellent pet and can be trained easily. Since ancient times cheetahs have been domesticated in Egypt and in India and other Asian lands as hunters and retrievers. These amazingly fleet creatures—they have been clocked at sixty miles per hour and it's believed they sometimes reach seventy-five—are rather like coursing hounds. They are kept, not in a cage, but simply on a chain. On a hunt the cheetah is hooded until the quarry is sighted; then the hood is removed and the cheetah dashes after the prey, knocks it down, and holds it by the throat. They have been used to kill coyotes in the United States. Like the dog's, the cheetah's claws are only partly retractile.

Once widespread in Africa and southwestern Asia, the cheetah is now so close to extinction that a conservation program aimed at saving these unique and wonderful animals has been established.

Genus *Felis* includes a number of unusual cats in addition to our domestic cat: the puma, the golden cats, the serval, the jaguarundi, the lynx, the bobcat, the caracal, the jungle cat, the ocelot, the margay.

The puma—or cougar, or mountain lion, as it is also called—is the second largest American cat (after the jaguar). Its body is long and lithe, with a six-foot frame and weight of one hundred and sixty pounds. This cat is very strong and can drag five times its own weight more than a hundred yards. It is rather oddly put together, with its hindquarters higher and more prominent than its head and chest, probably because it spends so much of its time leaping into trees and onto crags. It can spring twenty feet in one jump.

The puma is also one of the most misunderstood and maligned cats. It is often accused by ranchers in the United States of the wanton slaughter of domestic livestock. Although the puma will sometimes kill a calf, its usual prey is small mammals which are themselves serious pests, and so it is really helpful in maintaining the balance of nature and keeping down the farmer's worst enemies. It is one of the most timid of cats; there are scarcely any reliable accounts of a puma having attacked a man. In short, there is no reason for hunting the puma, except for the occasional cat that may become a persistent marauder.

The nonsense one hears about the puma and its "savagery" is appalling. I have personally enjoyed playing with a friend's pet puma, which acted like a kitten. Several members of the Long Island Ocelot Club, which takes in all the exotic cats, keep pumas as pets. Two members of the club, Ray and Daphne Ovington, reported in the club's newsletter an incident that must have enlivened things in Woodstock, New York. Mrs. Ovington wrote:

We were staying at a motel before we "closed" on our house. Ray was taking some boxes out to the car. Quick as a flash, before the screen door closed, Winnie [the cougar] dashed from across the room out the door, ran behind the motel, up the hill which was heavily wooded. She hid there. The forest ranger brought two of his best bobcat and coon dogs and tried to get her trail but of no avail. She had her collar on and we were afraid it would choke her with growth as it was already getting snug. She was afraid of people. Her instinct told her to lie low in the leaves or to run when approached. She was seen on someone's back porch several times. People were seeing her every day from their cars, crossing a road or walking around a corner of a house, but by the time they called us and we arrived, she was nowhere to be found. Finally we set a box trap with meat. After eleven days of being out, we found her sitting in the trap one evening. We brought her, trap and all, wild and frightened, to the house. She was very hungry and "beat" and she had grown quite a bit. We were worried about her disposition, but the next day she was nuzzling me and purring and seemed to be very happy to be home again. She is even more gentle and affectionate now than she was before.

The puma had one of the farthest ranges of any animal—from the Arctic to the Straits of Magellan, throughout the entire Western Hemisphere. Today it is generally believed by zoologists that the cougar is limited to the Canadian Rockies, the mountains of the western United States, and throughout most of Central and South America. There are also probably a few left in Florida and Louisiana. But that's not all. The mountain lion may be closer to some of our urban centers than we assume. In 1958 William V. Garner, professor of biology at Monmouth College, who has observed pumas in their natural surroundings, was startled to see a cougar on the shoulder of the Garden State Parkway near Long Branch, New Jersey, less than thirty miles from New York City. A New York businessman, Ludwig K. Moorehead, who collected reports of puma sightings in his area, had more than forty accounts in his file of cougars spotted in New York, New Jersey, Vermont, New Hampshire, and Massachusetts. There have also been well-authenticated sightings in Virginia, the Carolinas, Alabama, Missouri, and Minnesota over the past thirty years.

If pumas are about us, even in small numbers, one might expect to see them more often. But this is not always the case. D. D. McLean of the California Fish and Game Department, who regarded the cougar as "our least known large mammal," pointed out that "people living in lion country may go through an entire lifetime without as much as a fleeting glimpse of one of the big cats."

The golden cats are not found in America. They are two rather similar species of felines, one found in Asia, the other in central and west Africa, both about the size of a leopard—indeed, the Chinese call their golden cat *huang pao,* meaning "yellow leopard." There could be another reason besides their color for the name of these cats, for both species are an item of trade: the Chinese sell the bones of *huang pao* in their medicine shops, and some Africans chop the whiskers of their golden cats to make a poison said to be fatal to humans. (Whether it is fatal, and, if so, why, I don't know.)

The serval proves, beyond dispute, that cats, individualists that they are, will not permit themselves to be lumped indiscriminately together by taxonomists. This is a short-tailed cat with the long legs of a greyhound, and with good reason, for the serval lives on the open plains of equatorial Africa and runs down its quarry, usually small animals, birds, and lizards. Ignore its hide and its distinctly catty head, and the serval looks very much like a dog.

The jaguarundi is any of several varieties of closely related cats that can be found anywhere from the southwestern United States to southern Chile west of the Andes. They are also called the eyra, the colocollo, and (in Mexico) the otter cat. None of the jaguarundis looks very much like a cat; with their long bodies and tails, short legs, and small heads, they really appear more weasel-like than feline. As you might expect, they have caused another argument among zoologists, some of whom think they shouldn't be classified with the cats at all.

Indeed, there is very little agreement among the experts on this genus of cat. One eminent zoologist says the jaguarundi is "a ferocious, untamable creature," while another equally respected zoologist says the jaguarundi was domesticated by the Indians of Paraguay before the discovery of America. The latter would appear to be right, for many jaguarundis are now kept as pets, and their owners appear to be happy with them.

The lynx is another strange-looking cat. Its hindlegs are much longer than its forelegs, which gives it a peculiar posture, and its appearance is made still more remarkable by its stub of a tail, broad paws, extravagantly tufted ears, and profuse side-whiskers that look like the muttonchop whiskers once favored by portly gentlemen (and again in favor among some men). The lynx is found deep in the most remote forests of northern Europe and Asia. It is also found in North America, but rarely below the Canadian border, although a few have been sighted in Colorado and Oregon. The large pads on the lynx's feet enable it to run swiftly over snow after its favorite prey, the snow rabbit.

Like the other cats, the lynx is famous for its intelligence. The Czech writer Stanek, speaking of the lynx, asserts that in the Tatra Mountains of Slovakia he found the footprints of a lynx carefully placed inside the footprints of a bear for more than a hundred yards. This is said to be a favorite device of the lynx for baffling pursuers.

The bobcat is a variety of lynx that has a special attraction for Americans. It is a peculiarly American animal, being found throughout the United States, in southern Canada, and in northern Mexico. The Catskill Mountains of New York State were named for the bobcat by the explorer Henry Hudson (*Kaatskill* means Cat Creek). This cat is sometimes called a "catamount"—so is the puma, which makes for confusion—probably from the Spanish *gato monte* (woods cat). A more common name for it in the vernacular is "wild cat."

The bobcat is a pretty cat in its markings and its skull formation. It can be formidable, however; bobcats ranging in weight up to sixty-nine pounds and in length up to fifty-three inches have been killed by hunters.

Wrote historian John Lawson back in 1718:

This Cat is quite different from those in Europe; being more nimble and fierce, and larger; his Tail does not exceed four inches. He makes a very odd sort of Cry in the Woods, in the Night. He is spotted as the Leopard is, tho some of them are not (which may happen, when their Furs are out of Season). He climbs a Tree very dexterously, and preys as the Panther does. . . . He takes most of his Prey by Surprize, getting up the Trees which they pass by or under, and thence leaping directly upon them. Thus he takes Deer (which he cannot catch by running) and fastens his Teeth into their Shoulders and sucks them. They run with him, till they fall down for want of strength, become a Prey to the Enemy. Hares, Birds, and all he meets, that he can conquer, he destroys. . . . [His furs] are . . . used to line Muffs, and Coats withal, in cold Climates.

Bobcats, if taken young and reared in captivity, make excellent pets. Even when they are living in their natural wild state, bobcats often mate with domestic cats, and the offspring, too, are as engaging household company as any tabby. N. P. Kenoyer, writing in *Cats Magazine,* described such a mating:

It was early evening when we heard the unmistakable howl of Tabbette, our dark, striped cat. We rushed outside to see what neighbor's tomcat was courting our pet. We stopped short when we saw the two animals. It was not a neighbor's tom. The two cats faced each other, snarling and howling. Tabbette hugged the ground, her ears laid back tight against her head and her lips pressed against her teeth. This attitude was not unusual for her during this period, but her new, determined, prospective mate was. He was a young bobcat, long-legged, slim-bodied, with a mixture of stripes and spots running down his legs.

The account then reported on the results of the crossbreeding:

> Two months later Tabbette had five dark, tabby, stubby-tailed kittens. Some were tinged with reddish fur running along the soft undersides of their bellies. The tails were of different lengths but all bobbed. Their hind legs were unusually long and powerful and it became more apparent when they were old enough to run about. They hopped like rabbits except when they ran. There were tiny tufts of hair at each ear tip. They froze in cautious stance when startled. But they were deeply affectionate and wanted to spend all their time with us. They acted more like dogs than cats. They didn't even meow like a domestic cat. Their purr was heavy and deep-toned and they growled as they played. They began to hunt even before they lost their kitten roundness. We had no trouble finding homes for these little half-breeds. We kept a male kitten which we named Stubby.
>
> Stubby grew fast. By the time he was a year old he stood fourteen inches high and weighed ten pounds. He had a daily routine which he followed like a time clock. He was early for breakfast, eating little but always consuming a full saucer of milk. He loved cookies and crackers and would leave meat if he heard the sound of the cookie jar lid. He was fond of our boxer dogs and they liked him. If the dogs napped he always found them and curled up close to their warm bodies. He would sleep all day but he wanted out at night. He ranged between our barn and that of our neighbor. He kept both places free of mice.
>
> Stubby dispatched every tomcat who came within his boundaries. Our neighbor put out food for him but couldn't come within twenty feet without Stubby's racing away in the direction of home. Yet he liked people, if they were in our house. Visitors could expect to find him on their laps as soon as they sat down. But away from the house he would scream if cornered and his appearance was wild. However, the boys could pick him up anywhere. He chose our neighbor's Persian cat for a mate and soon there was a litter of short-tailed kittens. Stubby influenced the kittens with his conformation and disposition. Everyone who saw Stubby wanted one of his kittens. Now we are looking for a pure bobcat female for Stubby because, given a choice, we'd take a bobcat every time.

Another member of the lynx family is the caracal, a slender, long-eared, reddish-brown cat found in the drier areas of Africa, the Middle East, and India. (This cat should not be confused with the caracul, a sheep of central Asia which is known to many American women because its wool is often made into fur coats.)

Except for the cheetah, the caracal is the most aberrant of the cats. Its ears are tufted, like those of its lynx cousins, but it lacks the distinctive lynx sideburns. The tail is about nine inches long, a rather short appendage to a body about two and a half feet long.

In India this handsome cat has often been kept as a pet in wealthy households and is easily trained. A fast runner and remarkable jumper, the caracal is able to run down gazelles and even to catch birds on the wing by leaping six feet or more into the air to strike them.

There is one other cat in the lynx branch of the cat family: the jungle cat, also called the African wild cat. This cat, which probably is one of the progenitors of our domestic cat, is a remarkable example of how misleading feline nomenclature can be. This "African" wild cat is found mostly outside Africa. It is, to be sure, a native of the eastern part of North Africa, but it is also widely distributed from India, Sri Lanka (Ceylon), Burma, and Yunnan China west to the Caucasus, including the entire Middle East. It is *never* found in the jungles, as we customarily use that word, in the sense of a lush, humid, dense tropical forest. This cat is called the jungle cat because it prefers relatively open, hot, dry scrublands—and that's what the word *jangal,* from which "jungle" is derived, means in Hindustani.

This cat, described scientifically as *Felis chaus,* is found in several varieties, all of which are smaller than the other lynxes but larger than any of the other lesser cats. The largest form of the jungle cat is about thirty inches long and weighs up to twenty pounds. It has a rather wistful, haunting expression on its face, but this should not be permitted to encourage close approach by humans, for in captivity the jungle cat—or so some zoologists insist—remains shy of humans and untamed. (This is said incorrectly of so many other species of cat that one is inclined to doubt the accuracy of the statement when applied to the African wild cat, too.)

The African wild cat interbreeds freely with the domestic cat. Indeed, there is reason to believe that all the smaller cats with which we are now concerned have mated at various times with the domesticated animal. This is not to be wondered at, for these are the cats from which our domestic cat probably sprang. There are a number of cats that are believed to have had a part in the development of the household feline. The major wild cats in its lineage are assumed to be the Kaffir cat (*Felis lybica*), a related wild cat (*Felis ocreata*), both natives of Africa, and the European wild cat (*Felis silvestris*), which survives today in remote parts of Scotland and in the forests of central and eastern Europe all the way to Asia. All three of these cats are marked like tabbies.

There are many other small wild cats in various parts of the world. Precisely how many different kinds of small wild cats there are we don't know; often it is questionable whether a cat that has been captured or killed is a different species, a mutation, or simply a different color of a known species. These small cats include the tiny Sebala cat of the Kalahari Desert in Africa and several other desert cats, among them the long-haired manul (Pallas's cat) of central Asia, the sand cat of southern Russia, and the desert cat of Iran. Argentina boasts a long-haired, tabby-marked grass cat in the pampas. In southeast Asia there are two monochromatic little cats, the bay cat of Borneo and the flat-headed cat.

The ocelot and the margay are the most familiar of the small wild cats. Both are American cats. Their range is from the southwestern United States to southern South America. They are marked somewhat like leopards. The margay is about the size of a house cat. The ocelot ranges in weight from twenty to sixty pounds (which may indicate that what we believe to be a species is actually several species). The adaptability and tractability of the ocelot and the margay make these cats highly suitable as pets, with certain reservations (see Chapter 12).

Our own domestic cat (*Felis catus*) has been living with man for at least five thousand years. This may seem like a long time, but it is brief in comparison with the domestication of the dog, which probably occurred more than fifty thousand years ago. The cat may have been tamed first in the Nile Valley or simultaneously in various parts of the world; we really don't know. All that we do know for sure is that our oldest records of domesticated cats were found in Egyptian ruins. And we know that the house cat of the ancient Egyptians was somewhat like today's Abyssinian breed. (For a fuller discussion of the cat's history in its relationship with man, see Chapter 13.)

It was not until the fourth century A.D., or possibly a little earlier, that the word "cat" came into use. The origin of the word is, like almost everything else about the cat, shrouded in mystery, and yet it is an almost universal word. In literature the word first appears in the works of Palladius, who urges the use of the cat to protect artichoke gardens from rodents and moles; he calls the mouser *catus* (it was also written with two *t*'s in those days), and it is obvious that he didn't coin the word, but merely used a term already in popular use.

Today the word exists in recognizable form in many languages, including some which have no relationship to each other. Thus, the word is *kitt* in Arabic, *kadis* in Nubian, *kat* in Dutch, *katt* in Swedish, *gatto* in Italian, *gato* in Spanish and Portuguese, *kot* in Polish, *kots* in Russian, *keti* in Turkish, *cath* in Welsh, *kath* in Cornish, *chat* in French, *Katze* in German, *catua* in Basque, *kitta* in Armenian, and so on.

Linnaeus felt at home using *Felis catus* for the genus in 1758. Unfortunately, nobody seems to have noticed his designation of the domestic cat by that name, for in 1777 Erxleben called it *Felis domestica,* and so did Gmelin in 1788 and Fischer in 1829. By that time everybody was calling the wee beast *Felis domestica,* in public, at least—and then came the belated discovery by some taxonomical busybody that Linnaeus had been the first to slap a label on the creature, and that the label was *Felis catus.* Under taxonomical rules, the first name to be applied to any creature is its permanent, official tag, even if it is not particularly felicitous. So all the scientists had to discard the use of *Felis domestica* in favor of *Felis catus.*

But it wasn't that easy. The term *Felis catus* was already in use for another member of the genus, the European wild cat. If the domestic cat was to become *Felis catus,* obviously a new name had to be found for the wild cat. So it became *Felis silvestris,* a name first bestowed on it by Schreber in 1777. And thus this game of musical chairs appeared to have come to an end.

Not so. In recent years a movement has sprung up to change the names again. Some zoologists suggested that the whole process be revised, with the wild cat becoming *Felis catus* again, the domestic cat becoming *Felis domestica,* and the label *Felis silvestris* going into mothballs. Other zoologists suggested that the term *Felis catus* be extended to cover the wild cat as well as the domestic cat. But most of the zoologists, with the support of many cat fanciers, who were in danger of becoming thoroughly confused, decided that this sort of thing had gone on altogether too long. They decided that *Felis domestica* should not be resurrected and that the domestic cat should continue to be *Felis catus*. There the matter rests, at least for the present.

2. THE BREEDS

As centuries passed, and generation of cat succeeded generation, mutations occurred; changes took place from time to time in the genes of individual cats, altering the hereditary design passed on by the genes. Many of those mutations were harmful to the survival of cats, but nature, in its awesomely inexorable way, prevented the continuance of the dangerous mutations. Those which had no effect on survival, or which contributed to the ability of cats to stay alive under difficult conditions, became permanent features. This is, of course, the history of all life on earth.

Among domestic cats, this process resulted in a species of almost unbelievable variety of color, size, and structure. In some parts of the world certain strains—produced by mutations—struck the fancy of some cat owners. To perpetuate such a strain, the owner would segregate those cats so they could not breed with others. The resulting inbreeding accentuated the special qualities of the strain, and soon each generation bred true; that is, each litter of kittens could be counted upon to look very much like their parents. The strain was now a breed.

Most of our domestic cats, of course, belong to no particular breed, but to that great commonwealth of catdom which knows no law but the sovereignty of the individual. This same splendid independence is true also of those cats which can be classified within a breed, for nothing man has done over the long course of history has succeeded in changing the essential qualities of the cat—the intangible virtues that make it the embodiment of freedom.

If the presumptions about the origin of the domestic cat are correct—and that is a very big "if," given the uncertain history of the cat—the type we usually call "tabby" is the closest to the earliest domesticated cats of Egypt and western Europe. There are two forms of tabby, the blotched and the striped. R. I. Pocock (1863–1947), who was in his time probably the foremost expert on cats in the world, regarded the blotched variety (technically described as the *catus* pattern) as a mutation that "arose abruptly and fully developed" from the striped (or *torquata*) pattern.

The striped tabby has narrow stripes transversely or vertically arranged on the sides of the body behind the shoulders. Toward the rear end of the cat these markings have a tendency to break into shorter stripes or spots. There are ill-defined blackish markings toward the base of the tail. The blotched tabby, on the other hand, has broad stripes which usually are looped or spiraled behind the shoulders. There are generally three stripes on the back running to the root of the tail. "The two pattern-phases . . . are individually variable to a certain extent," wrote Pocock, "but one or the other can be detected in a majority of skins, at all events of European domestic cats, although the stripes on the body may be entirely suppressed in the *torquata*-phase, which is less stable than the *catus*-phase."

The tabby is only the basic cat. Throughout the world, cross-breeding with wild cats, adaptation of color and coat to environment, and the spontaneous development of mutants brought into being a myriad of different kinds of cats—short-haired, long-haired, curly-haired—of almost every imaginable color.

Pocock listed some of the varieties that he found: a tortoiseshell phase "supposed to have come from Spain," a blue-gray phase from Europe and Siberia, a red phase from the Cape of Good Hope, a black-and-yellow phase with pendulous ears from China, a reddish-yellow type with a long head and sharp snout from New Spain, a variety with a twisted tail "doubtless imported from Malaya, where the malformation is not uncommon," a blackish phase from South Africa, a gray-colored animal from Abyssinia, a black-and-white pattern from Japan, a piebald from the same country, a stunted-tailed cat of black and white, also from Japan, a fawn-and-black type from Thailand, and a black cat from southern Russia.

The world is full of many kinds of cats which are unfamiliar to most people in this country. For example, we know that there have been curly-tailed cats in China (whether these were a distinct breed or simply occasional mutants is not clear, however) and that Africa has the Mombas cat, which has very short, stiff hair with a few long hairs as eyebrows but no eyelashes.

There are also breeds of cats once known in America but no longer seen here. One of these was the Australian cat, which was not really Australian at all (the story of the cat is full of paradoxes). It was—or so it is generally believed—a mutation of the Siamese breed which was introduced into Australia and came to America by way of England. The cat, of varying colors, had very short fur, little or no whiskers, big ears, and a pointed head with a long nose. It was seen a good deal at cat shows a half-century or more ago.

Another breed that has vanished from the American scene is the Mexican hairless (sometimes called, rather chauvinistically, the *New* Mexican hairless cat). In all candor, it must be said that this is a loss that can be borne, for the hairless cat was surely one of the strangest and ugliest creatures ever bred. It looked somewhat like a cross between a cat and a rat, with big ears, a bare tail, and a hide like that of a boxer dog.

Today in America there are more than a score of recognized breeds. The number cannot be given with any exactitude because some old breeds are dropped from the stud books from time to time due to lack of interest, and new breeds are added to the stud books as breeders introduce them. Moreover, the various show-sanctioning associations do not agree with each other entirely on this matter of breed recognition, which is unfortunate. In Great Britain the Governing Council of the Cat Fancy is the single, supreme authority for British catdom. In the United States uniformity is maintained in the *dog* fancy by the American Kennel Club, but the cat fancy here is ruled by seven stud-book organizations, at latest count, and it sometimes gets a little confusing.

In the following pages of this chapter we shall discuss the breeds which are recognized by most of the cat fanciers' groups in America. Because it is not possible to publish each society's breed standards, which describe the ideal cat in each breed and set forth the most serious faults that may be encountered, we shall summarize standards of the Cat Fanciers' Federation (CFF). The standards of the other national organizations differ very little, if at all, from those of the CFF.

Charlie, nine-year-old female,
brown tabby shorthair,
owned by the author.
PHOTO: WILLIAM H. A. CARR

Bebe, nine-year-old female,
brown and orange tabby shorthair,
owned by the author.
PHOTO: WILLIAM H. A. CARR

Abyssinian: Champion Lion of Judah's Jubilee, nine-month-old female, bred and owned by Natalie del Vecchio, of Glen Gardner, N.J.
PHOTO: IVAN HELMRICH

Birman: Chez Romar, owned by Anna Bybee Grayson. PHOTO: CRESZENTIA ALLEN

British Short Hair: Double Champion Trafalgar's Indigo of K-La, blue male, bred by Mr. and Mrs. Joel Presser and owned by H. Edward and Kathleen A. Rohrer, K-La Cattery, East Petersburg, Pa.

Red Exotic Shorthair: Grand Champion Tamris Red Devil, owned by Mark Hannon.
PHOTO: CRESZENTIA ALLEN

OPPOSITE

TOP. *Burmese:* Casey Jones, owned by Mr. and Mrs. Roger Sanftner.
PHOTO: CRESZENTIA ALLEN

BOTTOM. *Color Point:* Grand Champion, owned by Mrs. Van Allen.
PHOTO: CRESZENTIA ALLEN

Havana Brown: Grand Champion Arocon's Mamaria, owned by Donna K. Fitzgerald. PHOTO: CRESZENTIA ALLEN

Korat: Akela, owned by Mrs. Carl Carlson. PHOTO: CRESZENTIA ALLEN

Maine Coon Cat: Orchard's Faux Pas, four-month-old male, brown mackerel with white, bred by Marion and Claudia Lively, Orchard Cattery, Pittsburgh, Pa. PHOTO: C. K. LIVELY

Brown Tortoiseshell Manx: Irish Stew, owned by Haine and Dick Gramling.

Egyptian Mau: owned by Chuck Wood. PHOTO: CRESZENTIA ALLEN

Oriental Shorthair: Gideion of Deejay, owned by Donald J. Ryan.
PHOTO: CRESZENTIA ALLEN

Persian Brown Tabby: Grand Champion Confetti Cake, owned by Judy
Hall. PHOTO: CRESZENTIA ALLEN

Black Persian Smoke: Grand Champion Chayenne of Polly Pur Jhan (Shy), owned by Mr. and Mrs. Thom O'Haro. PHOTO: CRESZENTIA ALLEN

White Persian Copper Eyes: Lady Luck, owned by Mr. and Mrs. Raymond Lock. PHOTO: CRESZENTIA ALLEN

Peke-faced Persian: owned by Seymour Millwain. PHOTO: CRESZENTIA ALLEN

In any breed a weak, receding, or protruding chin is considered a serious fault, as are jaw deformities and dental defects, such as the failure of the teeth to meet properly. It is expected, and accepted, that males may have "stud jowls"; that males may be larger than females; that there may be seasonal variations in the coat of any cat; and that, in kittens and young cats (up to twelve months), there may be faint tabby markings, undeveloped eye color, and undeveloped coat color.

Among the *disqualifying* faults for any cat are:

More or fewer than four toes on each back paw and five on each front paw.

Kinks in the tail.

Eye color outside the standard.

Crossed eyes or wall eyes, whether in one or both eyes.

White locket or white toes, if not part of the natural color pattern (the Rex, Manx, and Maine coon cat are exempted from this rule).

Deformity or disfigurement, whether hereditary, congenital, or acquired.

Markings outside the standard on all cats of the tabby variety.

Cats not amenable to handling, for all domesticated breeds of cat are expected to be gentle; pure-bred cats should be well balanced temperamentally as well as physically.

ABYSSINIAN

With cats nothing can be taken for granted. It would seem obvious that a breed named Abyssinian must have originated in Abyssinia, whose official name today is—as it was centuries ago—Ethiopia. This, however, is not the case; Abyssinian cats are unknown in Abyssinia. Indeed, there doesn't appear ever to have been a native breed in Ethiopia.

On the other hand, the Abyssinian cat certainly looks very much like the domestic cat of the ancient Egyptians. It is tempting to speculate that it may have been derived from two African wild cats, *Felis lybica* and *Felis ocreata*. There is no reason to believe that such a domesticated cat would not have been kept as a household pet in Africa.

One thing is known: the first Abyssinian in the Western world was taken to Great Britain in 1869 by an English army officer's wife who claimed to have obtained it in Abyssinia. So perhaps all the authorities are wrong.

Shortly after the turn of the century the first Abyssinians were imported to the United States from Britain. These cats are exotic-looking, active, and very friendly.

Head: Should show a modified, slightly rounded wedge without flat planes, the brow, cheek, and profile lines all showing a gentle contour. A slight rise from the bridge of the nose to the forehead, which should be of good size with width between the ears and flowing into the arched neck without a break. Muzzle not sharply pointed.

Ears: Large, alert, and pointed, broad at the base. Hair on ears very short and close-lying, preferably tufted at tips. Inner ear bare and open.

Eyes: Almond-shaped, large, brilliant, liquid, and expressive. Skull aperture follows the almond shape of the eye; that is, it should be neither round nor Oriental. The color of the eyes must be gold, green, or hazel, and the more depth and richness, the better.

Body: Medium long, lithe, and graceful, but showing well-developed muscular strength.

Legs and feet: Legs proportionately slim and fine-boned, with feet small, round or oval, neat, and compact.

Tail: Thick at the base, fairly long and tapering.

Color: Two colors are recognized, Ruddy and Red. In both colors, the lip and chin area is lightest in color, being cream or off-white, and this lighter coloring should be confined to lips, chin, and throat beneath the chin. Any white is unacceptable on the body, including belly spots, the area under the forelegs, and the groin. The *ticking** must be even, with double or more bands of color on each hair, over saddle sides and tail, without patching or irregularity. Darker shading is allowed along the spine if fully ticked.

Ticking, as used in the cat fancy, signifies a tip or touch of one color at the end of a hair of another color—for example, a black tip on a brown hair.

RUDDY is, as the name suggest
various shades of darker brow
and inside forelegs must be a ti
main body color, preferably unma
and inside forelegs must show no m
band of darker color at the tip of the
given to unmarked orange-brown (burn
nose leather is tile red. The paw pads
brown, with black between the toes and e
back of the hindlegs. The tail is tipped with
are tipped with black or brown. Pink on the
unacceptable.

RED is a dark sorrel; deeper shades are preferr
hairs are ticked with chocolate brown. The undersid
inside forelegs must be a tint to harmonize with the
body color. Undersides and inside forelegs should show
more ticking than a single band of darker color at the tip
the hair, preference being given to unmarked sorrel red.
The nose leather is rosy pink. The paw pads are pink with
chocolate brown between the toe and extending up the back
of the hindlegs. The ears and tail must be tipped with chocolate brown. Disqualifying faults are black or brown on the
pads or any black hair.

Coat texture: Silky and fine but dense and resilient to the
touch with a lustrous sheen. Medium in length but long enough
to accommodate two or more bands of ticking separated by
lighter bands.

Condition and balance: Lithe, hard, and muscular, giving a general appearance of activity, sound health, and general vigor.

Objectionable faults: Bars, rings, tabby markings, necklace.
Pure white on nostril, chin, or upper throat. Coldness or gray
tones in color. Cobby or rangy body. A tail that is scanty, whiplike, or abnormal. Short, heavy legs, splayed or pointed feet. A
round head, a long angular head, or an extremely wedge-shaped
head. Ears small or not well set. Pale or small eyes. Coarse, thin,
or long coat. A darker band on hair next to the skin.

Abyssinians are slow in maturing. Allowance is made, up to

⁓king, coat, leg bars,
⥁pper throat area.

now called,
⹃at fanciers
⁓minology.
⁓ any cat
⹃mestic
their
⹃quire
⹃ntry.
⹃void, although
⹃ come by. Domestic
, are to get, for they have
, ⹃ngenuity, and a sensible ir-
⹃ ceremony. The show cats of this
⹃⹃y bred and cultivated for generations,
⹃rthy elite of American cats.
⹃⹃ with cheeks well developed, especially in studs;
, allowance is made for immature animals. The head
⹃⹃d present a round-oval appearance when viewed from the
top. The muzzle should appear square but not foreshortened or
Peke-faced. The head must display a nose dip in profile.

Chin: Strong appearance, well developed, forming a perpendicular line with the upper lip.

Ears: Medium in size, proportionate to the size of the head,
rounded at the tips. The ears should be set straight up from the
outside of the head.

Eyes: The shape should be round, set to show breadth of nose.
The color must conform to requirements listed in coat color descriptions (see Color Descriptions on page 69). Where orange or
copper is called for, the color must be gold to copper.

Neck: Medium short, giving appearance of strength, proportionate to body.

Body: Well knit, powerful, showing good depth and full muscular chest. The back should be medium in length and level,
showing good muscle tone.

a ruddy brown, ticked with
or black. The undersides
t to harmonize with the
ked; and the undersides
e ticking than a single
air, preference being
sienna) color. The
are black or dark
xtending up the
black. The ears
ads is wholly

Legs and feet: The legs are approximately equal in length to the depth of the body. The feet are neat and well rounded.

Tail: The length of the tail should be proportionate to the body. The tail should be thick at the base, tapering gradually to a rounded tip. The tail should be carried level with the back.

Color: The coat color must be as set forth in the Color Descriptions on page 69. Allowance must be made for faint tabby markings on the tail and the legs in kittens and young cats. In Tortoiseshell, Tortoiseshell-and-White, and Blue-Cream, a slight amount of brindling is acceptable but not desirable.

Coat texture and length: Short, thick, and even in texture, the coat should have good body, giving a general appearance of shortness. It is somewhat heavier and thicker during the winter months. A double coat is a fault. In solid blues, allowance is made for a lack of luster in the coat.

Condition and balance: The cat should be hard and muscular, giving a general appearance of power and vigor. It should have "heft." Above all, the cat should be neat and clean.

BALINESE

These cats were dubbed Long-haired Siamese when they first appeared; like most new breeds, they began as mutants. Fuzzy white kittens were found in pure-bred Siamese litters by a couple of breeders at about the same time. Those breeders developed the mutants, which produced kittens like themselves. Many other breeders cultivated the breed, until it achieved official recognition in 1963. By that time the name of the breed had been changed to Balinese, because the breeders felt that these cats looked like beautiful and graceful Balinese dancers. In personality these cats are intelligent and fun-loving like their Siamese ancestors.

The standard for the breed ordains that the "type, conformation, and color shall be as close to the Siamese standard as possible, with the exception of a longer, flowing coat (two or more inches in length), and a generally heavier appearance." The coat texture should be silky. The acceptable coat colors are the same as those for the Siamese (see Color Descriptions on page 76).

The eyes should be clear blue, as deep as possible. The eyes may be slightly more round than those of a Siamese.

Any similarity to Persians is a fault.

BIRMAN

Also known as the Sacred Cat of Burma, the Birman is, nevertheless, not related at all to the Burmese as one might suppose, nor does it resemble that short-haired cat in any way. To the lay person, the most striking feature of the Birman is its color: the cat is a creamy gold longhair, with brown or blue points and white paws. The first of these cats were carried from Burma to France in 1919 by two men who had been given them by temple priests. In the early 1960s Birman cats were imported into Great Britain and America.

There is a legend attached to these cats. According to this tale, a temple priest was praying before the golden statue of a goddess with a beautiful white temple cat at his side, when bandits attacked the temple and killed the priest. As life left the priest's body, the cat put its paws on the fallen man and faced the goddess's statue. At that moment, the goddess caused the cat's fur to turn golden like her statue, but as a symbol of fidelity the four paws remained white where they had rested lovingly on the slain priest's body.

Head: The skull must be strong, broad, and rounded. The forehead slopes back. There is a slight flat spot just in front of the ears. The nose is Roman in shape, medium in length. The nostrils are set low on the nose. The cheeks are full and the jaws heavy. The chin is full and well developed, forming a perpendicular line with the upper lip. The ears are medium in length. The eyes are almost round. A Siamese-type head is frowned upon.

Eye color: Blue, the deeper the better.

Type: The body is long but stocky. The legs are medium in length and heavy. The paws are large, round, and firm. The preferred color for the paw pads is pink. The tail should be medium in length, in pleasing proportion to the body.

Color and gloving: The body is an even color with subtle shading when allowed. There should be a strong contrast between the body color and the points. The mask, ears, legs, and tail must be dense, clearly defined, and all of the same shade. The mask covers the entire face, including the whisker pads, and is connected to the ears by tracings. No ticking or white hairs are allowed in the *points* * except the paws. The front paws have white gloves ending in an even line across the paw at the third joint. The back paws have a white glove that covers the entire paw and must end in a point, called laces, that goes up the back of the hock.

Coat and condition: The fur is long and silken in texture, with an abundant ruff around the neck. The fur is slightly curly on the abdomen and of such a texture that it does not mat or tangle.

Birman colors:

SEAL POINT: Body even, pale fawn to cream, warm in tone, shading gradually to lighter color on the abdomen and chest. Points (except gloves) must be a deep seal brown; the gloves, pure white. The nose leather is the same as the points.

BLUE POINT: The body is a bluish white, cold in tone, shading to almost white on the abdomen and chest. The points (except the gloves) are a deep blue; the gloves, pure white. The nose leather is slate color.

CHOCOLATE POINT: The body color is ivory with no shading. The points (except gloves) are milk chocolate color, warm in tone; the gloves, pure white. The nose leather is cinnamon.

LILAC POINT: The body is a cold glacial tone, verging on white, with no shading. The points (except gloves) are a frosty gray, with a pinkish tone; the gloves, pure white. The nose leather is lavender.

BRITISH SHORT HAIR

This is the British version of the American Short Hair. Cats have been in Britain at least since Roman times, if not earlier, and the

---

* The points, in the terminology of cat fanciers, refer to the darker coloration sometimes seen on the face, paws, ears, and tail of certain breeds, like the Siamese.

British Short Hair is the end result—and a splendid product it is, a sturdy, no-nonsense, quiet sort of cat. It is a cat that deserves more popularity than it has gained, up to now, in America.

Head and neck: The head is very broad and massive, with well-rounded contours. The cheeks are well developed. The nose is short and broad. The cat must have a good muzzle. The neck is short and bull-like, particularly in males.

Ears: The set is important. The ears should be small to medium in size and set far enough apart that the base of the inner ear is perpendicular to the outer corner of the eye. They should be broad at the base and slightly rounded at the tip.

Eyes: The opening is large and round, set well apart to show the breadth of the nose. The eye color must conform to the requirements of the coat color (see Color Descriptions on page 69).

Body and tail: Medium to large. The shoulders are broad and flat. The hips are the same width as the shoulders. Males should be more massive than females. The chest is full and rounded. The body is well knit and powerful. The tail is thick at the base with a slight taper; its length is in proportion to the body.

Legs and feet: The legs are of good substance and in proportion to the body, giving it the appearance of being carried low to the ground. The feet and toes must be well rounded.

Color: See Color Descriptions on page 69.

Coat length and texture: The coat should be short, dense, and resilient; not woolly, open, or double-coated.

Condition and balance: Very hard and muscular, without indication of fat, giving a general appearance of activity.

BURMESE

In 1930 a San Francisco doctor imported from India to the United States a cat that some other fanciers believed to be an unusually dark Siamese. The doctor disagreed, and he was able to establish the breed, which for some now-unknown reason acquired the name of Burmese, although there has never been any proof that the breed originated in that country.

No matter; the cat is here, and it is surely one of the most lovable of all the breeds. One of the most affectionate, too—so affectionate that some people find the cat's manifestations of love almost more than they can cope with. But most humans are delighted by the warmth, brightness, and rationality of the Burmese. (See page 61 for more about the Burmese.)

There are three Burmese colors recognized in America today: sable, blue, and champagne. The British have five other colors: cream, blue-cream, red, tortoiseshell, and lilac.

"The overall impression of the ideal Burmese," says the CFF's standard, "is that of a compact, muscular, satin-coated cat of rich solid color and substantial bone structure with surprising weight for its size. Its cobby body, inquisitive, sweet-faced expression, and bear-like walk make it a unique breed."

Head and ears: The head and face should be round and full without flat planes whether viewed from the front or the side. There should be considerable width between the eyes. The muzzle is short, broad, and well developed. In profile, there must be a definite nose break. The ears are medium in size, tilting forward with slightly rounded tips.

Eyes: These should be large, round in aperture, and set far apart. The color of the eyes ranges from yellow to gold; the greater the depth and brilliance, the better.

Body, legs, and feet: The body should be medium in size, compact, and muscular, with stocky boning. The structure is broad and short-coupled, with a broad, rounded chest, heavy flanks, and level back. The neck is short and thick. The legs, set wide apart, are sturdy and proportionately short with solid round feet. The claws may be partially nonretractable.

Tail: The tail is proportionately short and heavily muscled with a blunt end.

Color: There is sometimes a slight shading on the face and ears; this is acceptable. Such shading tends to be more prominent on the blue and champagne.

Coat: Fine, short, close-lying, and glossy.

Condition: The cat should be hard and muscular, with no evidence of obesity, paunchiness, weakness, or apathy.

Burmese colors:

SABLE: The mature specimen should be a rich, warm brown, shading almost imperceptibly to a slightly lighter hue on the underparts, but otherwise without markings of any kind. Allowance is made for lighter color in kittens and adolescents. The leather is dark brown.

BLUE: The mature specimen should be a rich, sound, even blue-gray of a velvety texture characterized by a high sheen on the coat giving the illusion of iridescence. The underside is slightly paler than the back. The nose leather is blue-gray. The footpads are blue-gray with a possible pinkish tinge.

CHAMPAGNE: The mature specimen should be a sound, warm beige, shading to a pale gold-tan underside. A gradual darkening is allowed in older specimens, the emphasis being on evenness of color. The footpads are a warm, pinkish tan. The nose leather is light warm brown.

COLORPOINT SHORT HAIR

The Colorpoint Short Hair is an artificially developed variety of Siamese, although this cat is now a distinct and separate breed. Because the Colorpoint is bred to Siamese type, the Siamese standard (see page 61) applies, except for the distinctive point colors and patterns.
  Color descriptions:

RED POINT: The body is clear white, with any shading in the same tone as the points. The points are deep orange-red. The nose leather is flesh-colored or coral pink; so are the paw pads. The red is a color slow to develop; it often requires two years for full development of color intensity.

CREAM POINT: The body is clear white, with any shading in the same tone as the points. The points are apricot. The nose leather ranges from flesh-colored to coral pink.

LYNX POINT (OR TABBY POINT): The mask consists of vertical stripes or an intricate letter "M" on the forehead, horizontal stripes on the cheeks, and dark spots at the base of the whiskers. The bridge of the nose may have a shading of

gray or fawn gold. The ears are solid color, usually with a
thumb mark of paler color on the back of each ear. The
nose leather may be solid color, the same as the corresponding color of Siamese, or pink outlined in point color.
The paw pads should correspond with the points. The legs
have irregular bracelet bars of point color, the color being
darkest on the heels and the webbing of the toes. Allowance
is made for fainter point markings in young cats, particularly in Chocolate or Lilac. The tail is evenly barred in point
color, with the tail tip end in the deepest point color (Seal
with black tip; Chocolate with chocolate tip; Blue with dark
blue tip; and Lilac with silvery-gray tip).

SEAL LYNX POINT: The stripes are dark seal brown or
black. The ears are dark fawn to seal, shading to black at
the tips; the ears may have paler fawn thumb marks. The
body is cream or pale fawn, shading to lighter color on
the abdomen and chest. The body shading may take the
form of ghost striping (barely visible tabby markings).

BLUE LYNX POINT: The stripes are blue-gray. The ears
are deep blue-gray; they may have thumb marks. The
heel and the tail tip are dark blue-gray. The body ranges
from bluish white to platinum gray, cold in tone, shading
lighter color on the chest and abdomen. The body shading may take the form of ghost striping.

CHOCOLATE LYNX POINT: The stripes are the color of cinnamon or milk chocolate, in warm tones. The ears, too,
should be a warm brown, the color of chocolate; they may
have a paler thumb mark. The heels and the tip of the
tail also are the color of chocolate, a warm, rich brown.
The body is ivory. The body shading may take the form
of ghost striping.

LILAC LYNX POINT: The stripes are frosty gray with pinkish tone bars. The ears are frosty gray, too; they may
have paler thumb marks. As you might expect, the heels
and the tail tip are frosty gray also, but the body is glacial
white. In this coloring, too, the body shading may take
the form of ghost striping.

RED LYNX POINT: The stripes, the ears, the heels, and the tail tip all must be deep orange-red. The ears may have paler thumb marks. The body is white. As in the other varieties, the body striping may take the form of ghost striping.

TORTIE POINT: Of course, "Tortie" means Tortoiseshell. In this variety, the color patching is restricted to the points and should be mottled with clear bright patches of red and/or cream. The cat should not be brindled. Both colors should appear in all points, particularly in the mask, and the characteristic blaze is highly desirable. Faint mottling is allowed in the body color of older cats. The footpads and the nose leather should match the corresponding color of Siamese, but may have clear pink patching where the point mottling extends into the paw pads.

SEAL TORTIE POINT: The points should be a deep seal brown, uniformly mottled with red and cream. A blaze is desirable. The body ranges from pale fawn to cream, shading to lighter color on the chest and the abdomen.

CHOCOLATE CREAM POINT: The points are a warm cinnamon in color, uniformly mottled with cream. A blaze is desirable. The body ivory, mottled in older cats.

BLUE CREAM POINT: The points are blue-gray, uniformly mottled with cream. A blaze is desirable. The body ranges from bluish white to platinum gray, cold in tone, and shading to a lighter tone on the chest.

LILAC CREAM POINT: Points frosty gray, uniformly mottled with cream; a blaze is desirable. Body glacial white, may be mottled in older cats.

(Note: Chocolate, Lilac, and Blue Cream Points may be uniformly mottled with both red and cream in the points.)

SEAL POINT: Points deep seal brown. Body is an even pale fawn to cream, warm in tone, shading gradually into lighter color on the chest and stomach. The nose leather and paw pads are a deep brown or black.

CHOCOLATE POINT: The points are milk chocolate, warm in tone. The body is ivory with no shading. The nose leather and paw pads are cinnamon pink.

BLUE POINT: The points are deep blue. The body is bluish white, cold in tone, shading gradually to white on the chest and stomach. The nose leather and paw pads are slate color.

LILAC POINT: The points are frosty gray with pinkish tone. The body color is a glacial white with no shading. The nose leather and paw pads are lavender pink.

TORBIE POINT: This is a lynx point pattern of any color overlaid with clear patching of red and/or cream on the points. The nose leather and paw pad color must correspond with the basic point color.

EGYPTIAN MAU

In the early 1950s an unusual pair of cats was brought to the United States from Cairo by way of the Lebanese Embassy in Rome. From that beginning, the Egyptian Mau breed has been developed in America. (In Great Britain a similar breed has been established by selective breeding of Siamese and Havana Browns, but the resulting cat doesn't look quite the same as the American version of the Egyptian Mau, although the breed bears the same name in the United Kingdom.) It is a quiet, intelligent animal which should achieve considerable popularity as it becomes better known.

The Egyptian Mau conformation strikes a balance between the cobby heftiness of the American Short Hair and the tubular svelteness of the Oriental types. A large, well-balanced cat with a somewhat wild look about it is preferred. With age, the males tend to develop very muscular necks and shoulders and broad heads. The female may be considerably smaller.

Head: Should have a modified, slightly rounded wedge without flat planes, the muzzle definitely not pointed. There should be a slight rise from the bridge of the nose to the forehead, and the forehead must be of good size, with ample width between the ears and flowing into an arched neck without a break.

Ears: Alert, large, and pointed; broad at the base and upstanding. The hair on the ears is short and close-lying. The inner part of the ear has a delicate shell-pink color, almost transparent and tufted. The tips of the ears may have hair tufts as well.

Eyes: Very large Egyptian slanting oval cut. The color is green, but may flash to amber and back without warning.

Body: Long and graceful, showing well-developed, muscular strength.

Legs and feet: The body is positioned high on the legs, with the back legs being proportionately longer, giving the appearance of being on tiptoe when standing upright. The front feet are small and dainty, and oval in shape. The toes on the hind feet are very long.

Tail: Thick at the base, long and tapering.

Coat and texture: The coat is silky and fine in texture, but dense and resilient to the touch with a lustrous sheen. Hair medium in length, but long enough to accommodate two or more bands of ticking, separated by lighter bands.

Pattern: The markings on the body must be spotted; these markings may vary in size and shape, but preference will be given to round, evenly distributed spots. The spots should not run together or in a broken line pattern. A dorsal stripe runs the length of the body to the tip of the tail; ideally, this line is composed of spots on the body. The legs are barred. On the upper chest, there are one or more necklaces, preferably broken in the center. There should be good contrast between color and the markings. The forehead is barred with the characteristic "M" and frown marks. The cheeks are barred with a mascara line starting from the outer corner of the eye and continuing along the contour of the cheek to the back of the head. A second line starts at the center of the cheek and curves toward the upper mascara line, almost meeting it below the base of the ear. The underside of the body is to have vest buttons dark in color against the background. The tail is heavily banded and has a dark tip.

Color:

BRONZE: The ground color is light bronze, ticked with varying shades of darker brown, the ticking being darkest on the saddle and lightening to a tawny buff on the sides. The underside fades to a creamy ivory. The backs of the ears are tawny pink and are tipped with a deep dark brown. The nose leather is brick red. The bridge of the nose is ocher. The paw pads are black or darkest brown, with black between the toes and extending up the backs of the hindlegs. There is pale creamy white on the chin, the upper throat area, and around the nostrils. All the markings are dark brown and show good contrast against the lighter ground color.

SILVER: The ground color is a pale, clear silver. The chin, the upper throat, and the area around the nostrils are the lightest in color. Stomach is a pale silver. The markings are charcoal, proportionately darker than the ground color. The paw pads are black. The nose leather is brick red. The eyes, nose, and lips are outlined in black.

SMOKE: The undercoating is a pale, clear silver. The chin, upper throat, and the area around the nostrils are lightest in color. The markings are jet black on a charcoal ground color. The paw pads are black; so is the nose leather. The eyes, nose, and lips are outlined in black.

EXOTIC SHORT HAIR

This breed, first accepted by one of the associations in 1967, was developed in the United States by Mrs. Jane Martinke, who once described it as a "mod Persian in a mini-skirt." It was founded on a hybrid, a cross of a shorthair and a Persian. The result is an animal with fairly short, plushlike hair. It is a lovely creature to touch, as well as to see.

Head: Round and massive, with great breadth of skull. The face must be round, and the same is true of the underlying bone structure. The head is well set on a short, thick neck. The nose is short, snub, and broad. The cheeks are full. The jaws are broad and powerful. The chin is full and well developed. The ears are small, round-tipped, tilted forward, and not unduly open at the base; they are set far apart and low on the head, fitting into the rounded contour of the head. The eyes are large, round, and full; they are set far apart and are brilliant, giving a sweet expression to the face.

Eye color: The eye color must conform to the requirement for coat color, as indicated in the Color Descriptions, page 69.

Body, legs, and feet: Cobby type, low on the legs, deep in the chest, and equally massive across the shoulders and rump, with a short, well-rounded middle piece. Large or medium in size. Quality, however, is the determining consideration, rather than size. The back is level. The legs are short, thick, and strong. The forelegs are straight. The paws are large, round, and firm. The toes are carried close. The tail is short but in proportion to the body length; it is carried without a curve and at an angle lower than the back.

Color: The same colors as for Persians, except that Peke-faced types and bi-colors are not permitted.

Coat: Medium in length, soft in texture.

HAVANA BROWN

Sleek, lithe, playful, and affectionate, this green-eyed beauty is sometimes confused with the Burmese by people who are not experts on cats, but its coat is darker than that of a Burmese, and the pads of its feet are pink. The Havana Brown was developed in Britain in the early 1950s, and a decade later cats of this breed began winning at cat shows in the United States. It is still a stranger to most American cat lovers, but its popularity seems likely to increase as its virtues become more widely known.

Head: Longer than it is wide, with a distinct stop (that is, depression between the forehead and the nose) at the eyes. The head narrows to a rounded muzzle with a slight break behind the whiskers. Allowance will be made for sparse furnishing on the lower lip. Siamese type and the lack of a stop are viewed with disfavor.

Whiskers: Brown, the same shade as the coat. White whiskers are frowned upon.

Ears: Large and round-tipped, with very little hair inside or outside. The ears should be wide set but not flaring.

Eyes: The color should be chartreuse green, with darker green preferred. The shape should be oval.

Neck: Proportionate to the body. A short neck is objected to.

Body: Medium length, firm, and muscular. Siamese body type is a fault.

Legs and feet: Proportionate to the body, with the hindlegs slightly higher than the forefeet. The paws are oval, with the pads pinkish rose.

Tail: Medium in length and in proportion to the body. Objection is made to tails that are thick or short, kinked, or Siamese type.

Color: A shade of rich, warm, mahogany brown. The entire coat should be the same shade of brown to the skin. The nose leather must have a rosy tone. The standard disapproves of any other than solid color, and of black pads or nose leather.

Coat: Medium in length; smooth. The coat must not be dull, open, or too close.

Condition and balance: The coat must be glossy. The eyes must be clear. The cat should not be too fat or undernourished.

HIMALAYAN

One of the most striking in appearance of all the longhairs, the Himalayan has the coloring of a Siamese with the rich, fine coat of a Persian—an appearance that seems understandable in the light of the breed's ancestry, for it was developed from Siamese-Persian hybrids. In Great Britain the breed is called the Color-point Long Hair.

Before World War II Mrs. Virginia R. Cobb and Dr. Clyde E. Keeler conducted some genetic experiments with Siamese cats. These included crossing the Siamese with longhairs. The Siamese color proved recessive. On the other hand, the short hair appeared dominant over the long hair. The kittens all took their color from the long-haired parent and their type of coat from the Siamese parent. By mating the kittens to each other, however, the experimenters were able to produce a cat that was, essentially, a long-haired Siamese.

The experiments were then abandoned, to the relief of Siamese fanciers, including Brian A. Stirling-Webb of England, who regarded the entire matter as nothing less than a desecration of their breed. In 1947, however, Stirling-Webb came across a stray longhair that was Siamese in coloring but a true Persian in type. This beauty so intrigued Stirling-Webb that he began breeding experiments to try to develop such a cat.

About the same time in America, Mrs. Marguerita Goforth, having seen a mixed Siamese-longhair, began to wonder about the possibilities of developing a strain of true longhairs with Siamese coloring. She knew nothing about Stirling-Webb's work, and he was unaware of hers. In 1955 the Governing Council of the Cat Fancy in the United Kingdom recognized Stirling-Webb's cats, which had now produced the third true-breeding generation, as a new breed. Two years later the Goforth first list of Himalayans was recognized by one of the American associations; this was soon followed by other organizations.

The American cats of this breed were named Himalayans not because they came from that mountain range—as we have seen, they didn't—but because the color pattern is similar to that of the Himalayan rabbit.

The Himalayans are a little more active than other longhairs, but have the gentle voice of the Persian, not the loud and imperative voice of the Siamese.

Head: Massive, with great breadth of skull. In full face, it should measure as great a distance as the full length from top of head to tip of muzzle; the jaws are broad and powerful, the cheeks full and prominent. The short nose should be almost as broad as long. A break between the eyes is desirable. Faults to be avoided: a long, narrow head; a long, Roman nose; a thin muzzle; an overshot or undershot jaw; bite deformity.

Ears: Should be small, round-tipped, set wide apart, tipping forward, and not unduly open at the base. Faults include large, pointed ears and ears slanting out from the head or set too close together.

Eye opening: Should be round and large. Apparent obstruction of the tear drainage ducts is a serious fault. Objections: small eyes or eyes set on the bias or close together.

Eye color: Must conform to the requirements for coat color (see Color Descriptions on page 76). Objection: pale eye color.

Body, legs, and feet: The back should be short and level. The cat is massive across the shoulders and rump with a well-rounded midsection and deep in the chest. The neck should be short and powerful, providing adequate support for the head. The body should have heavy bone and good muscle tone. The cat should be medium to large. Judges view with disfavor Himalayans with narrow chests, long backs, slab flanks, and long, thin necks.

The legs should be short, thick, and heavily boned, having a height at the shoulders and the rump about equal to the length of the back. In front view, the forelegs should slant very slightly inward from breadth of chest, adding to the cat's sturdy appearance. From the rear, the legs are straight.

The feet should be large, round, and firm, with the toes close together.

Objections: light-boned; long legs; bow legs; oval feet.

Tail: Should be short in proportion to the body. It is carried without a curve at an angle lower than the back but not trailed when walking. Objection: long tail.

Coat: Should be long, fine in texture, soft, glossy, full of life. It should stand off from the body, and should be long all over the body, including the shoulders. The ruff should be immense and continue in deep frill between the front legs. The ear tufts should be long and curved; the toe tufts, long. The tail plume should be very full.

Color: See Color Descriptions on page 76.

Condition: Firm in flesh, not fat. Well presented.

Balance: In general appearance, the Himalayan should be a well-balanced cat, medium to large in size, heavily boned, short-coupled, and broad through the chest and rump with short, sturdy legs, the whole type giving the impression of robust power.

Note: The general Himalayan standard is to be observed in conjunction with the specific standard for the color class. In comparing cats of different colors, that cat shall be preferred which most nearly achieves the ideal within the potential for its color.

It is particularly desirable to eliminate rangy, flat-sided, narrow-chested, long and spindle-legged, long-tailed cats with long noses, large ears, pointed and upright, eyes set on the bias or close together, receding chins, light bone, and a general "foxy" face. Any suggestion of Peke-face is a serious fault.

KORAT

Shortly after the turn of the century, word spread in Britain and America about a silver-blue breed of cat in Thailand (or Siam, as it was then called). During the 1930s a few of these cats are said to have been brought into the United States, although none was ever exhibited at a show. After World War II Jean L. Johnson went with her husband to Bangkok. The American couple decided that this sojourn in the homeland of the Siamese cat provided an excellent opportunity to get a cat of that breed.

"We turned first to our new Siamese friends," Mrs. Johnson recalled later in an article in *Cats Magazine*. "Strangely, they did not seem to know anything about the cat as we described it!" (For good reason—see page 60.)

The Johnsons' friends did, however, tell them about a Siamese cat that was solid gray and could only be found on the Korat Plateau, a wild and sparsely populated plain far away to the northeast of Bangkok. Even there, they said, the Johnsons probably wouldn't be able to buy one of the cats because the local people prized them too much. These Korat cats, solid silver-blue with amber-green eyes, were rare and were "given only to the highest officials as a token of high esteem and affection." In six years of residence in Thailand the Johnsons were unable to obtain such a cat.

In 1959, after the Johnsons had left Thailand and returned to the United States, a Siamese friend managed to obtain a Korat male and female for Mrs. Johnson. The cats were bred successfully and soon a breed club was formed. By 1965 the breed had won recognition from one of the national organizations, and others soon followed suit.

Korats are said to shed very little hair.

The Korat is a solid blue cat with a heavy silvery sheen; it is medium-sized, muscular, with smooth, curved lines and has huge, prominent, luminous green or amber-green eyes, alert and expressive.

Head: When viewed from the front, or looking down from just back of the head, the head is heart-shaped, with breadth between and across the eyes. The eyebrow ridges form the upper curves of the heart, and the sides of the face gently curving down to the chin complete the heart shape. Objection: any pinch or narrowness, especially between or across the eyes.

In profile there is a slight stop between nose and forehead, and the tip of the nose just above the nose leather has a lionlike downward curve. Objections: a nose that appears long in proportion to the head or appears short enough to give the head a squashed-down look.

The chin and jaw are strong and well developed, making a balancing line for the profile and properly completing the heart shape. They should be neither squared nor sharply pointed. The cat should not have a weak chin that gives the head a pointed look.

The ears are large, with a rounded tip and a large flare at the base. The ears are set high on the head, giving an alert expression. The insides of the ears are sparsely furnished. Hairs on the outside of the ears are extremely short and close.

Eyes: Large and luminous, particularly prominent, wide open, and oversized for the face. The eye aperture, round when fully open, has an Asian slant when closed or partially closed. Objections: small or dull-looking eyes.

The preferred color for the eyes is brilliant green; an amber cast is acceptable. Kittens and adolescents have yellow or amber to amber-green eyes. The eye color is not true until the cat is mature, usually at two to four years of age.

Body and tail: The body is semi-cobby (that is, neither short-coupled like the Manx nor long like the Siamese), muscular, and supple, with a feeling of hard-coiled "spring" power and unexpected weight. Males must look powerful and fit. Females should be smaller and dainty; medium and well curved describe the body size and shape. The legs are well proportioned to the body, and the feet are oval.

The tail is medium in length, heavier at the base, and tapering to a rounded tip.

Color: Silver blue all over, tipped with silver, the more silver tipping the better. There are no shadings or tabby markings. Where the coat is short, the sheen of the silver is intensified. Objection: coats with silver tipping only on the head, legs, and feet.

The nose leather should be dark blue or lavender.

The lips are dark blue or lavender.

The paw pads are dark blue ranging to lavender with a pinkish tinge.

Coat: The hair is short to medium in length, glossy and fine, lying close to the body. The coat over the spine is inclined to break as the cat moves.

Condition: Perfect physical condition; muscular; alert appearance.

MAINE COON CAT

Ask any New England hunter and he'll tell you all about how the Maine coon cats result from the crossbreeding of cats with raccoons. It's a fanciful idea, but totally false. Raccoons belong to a completely different division of animals (they're closer to dogs than to cats, but they can't mate with dogs, either), and such a crossbreeding is, literally as well as figuratively, inconceivable.

In fact, nobody knows where the Maine coon cat came from. Some believe that it descended from long-haired tabbies that went feral (wild) centuries ago, after the early settlers brought them here. Others theorize that New England sea captains brought back long-haired cats from their voyages, and that these mated with local cats.

One thing is sure: the Maine coon cat has been established for a long time in America. A century ago these cats were being exhibited in shows. After a period of obscurity, they have been growing more popular again, and with good reason. They are sound, handsome, companionable little animals.

Head: Medium in width, except in the older, more developed studs, where it should be broader. The cheek bones are high. The nose and face are medium long, with the appearance of squareness to the muzzle. The chin is firm and in line with the upper lip and nose. There is little or no break in the nose. Objections: short, flat face, or long pointed nose; undershot chin.

Ears: Large in size, wide at the base, set high and well apart.

The ears should taper to a point and be tufted. Objections: short, rounded, narrow set, or untufted ears.

Eyes: Large and wide set. Slightly oblique setting. The eye color should be shades of green and/or gold. In white cats, eye color may also be either blue or odd-eyed. Clarity of color is desirable. Objections: narrow or very slanted eyes; dull eye color.

Neck: Medium long, giving the appearance of length to the body. In the older, more mature cats, especially the studs, the neck should be thick and muscular, giving the appearance of power and strength.

Body: Muscular, powerful, and long. The cat should be medium to large in size. Females are slightly smaller than the males. The body should present a rectangular profile. When viewed from the rear, there should be a definite squareness at the rump. Objections: short, cobby body; delicate bone structure; rounded rump.

Legs and feet: The legs are substantial, muscular, and wide set, of medium length and in proportion to body length. The paws should be large, round, and well tufted. Objections: short legs; untufted paws.

Tail: Long and flowing. Wide at the base, it should taper toward the tip.

Coat: The fur on the front shoulders is shorter and should become longer along the back toward the tail, ending in a shaggy heavy coat on the britches. The sides of the cat's coat should gradually get longer until the stomach is reached, where it should be long and full. A full ruff is not expected; however, there should be a slight frontal ruff beginning at the base of the ears. The fur on the tail should be long and flowing. Feet and ears should be tufted. The coat should be of a fine texture, but heavy, and should fall smoothly. The coat should have a lustrous sheen but should not be excessively oily or dull. A slight undercoat may be carried. This is the optimum coat and will vary with the climate. Cats should not be penalized for less than a full coat during the warm season nor shall they be penalized for a very full coat. Objection: even length of coat.

Condition: Solid, firm, and muscular. Should be presented in a well-groomed manner.

Color: See Color Descriptions on page 69. In addition to the colors set forth there, Parti-Color is permitted. Parti-Color must be as set forth for the corresponding Tabby, with or without white on the face. The Parti-Color must have white on the bib, belly, and all four paws. White on one-third of the body is desirable.

For all other colors, there may be white trim around the chin and lip line, except in solid color cats other than white. Wins not to be withheld for buttons and lockets.

MANX

The Manx is one of the most interesting and unusual of all the cats. Lively, extremely brave, patient and skillful hunters, and affectionate comrades, young Manx are as famous for their rabbity hop as for their taillessness. The rabbity hop, however, usually disappears as the Manx matures. Some people say the Manx is a cat-rabbit cross, but this is a biological impossibility.

Tailless cats are known in many parts of the world—Korea, Japan, southeast Asia, the South Sea islands, southern Russia, and so on. How these cats got to the Isle of Man, a 221-square-mile island in the Irish Sea off the northwest coast of England, remains unknown. Legend says that a ship from the Spanish Armada which was wrecked on the island brought a tailless cat with it (although tailless cats are a rarity in Spain). Manx folk generally have believed that the tailless cat was brought to their island from the distant East long centuries ago.

However, since the tailless cat, wherever it is found, is clearly a mutant, it may well have originated right on the Isle of Man. The genetic effect of taillessness is incompletely dominant, which means that the mutation tends to, but does not always, perpetuate itself when these cats are bred with cats which do have tails. This is fortunate, for a lethal factor is involved in the genetic makeup of the Manx. Breed tailless Manx to tailless Manx, and the third generation will produce feeble kittens. The kittens of the fourth generation will all be born dead. But not all Manx are tailless, or "rumpies," as the islanders call them. In a Manx litter some may be tailless, some may have a stub of a tail (they're called "stumpies"), and some may even have complete tails.

Head and ears: The head should be slightly longer than it is broad, with prominent cheeks, which make the head appear round. Stud jowls are allowed in the male. There should be a break at the whiskers. The nose is slightly longer than that of the American Short Hair, but with no suggestion of snippishness. The ears are medium in size, wide at the base and tapering gradually to a rounded tip with sparse furnishings inside. Tufts are allowed at the tip of each ear; these may make the ear appear pointed. The ears are rather widely spaced, set slightly outward, and, when viewed from behind, resemble the rocker of a cradle from tip to tip. The head shape, ear set, and eye set give the Manx a unique look. Objections: foreshortened head; short nose; heavy furnishings inside ears; ears that set straight up; ears high on the head.

Eye shape and set: Round and full, set at a slight angle toward the nose. The ideal eye color conforms to the requirements of coat color (see Color Descriptions on page 69). In the Manx, the eye color is secondary, but prime consideration must be given to eye color when all other points are equal. Objection: eyes set straight across in the head as in Persians.

Body, legs, and feet: Firm, sturdy, heavy bone structure; substantial girth, compact, muscular, and well developed in mature adults. The body is broad and barrel-chested, set between short forelegs; the rear legs are longer. The neck is short, almost as broad and round as the shoulders to the back of the head. The back is short, rising from the shoulders to the roundness of the rump. The feet are round and firm. In mature adults, the males are larger than the females. Some indication of skin stretch is allowed between the rear legs and the stomach line because the Manx more often jumps from a sitting position than any other position; its method of running also contributes to skin stretch. Objections: narrow, shallow, long, or rangy body; level back.

Height of hindquarters: The hindquarters and rump should set higher than the shoulders on well-developed hindlegs of substantial bone, straight when viewed from the rear, and longer than its forelegs. In well-developed adults, a slight pigeon-toed attitude, when viewed from the rear, is allowed. The hair will often be worn on the lower part of the leg below the hock because the Manx rests on this part as often as it does on its paws; therefore, the cat should not be faulted for this. Objections: fine-boned and short hindlegs. Withhold wins for: bowed or cow-hocked (knock-kneed) hindlegs; inability to support the hindquarters or stand on the hindlegs, indicated by the rear legs parting in spread-eagle fashion or falling to either side, all of which indicate severe physical deformity of the hindquarters as well as deformed or incomplete spinal development.

Roundness of rump: The ideal would be perfectly round.

Depth of flank: The flank should have greater depth than in any other breed, adding to the short, cobby appearance. The depth of the flank, height of the hindquarters, shortness of forelegs, and the shortness and rise of the back to the roundness of the rump produce a typical Manx. The hopping gait should be allowed in kittens and very young immature adults. Withhold wins for: hopping gait in adult Manx indicating lower and upper leg bone fusion and deformity as indicated under Withhold Wins for hindquarters.

Taillessness: Must be absolute in a show specimen. It is desirable that there be a depressed hollow at the end of the back bone where the tail would begin in other breeds. Sometimes there is a slight rise at the end of the spinal column because of the presence of undeveloped cartilage or bone; in kittens and immature adults this may be movable and should not be considered a fault. In mature, well-developed adults, this rise should not move or prevent continuous tracing of the roundness of the rump by the hand. Objections: cartilage or bone movement; broken tracing of the rump by the hand to be considered a serious fault. Note: excessive manipulation and pressing at the base of the spine is forbidden.

Color and markings: All colors are recognized, including ticked Tabbies and Parti-Colors. Awards are not to be withheld for lockets or a button. Withhold wins for: any combination of eye color and coat pattern resembling or identical to Siamese or Colorpoint Short Hair.

Double coat: The double coat is an absolute in a show specimen. The coat should have a soft, well-padded quality because of the longer outer coat and the thick, close undercoat. Withhold wins for: lack of double coat, indicating mixed ancestry.

Condition: The overall appearance should be that of a well-developed, compact, muscular cat of substantial girth, well fleshed but not fat. The head, neck, body, and legs should blend smoothly.

Note: Manx are slow in maturing, and allowance should be made in kittens and young adults. The average male reaches maturity at about thirty-six months, whereas the female reaches maturity at about twenty-four months. Early overall development is not unusual in both sexes.

ORIENTAL SHORT HAIR

This new breed—it was accepted for championship competition in 1976 by one of the national organizations—is the product of more than two decades of development by breeders in America and Europe. What they set out to do was to produce a cat having the long, fine, angular lines of the Siamese but having conventional color patterns rather than point restriction. The result of the breeders' work is a vigorous, healthy breed of such high quality that in Europe, where the breed was accepted for competition before it was in America, Oriental Short Hairs began taking Best in Show wins shortly after the breed was recognized.

Head: The shape is a long, tapering wedge, starting at the nose and flaring out in straight lines to the tips of the ears, forming a triangle with no break at the whiskers. The nose is long and straight, a continuation of the forehead with no break. The skull is flat. In profile, a long, straight line is seen from the top of the head to the tip of the nose. The muzzle is fine and wedge-shaped. The chin and jaw are medium in size. The tip of the chin lines up with the tip of the nose in the same vertical plane. There should be no less than the width of an eye between the eyes. When the whiskers are smoothed back, the underlying bone structure is apparent. The head, overall, is medium in size, in good proportion to the body. Objections: round or broad head; short or broad muzzle; a bulge over the eyes; a dip in the nose; a receding or massive chin.

Ears: Strikingly large, pointed, wide at the base, continuing to the line of the wedge. Objections: small or short ears.

Eyes: Almond-shaped; medium size; slanted toward the nose in harmony with the lines of the wedge. Objections: small, round, bulging, or receding eyes; unslanted eye aperture.

Eye color: Green; amber is permitted. In white cats, the eyes may be green or vivid blue. Odd-eyed whites are not permitted. Objection: pale eye color.

Neck: Long and slender. Objections: short or thick neck.

Body: Medium in size, long and svelte. A distinctive combination of fine bones and firm muscles. The shoulders and hips continue the sleek lines of the tubular body. The hips should never be wider than the shoulders. Abdomen tight. Objections: cobby, short, thick, or flabby body; belly pouch.

Tail: Narrow at the base, thin, long, and tapering to a fine point, giving the effect of slenderness and length. Objections: thick base; nontapering tail.

Legs and feet: The legs are long and slim. The hindlegs are longer than the front, but in good proportion to the body. The paws are small and dainty, oval in shape. Objections: short legs; heavy leg bones; large or round feet.

Coat: Short, fine-textured, glossy, lying close to the body.

Condition: Hard and muscular, with no indication of fat or emaciation. An appearance of health and vitality.

Balance: A svelte cat with long, tapering lines, very lithe, but muscular. Overall appearance of a well-balanced, medium-sized cat. Males may be somewhat larger than females. The cat should not be too small or too large. Miniaturization must be considered a serious fault.

Color:

CHESTNUT: Rich chestnut brown, sound throughout. Whiskers and nose leather the same color as the coat. Paw pads are a pinkish shade.

LAVENDER: Frost gray with a pinkish tone, sound and even throughout. Nose leather and paw pads: lavender pink.

CHESTNUT SMOKE: White undercoat, deeply tipped with brown. The cat in repose appears brown. In motion the white undercoat is clearly apparent. The points and mask are brown, with a narrow band of white at the base of the hairs next to the skin which may be seen only when the fur is parted. Nose leather: pinkish shade. Paw pads: pinkish shade.

LAVENDER SMOKE: White undercoat, deeply tipped with red. The cat in repose appears red. In motion the white undercoat is clearly apparent. The points and mask are red with narrow band of white at base of hairs next to skin, which may be seen only when the fur is parted. Nose leather, rims of eyes, and paw pads are rose.

EBONY TABBY: The ground is a brilliant coppery brown. The markings are dense black. The lips and chin are the same shade as the rings around the eyes. The back of the leg is black from paw to heel. The nose leather is brick red. The paw pads are black or brown.

CHESTNUT-TORTIE: Chestnut brown with unbrindled patches of red and cream. Patches are clearly defined and well broken on both body and extremities. A blaze of red or cream on the face is desirable.

LAVENDER-CREAM: Lavender with patches of solid cream. Patches are clearly defined and well broken on both the body and the extremities.

For other color descriptions, see Color Descriptions on page 69.

PERSIAN

Cat fanciers have been speculating about the origin of long-haired cats for a long time. The type could have developed through selective breeding, beginning with mutants. The Tibetan temple cat, for instance, probably came into being this way, its long coat being peculiarly suitable to the cold climate in which these cats lived.

Many zoologists, on the other hand, are inclined to wonder whether the manul, also known as Pallas's cat (see page 17), might not have been one of the ancestors of the longhairs. The manul, about the size of a domestic cat, is a beautiful creature. It has very long, fine hair, faintly dotted on a ground of grayish-brown. It has side-whiskers that are not as prominent as those of a lynx. It is found from the Caspian Sea to Tibet, and north to Siberia, but always in the mountains and the high plains, where the temperatures are low. The Caspian Sea, of course, is the northern frontier of Iran, ancient Persia.

More than four hundred years ago the first Persian cats arrived in western Europe; from there they were brought to America. Over the years they have established themselves as the showiest, most imperial of cats.

Head: Massive, with great width of skull. In full face, it should measure as great a distance as the full length from top of head to tip of muzzle. Jaws must be broad and powerful, with full and prominent cheeks. The forehead should be rounded. The nose should be short and almost as broad as long. A break between the eyes is desirable. Objections: long, narrow head; long, Roman nose; thin muzzle.

Ears: Small, round-tipped, tipped forward, and not unduly open at the base. The ears should be set wide apart, this width giving the appearance of a broad, almost level top of head. Objections: large, pointed ears; ears slanting out from the head or set too close together.

Eye opening: Large and round. Apparent obstruction of the tear drainage ducts is a serious fault. Objections: small eyes; eyes set on a bias or close together.

Eye color: Eye color must conform to the requirement for coat color (see Color Descriptions on page 69). Objection: pale eye color.

Body, legs, and feet: The back should be short and level, equally massive across the shoulders and rump, with a well-rounded midsection. The cat must be deep in the chest. The neck should be short and powerful, providing adequate support for the massive head. The body should have heavy bone and good muscle tone. The cat should be medium to large in size, but there should be no sacrifice of quality for mere size. Objections: narrow chest; long back; slab flanks; long and thin neck.

The legs should be short, thick, and heavily boned, having a height at the shoulders and the rump about equal to the length of the back. In a front view, the forelegs should slant inward slightly from the breadth of the chest, adding to the cat's sturdy appearance. When viewed from the rear, the legs are straight.

The feet should be large, round, and firm, with the toes close together. Objections: light-boned, long legs; bow legs; oval feet; splayed toes.

Tail: Should be short in proportion to the body and carried without a curve at an angle lower than the back, but the tail should not be trailed when walking. Objections: long tail; pointed tail.

Coat: Long, fine in texture, soft, glossy, and full of life, the coat should stand off from the body. It should be long all over the body, including the shoulders. The ruff should be immense and continue in a deep frill between the front legs. The ear tufts should be long and curved, and the toe tufts long. The tail plume should be very full.

Condition and balance: The cat should be firm in flesh, not fat, and well presented. In general appearance, it should be a well-coupled cat, medium to large, heavily boned, and broad through the chest and rump, with short, sturdy legs—the whole type giving the impression of robust power. Any suggestion of Peke-face, in other than the recognized varieties, is a serious fault.

It is particularly desirable to eliminate rangy, flat-sided, narrow-chested, spindle-legged, long-tailed cats with long noses, large ears, pointed and upright, eyes set on a bias or close together, receding chins, light bones, and a general foxy face.

Color:

CHINCHILLA GOLDEN: Red gold, shading to a seal brown or black at fur tips, end of tail, and "M" on forehead. Cream-gold ruff. Nose leather: deep rose. Eyes and nose outlined in seal brown or black. Eye color: vivid emerald or deep aquamarine.

SHADED GOLDEN: Cinnamon brown, shading to seal brown or black at fur tips, end of tail, and "M" on forehead. Cream beige or warm cream on muzzle, chin, and ruff. Nose leather: deep rose. Eyes and nose outlined in seal brown or black. Eye color: vivid emerald or deep aquamarine.

GOLDEN SMOKE: Undercoat hot cream or light, bright cinnamon. Top coat: seal brown to black. Ruff: hot cream or bright, light cinnamon. Nose leather: deep rose. The masked face is seal brown or black. Eye color: vivid emerald or deep aquamarine.

GOLDEN TABBY (also called CLASSIC or MACKEREL): Ground color cinnamon-honey toned to cream-colored. Tabby markings seal brown or black. The muzzle, chin, and ruff are honey toned. Nose leather: deep rose. Eyes and nose rimmed with black or seal brown. Eye color: vivid emerald or deep aquamarine.

For remaining colors, see Color Descriptions on page 69.

PEKE-FACED PERSIAN

This breed was recognized to take in those Red, Red Tabby, and Red Mackerel Tabby longhairs that began to produce heavy-jowled offspring. By 1938 there was at least one Peke-faced champion in the United States. This variety has, if anything, lost a little popularity in America over the past forty years, and it is not recognized abroad.

The only colors accepted are Red, Red Tabby, and Red Mackerel Tabby. These cats should resemble the Pekingese dog which gives the cat breed its name. There is a cascading of skin under the eyes. The nose must be very short, with a deep stop or indentation between the eyes. The forehead curves outward with an indentation or depression in the bone above the eyes and below the forehead; there is a depression in the bone on each side of the nose. The chin does not align with the outer line of the face and cheek bones, which causes a "pinch." The chin appears and feels as if it were separated from the rest of the cheek and face. On the broad muzzle, a wrinkle runs from the inside corner of the eye to the outside corner of the mouth. The eyes are large, very round, set wide apart, very prominent, and have a different expression from that of the standard Persian. Objections: crooked underjaw; large upright ears, too closely set; eyes too small and closely set, or not prominent enough to give the characteristic "owl-eyes" appearance; excessive protrusion of eyes, giving pop-eyed appearance. Withhold wins for: tooth irregularities; deformities of the mouth and chin; nose so deformed as to cause chronic sniffles or eye discharges.

RAGDOLL

One of the newest breeds, the Ragdoll is a big, moderately long-haired, even-tempered cat, generally regarded as one of the most agreeable and easily handled of cats.

Head and neck: Head is broad between the ears and eyes. The forehead slopes gradually down to a rounded chin. There is a flat spot on the top of the head that extends for a short distance toward the eyes. Nose: medium in length, with a gentle break between the eyes. Cheeks are well developed; whiskers are long. The chin should be well developed, with a medium jaw. The neck is strong, heavy set, and quite short. There is a full and fluffy ruff over a well-expanded breast bone.

Ears and eyes: The ears are of medium length. They are set high on the head with a slight tilt forward. Each ear is broad at the base, with a slightly rounded tip. Ticking is allowed on the ears. Eyes are large and round. The eyelids have a slight upward tilt at the outer edge.

Body and tail: The body is extremely heavy in the hind section and there is a large loose muscle on the underside of the belly. The females are noticeably smaller in height, weight, and length than the males. Mature males are very long and much huskier than the females. The rump is higher than the shoulders. The head is slightly higher than the rump. The tail is long and full and in proportion to the body length.

Legs and feet: Long and heavy. The back legs are longer than the front. The fur on the back legs is thick and featherlike. There are tufts between the toes.

Coat: The fur must be thick and soft, similar to rabbit fur. The coat is medium long to long. Allowance should be made for seasonal variations in thickness and length.

Condition and balance: This cat is placid by nature. It is calm, alert, affectionate, and intelligent. It has a gentle voice, which it seldom uses. Eyes: bright. The cat is solid and firm, giving the impression of a graceful and flowing movement. The cat should be presented in a well-groomed manner.

Color:

BI-COLOR: Body colors may be Seal, Blue, Chocolate, or Lilac. The mask and ears are clearly defined. The white color of the mask starts at a point in front of the ears and extends down in a line through the middle of the eyes, then sweeping toward the back of the chin into the ruff. It presents the appearance of an inverted "V." The color of the inverted "V" portion of the face, stomach, legs, feet, and ruff is snow white. The body has a random amount of color patches of any shape; the ratio may be of any percentage. The nose leather and paw pads are pink. Eyes: blue, the bluer the better.

COLORPOINT: The body color may be Seal, Blue, Chocolate, or Lilac. The color of the points (ears, mask, and legs) must be well defined. The mask covers the cheeks, the whisker pads, the nose, and the area under the eyes with a streak of color extending upward to the forehead, but not past the middle of the ears. The ruff may be a lighter shade or the same shade as the body color. The body and tail color should be a slight contrast to the point color. The nose leather and paw pads are dark. Eyes: blue, the bluer the better.

MITTED: The body color may be Seal, Blue, Chocolate, or Lilac. The body color is similar to that of the Colorpoint Ragdoll, except that there are mittens on the front legs and boots on the back legs. The mittens are scalloped and evenly matched on the front feet. On the back there are evenly matched short boots at least up to the knee but no higher than mid-thigh. There are no scallops on the boots. The ruff is white, gradually blending into the body color. The body and tail color show a slight contrast to the point color. The stomach has a white band of color, varying in width, extending from the chin to the base of the tail. Nose leather: dark. Paw pads: pink. Eyes: blue, the bluer the better.

REX

The history of the Rex dates back only to 1950, when a litter of curly-coated kittens was born in England. The breeder, who was familiar with the wavy-haired Rex breed of rabbits, gave the same name to the litter of kittens. Other curly-coated mutations came to light in Germany and in the United States. Through the efforts of breeders in several countries, the Rex was soon established as a true-breeding cat. There are two Rex types in Britain, named Cornish Rex and Devon Rex for the areas in which they were developed. The American breed is closer to the Cornish than to the Devon variety.

This should become an extremely popular breed, for it does not shed hair. The reason for this endearing characteristic is that the Rex has only an undercoat. It even lacks guard hairs, the coarse hairs covering the underfur of many cats. Because it lacks an outer coat, the Rex should be rubbed daily with a soft cloth or other soft material. Otherwise, the coat may begin to feel oily or dirty.

When handled, the Rex feels firm and, because of its short coat, warm to the touch. Viewed as a whole, the cat should be well knit and smooth, and each part should be in good proportion.

The standard for the breed emphasizes that "the coat is the singular and most important feature of the Rex cat."

Head: Comparatively narrow, longer than it is wide. The muzzle is well defined, with a distinct whisker-break. The chin is well developed, forming a straight line with the tip of the nose. The whiskers and eyebrows are usually curly.

Ears: The ears are large, wide at the base, taller than they are wide. The ears come to a modified point. They are placed high on the head and stand erect, with the outer edges nearly parallel and continuing a straight line from the jowl. Ears may be bare.

Eyes: Set a full eye's width apart. They are medium in size and oval in shape, with a slight upward slant. The color should be clear and appropriate to the coat color.

Body: Small to medium in size, delicate throughout, with a long, slender body and neck. The male is larger than the female and may appear heavier. The fine bones are covered with very firm muscle, giving the cat a well-rounded appearance rather than an angular appearance. A Rex in good condition has a firm, lean, muscular body.

Back and body arch: The back is slightly arched with the body following the upward curve showing tuck-up. The shoulders are well knit and the rump rounded and well developed.

Legs: Very long and slender, with dainty paws.

Tail: Long, slightly tapering, and extremely flexible. The end of the tail is normally curved upward when carried down; when up, it is frequently looped. The tail is sometimes tipped with a tuft or wave. Cats are not penalized for a tail which has a bare upper surface.

Color and markings: Any color or combination of colors or patterns is permitted.

Coat: Extremely soft and silky. The coat must be completely free of coarse or guard hairs. It should be short and dense. Tight uniform marcel waves or uniform curls extend from the top of the head, across the back, sides, and hips, and continue to the tip of the tail. The fur under the chin and on the chest and abdomen is even shorter and should be noticeably wavy; it is often tightly curled.

Condition and balance: Firm and muscular. Lack of condition shows in flabbiness, loss of coat quality, and a dull look in the eyes.

RUSSIAN BLUE

This is the alley cat of Russia, often called the "Archangel cat" by British sailors who carried it home on their ships from that northern port. Or perhaps one should say that this is one of the theories to account for this handsome beast.

"Maltese" is another, now passé, name sometimes bestowed on this cat. Since Malta is a long way from Russia, it would seem that there is a certain amount of confusion surrounding the question of this cat's origin.

Regardless of its origin, however, the Russian Blue is an uncommonly graceful, courageous, noble animal whose loyalty must be experienced to be believed. The Russian Blue is not seen very often these days, but in the past few years there have been a few welcome signs that its popularity may be slowly increasing. It certainly deserves wider acceptance than it has received, for it is a splendid breed.

The Russian Blue is very distinctive; the truest criterion is its soft, lustrous, bright blue double coat. Gentle, refined, shy, and often playful in manner, the Russian Blue has a voice that is soft and sweet. These cats are very slow in maturing, so allowance is made by judges when considering eye color and density of coat in adolescents.

Head and neck: The forehead is high. The top of the skull is flat and narrow, smoothly curving into the back of the neck. The face is broad at eye level and looks even more broad because of the thick fur at the side of the head. The straight nose, of medium length, looks upturned from almost any view except in profile, because of light reflection. The neck is long but does not appear so in repose because of the thick fur. The heavy whisker pads may appear puffed, thus giving the impression of a pinch; when the whiskers are drawn down, the true profile appears.

Ears: Rather large, almost as wide at the base as they are tall, and set far apart as much into side as top of head. The ears look pointed because the hair tufts finish off where slightly rounded tips stop. Heavy inside furnishings cover approximately one-half of the otherwise bare, almost translucent ear area. The outside of the ears is completely covered with short, fine hair.

Eye shape and set: Almost round, just oval enough to show an Oriental slant. The eyes are set at least one and a half eye-widths apart.

Eye color: As vividly green as possible at maturity. Kittens and adolescents have yellow eyes, but by four months a green ring should have appeared around the pupil. Cats whose eyes are not completely vivid green should be penalized, the amount determined by the quantity and vividness of green, as well as by the age of the cat. Withhold wins for: no green in eyes of cats two years of age or older.

Body: Fine-boned, long, and graceful. Appears heavier in repose, because of supple skin and the lie of the thick coat. Muscular in the manner of a swimmer rather than that of a wrestler.

Legs and feet: Long, fine-boned legs with small, neat, well-rounded feet.

Tail: Straight, rather long, and tapering from rather thick base.

Coat and texture: The double coat should be short, very dense, fine, and plushlike. The coat lies out from the body because of the thick undercoat. The coat may best be felt by stroking toward the head.

Color: Coat should be even, bright blue throughout, with lighter, lavender color preferred. Guard hairs shade to silvery blue tip, giving the coat a lustrous appearance. Nose leather: charcoal gray. Body skin is pale blue. Pads may vary from pink-mauve to charcoal gray. Withhold wins for: white anywhere in the coat.

Condition and balance: Well balanced and healthy.

SIAMESE

One of the most unexpected facts about the Siamese cat is that it is not the common cat of Siam (Thailand) and probably was not originally native to that country. In fact, the Thai people often called it "the Chinese cat." Nothing is dependable in this world.

The Siamese cat undoubtedly originated as a mutation somewhere in the Far East. Siamese royalty, attracted by the unusual and attractive color patterns, bought all of these cats that could be found at inflated prices and proceeded to breed them. By 1830, at the latest, the breed was well established in Thailand.

In 1884 the Siamese royal family gave two of the cats to the British Resident in Bangkok, Owen Gould, who took them home with him and exhibited them at a cat show the following year in London. They aroused so much interest that several other pairs were imported to England in the next few years. About 1895 the first Siamese were imported into the United States, where they took hold immediately. For more than a quarter of a century there have been more Siamese cats in this country than in Thailand.

From a breeder's point of view, these cats have a couple of faults that must be guarded against carefully: a kink in the tail (common to many of the cats from southeast Asia) and crossed eyes. From a pet owner's point of view, they have one drawback: their fondness for "talking"—meowing in a clear, high, articulate voice that is unlike the call of any other breed except the Burmese. It is a sound that can be somewhat nerve-wracking after a while to some people.

But this is a small price to pay for the pleasure of sharing one's home with a Siamese cat, one of the most playful, gay, intelligent, companionable, and affectionate of all cats—indeed, of all animals. Siamese not only love to talk, they love to listen, too, to take part in conversations. They are mischievous and clever and curious. They quickly become part of one's family.

The Siamese and the Burmese breeds are closely related. As Sinnott, Dunn, and Dobzhansky have pointed out, "one of the alleles [alternate forms of the genes] of the albino series gives the so-called Siamese color highly prized by cat fanciers." The Burmese, too, belong to this albino series. Phyllis Lauder says that Burmese is dominant to Siamese, and two cats both carrying genes for Burmese and Siamese will produce three Burmese kittens to one Siamese—the Mendelian 3:1 ratio.

Head: Should be long and evenly proportioned, narrowing in perfectly straight lines to a fine muzzle. A wedge as viewed from the top or front is created by straight lines from the outer ear bases along the sides of the muzzle without a break in the jaw line to the whiskers. The skull is flat and the nose is a continuation of the forehead (the forehead being that area between the top of the eye opening and the bottom of the inside of the ear opening). In profile, a straight line, without a dip or a rise, is seen from the center of the nose to the bottom of the chin (the chin to be included in the profile picture). Objections: round or broad head; short or broad muzzle; bulging forehead; receding chin; Roman nose.

Ears: Alert and large to go with the overall dimensions of the other parts of the head (that is, the longer the head, the larger the ears), wide at the base and pricked slightly forward as if listening. The ears should be set, not too flared nor too high on the head, but as a definite continuation of the line of the wedge. The ears should complete the narrow triangle formed by the head, the apex being at the muzzle, the base the imaginary line from ear tip to ear tip. Objections: small or short ears; exaggerated spacing between the ears making them "fly"; ears too closely set giving the "donkey" effect; ears too short or too large which put the head out of balance.

Eye shape: The eyes should be almond-shaped, with an Oriental slant toward the nose, in harmony with lines of wedge and ears. Objections: round, small, or unslanted aperture.

Eye color: Clear, brilliant blue, the deeper the better. Objection: pale eye color.

Neck: Should be long and slender and carried to display length, not drawn in between the shoulders. Objections: short or thick neck.

Body: Medium in size, dainty, long, lithe, and svelte; the appearance of solid weight, firm and muscular, without excessive bulk. The overall body structure should be fine-boned. Objections: cobby, short, thick, or flabby body, or a belly pouch.

Tail: Should be narrow at the base, long, tapering, and whippy, giving the effect of slenderness and length. (The tail, when brought down along the hindleg, should reach the tip of the foot, or when brought alongside the body, should reach the shoulder.) The tail must be in balance with the size of the cat.

Legs and feet: Long and proportionately slim. The hindlegs are longer than the front legs. The legs must be proportioned to carry body weight and length gracefully. The feet are proportionately small and oval in shape. Objections: short legs; heavy leg bones; large or round feet.

Coat: Should be very short and fine in texture, glossy and close-lying. Withhold wins for: coat that has been sanded or shaved.

Body color: Should be even, with slightly darker shading across the shoulders, back, and top of hips, shading into lighter color on the chest and belly; darker color allowed for older cats. The kittens are generally lighter in color. Allowance is made for nursing spots on females. Objections: uneven body color or shading; dark spots on belly; hip spots; tabby or ticked markings. (See Color Descriptions, page 76.)

Points: The mask, ears, legs, feet, and tail should be clearly defined in darker shade, but merging gently into body color on legs. Except in kittens, the mask and ears should be connected by tracings. Objections: complete hood (a continuation of or an extension of the point coloring over the top of the head, around the sides, and under the throat; the mask, instead of fading away gradually at the throat, makes a distinct change of color so it would appear that a hood were tied under the head; tracings to the ears are lost as the mask continues up between the ears); light hair in points; bars or tabby markings. Withhold wins for: white toes or definite patches of white (a sprinkling of white hairs in the points or light whisker pads probably due to past illness, not to be confused with definite spots or patches).

Condition: Hard and muscular, with no indication of fat or emaciation. An appearance of good health and vitality.

Balance: The overall appearance should be of a well-balanced cat. The cat should "fit together"; if extreme in one part, all parts should be extreme or it is out of balance.

SOMALI

One of the newest breeds, the Somali is an amiable, lively, intelligent cat of good size, with a soft coat of relatively long hair. This is an unusual, handsomely colored cat, whose grace is sure to delight the esthetic sensibilities of any cat lover.

The overall impression of the ideal Somali is that of a well-proportioned, medium to large cat with firm muscular development. It is a lithe animal and shows an alert, lively interest in its surroundings. It has an even disposition and is easy to handle.

Head: A modified, slightly rounded wedge without flat planes; the brow, cheek, and profile lines all show a gentle contour. There is a slight rise from the bridge of the nose to the forehead, which should be a good size with width between the ears, flowing into the arched neck without a break.

The muzzle follows gentle contours in conformity with the skull, as viewed from the front and in profile. The chin is full, neither overshot nor undershot, having a rounded appearance. The muzzle must not be sharply pointed. There should not be any evidence of snippiness, foxiness, whisker pinch.

Ears: Large, alert, and moderately pointed; broad and cupped at the base. The ears are set on a line toward the rear of the skull. The inner part of the ear should have horizontal tufts that reach nearly to the other side of the ear.

Eye shape: The eye is shaped like an almond; it is large, brilliant, and expressive. The skull aperture is neither round nor Oriental. The eyes are accented by dark lid skin, encircled by a light-colored area. Above each eye there is a short, dark vertical pencil stroke, with a dark pencil line continuing from the upper lid toward the ear.

Eye color: Gold or green, the more richness and depth of color the better.

Body: Medium long, lithe, and graceful showing well-developed muscular strength. The rib cage is rounded. The back is slightly arched, giving the appearance of a cat about to spring. The flanks are level with no tuck-up. The conformation strikes a medium between the extremes of cobby and svelte, lengthy types.

Legs and feet: The legs are in proportion to the body. The feet are oval and compact. When standing, the Somali gives the impression of being nimble and quick.

Tail: The Somali has a full brush, thick at the base and slightly tapering. The length of the tail should be in balance with the body.

Coat: Very soft to touch, extremely fine-textured and double-coated. The denser the coat, the better. The coat should be medium long, except over the shoulders, where a slightly shorter length is permitted.

Condition: The cat should give the appearance of activity, sound health, and general vigor.

Color:

RED: Warm, glowing red, ticked with chocolate brown. Deeper shades of red are preferred. Ears and tail tipped with chocolate brown. Paw pads: pink with chocolate brown between the toes and extending slightly beyond the paws. Nose leather: rose pink. The ticking begins at the skin, with the red tone alternating with the chocolate brown.

RUDDY: The overall impression is that of an orange-brown or ruddy color tipped with black. The color has a radiant or glowing quality. Darker shading is allowed along the spine. The underside of the body and the insides of the legs, as well as the chest, should be an even ruddy tone harmonizing with the top coat; there should be no ticking, barring, necklaces, or belly spots. The nose leather is tile red. Paws are black or dark brown. White or off-white is to be found on the upper throat, lips, and nostrils, and nowhere else.

The tail continues the dark spine line, ending in black at the
tip. There is a complete absence of rings on the tail. Preference is given to unmarked ruddy color. The ears are tipped
with black or dark brown. The ticking begins at the skin,
with the ruddy tone alternating with the black.

Objections: cold gray or sandy tone to coat color; mottling or
speckling on unticked areas; necklaces; leg bars; tabby stripes or
bars on the body; lack of desired markings on head or tail.

Withhold wins for: white locket or groin spot, or white anywhere on the body other than nostrils, chin, and upper throat;
wrong color in paw pads or nose leather; unbroken necklace.

Note: The Somali is extremely slow in showing mature ticking,
and allowances should be made for kittens and very young mature cats.

TONKINESE

In the 1950s breeders in Great Britain and America began to
work toward developing a new breed which, they hoped, would
combine the best of two outstanding breeds, the Siamese and the
Burmese (genetically, the two breeds had much in common—see
page 61). The result of those breeding efforts was the Tonkinese, which comes in any of four colors and is a splendid cat in
any of them.

For many years I had a Siamese-Burmese cross which was part
of the early breeding experiments, and a sweeter animal, or a
more enjoyable, intelligent companion, never existed. The Tonkinese are playful like the Siamese, but as affectionate as the
Burmese. They are sleek, elegant, debonair creatures.

Head: Should show a modified wedge. The muzzle is squarish,
with a slight rise from the bridge of the nose to the forehead.
The forehead is of good width between the ears. Objections:
round head; sharply pointed muzzle.

Ears: Medium in size; softly rounded and pricked forward.
Objections: small, short ears; large ears.

Eyes: Almond-shaped, slightly Oriental, set well apart, and in
proportion to the rest of the head and ear set. Objection: round
eyes. Color: blue-green, various intensities.

Body, legs, and feet: Body is medium in size, elegant and well muscled. The legs are slim, with the hindlegs slightly longer than the front. The paws are oval and dainty. Objections: broad or short body structure (cobbiness); fine-boned body; short, thick, or extremely long neck; short or heavy legs; round feet.

Tail: Medium to long, and tapering. Wider at the base than at the tip. Objections: narrow at the base; whippy, short, thick, or blunt.

Coat: Short, fine, and glossy; close-lying.

Condition and balance: Excellent physical condition and well muscled. The overall impression is of all the physical aspects complementing each other to present a pleasing-looking animal.

Color: In the mature specimen, the body should be a rich, sound color with shading to a slightly lighter hue on the underparts. Allowance is made for lighter color on kittens. Darker body color is allowed on older cats. Objections: irregular color shading; barring; white patches or spots.

As to points: the mask, ears, legs, feet, and tail should be clearly defined in darker shade but merging gently into the body color on the legs. Except in kittens, the mask and ears should be connected by tracings. Objections: complete hood (a continuation of or an extension of the point coloring over the top of the head, around the sides, and under the throat; the mask, instead of fading away gradually at the throat, makes a distinct change in color so that it would appear that a hood were tied under the head; tracings to the ears are lost as the mask continues up between the ears); light hairs; barring in points (allowance to be made for kittens).

NATURAL MINK: The body is a rich, warm brown. The points are a dark chocolate to sable. Leather: dark brown.

HONEY MINK: The body is a warm, ruddy brown with a reddish cast. The points are a rich chocolate brown. Leather: medium dark brown.

CHAMPAGNE: The body is a soft, warm beige; this gradually darkens in older cats. The points are a warm, light brown. Leather: pink to cinnamon. Withhold wins for: lack of definite leg gauntlets.

BLUE: The body varies from a soft blue-gray to a medium blue-gray. The points are a medium blue to slate. Leather: blue-gray. Withhold wins for: lack of definite leg gauntlets.

TURKISH ANGORA

In the discussion of the Persian cat (page 51), it was pointed out that some theorists think that long-haired breed may have descended from a wild cat called the manul, or Pallas's cat, whose range includes the Caspian Sea, the south shore of which is in Persia (Iran). Iran's neighbor to the west is Turkey, whose capital, Ankara, was formerly called Angora.

At one time it was assumed that Angora and Persian were simply different names for the same long-haired cats, but this is not so. A half-century ago Helen Winslow, writing about the long-hairs of her day, specifically mentioned the differences between the two breeds, although it was only a few more years until another cat fancier, Frances Simpson, was obliged to write, "The distinctions between Angoras and Persians are of so fine a nature that I must be pardoned if I ignore the class of cat commonly called Angora, which seems gradually to have disappeared from our midst."

As a comparison of the Angora standard with that of the Persian will show, there are distinct differences between the two breeds. However, in years past the two were often interbred, and when that happened, the Angora characteristics tended to disappear and the Persian dominated. In time, true Angoras vanished from the Western world.

In 1963 a pair of cats were carried from Turkey to the United States, where they excited a good deal of comment. They were true Angoras of a type not seen in the West for many years, and they came from the Angora cat colony maintained for a long time in the Ankara zoo. The pair were imported by Colonel and Mrs. Walter Grant, who later brought still another pair to the United States.

In personality and temperament the Angora is second to none. It is likely to enjoy increasing popularity in the years ahead.

Head: In size, it is small to medium. The shape is a moderate wedge, wide at the top, tapering to a rounded chin. Allowance is made for a wider head and for jowls in mature studs. The chin is gently rounded. The tip of the chin should form a perpendicular line with the nose and lips. The nose is medium long and straight. A slight curve is allowed, but no break. The ears are large, tall, and straight, wide at the base, and pointed and tufted. The ears are set high on the head. The eyes are large, slightly rounded; almond-shaped, they slant upward slightly. The neck is slim and graceful, giving the impression of length; the neck must be in proportion to the body.

Body: Females are medium in size; males are slightly larger. Type should not be sacrificed for size. Bone type: medium. The torso is long and graceful, showing well-developed muscular strength. The body is set high on the legs. Chest: slender and deep. The rump is slightly higher than the shoulder. The legs are long and slender. Hindlegs are longer than the forelegs. Paws are small and rounded, well tufted. Tail: long and tapering, carried lower than the body but not trailing.

Coat: The fur is shorter on the shoulders, gradually becoming longer toward the back, on the undersides, britches, and ruff. The tail fur should be full and plumelike in appearance. The texture is fine and silky, with a wavy tendency on the undersides. The coat has a silklike sheen.

Color: See Color Descriptions on page 69. In whites, eye color may be blue, odd, or amber. A greenish cast in amber eyes does not constitute a reason for withholding a win.

Balance: The Angora is a long, well-proportioned, solid cat with a lithe, graceful appearance. The cat gives an appearance of flowing motion.

Objections: any extremes in type tending toward the Persian in any particular way, or toward the Siamese, other than length of body, tail, or legs.

Rex: Lily, owned by Kenneth Withstandley. PHOTO: CRESZENTIA ALLEN

Russian Blue: Grand Champion, owned by Mr. Stack. PHOTO: CRESZENTIA ALLEN

Blue Point Siamese: Jessie, owned by Martha Gutnecht. PHOTO: CRESZENTIA ALLEN

Seal Point Siamese: Sia Ti's Blue Jessie of Dei-Jai, with her kittens, owned by Doris J. Thoms, Dei-Jai Cattery, Hackettstown, N.J.

Somali: Champion Lapinchat Hercules, ruddy male, bred and owned by Andrea Zaun Balcerski, Lapinchat Cattery, Detroit, Mich.
PHOTO: JIM BALCERSKI

Tonkinese: owned by Dian Jensen. PHOTO: CRESZENTIA ALLEN

Turkish Angora: owned by Mr. and Mrs. Glen Hendrickson. PHOTO: CRESZENTIA ALLEN

Bombay: Escalita of Baloff, owned by Carol B. Kirchoff. PHOTO: CRESZENTIA ALLEN

Chartreux: Champions Arista Kia (top) and Arista Kallista, owned by Genevieve A. Scudder, Arista Cattery, San Diego, Calif.

Black and White Japanese Bobtail: owned by Elizabeth Feret. PHOTO: CRESZENTIA ALLEN

Classic Brown Tabby Scottish Fold: Kinsey, owned by Sally Wolf Peters.
PHOTO: CRESZENTIA ALLEN

COLOR DESCRIPTIONS

AMERICAN SHORT HAIR, BRITISH SHORT HAIR, EXOTIC SHORT HAIR, MAINE COON, MANX, ORIENTAL SHORT HAIR, PERSIAN, REX, TURKISH ANGORA

BI-COLOR

Limited to black with white, blue with white, red with white. Both colors are to be well distributed, clearly marked and well defined, and/or well-broken patches with white. Markings and/or patches are distinct and well distributed, almost forming a pattern as though the patches or markings were painted on. Eye color—brilliant orange or copper. Judges should take into consideration that the bi-color pattern or markings can vary considerably and still fit the standard.
Objections: pale eye color and all color faults listed in the solid colors with the exception of white in color areas, which is not a fault in the bi-colors.
Withhold wins for: white locket or white toes on any Persian cat, for this is not true bi-color other than when a part of the natural pattern.

BLACK

Lustrous jet black, sound from roots to tip of fur. Eyes copper to deep orange. Leather black.
Objection: smoky undercoat.

BLACK SMOKE

So heavily tipped with jet black, it appears as a solid black cat. Except for the lighter undersides (may appear silver gray, shading down to white), the undercoat of white will not show until the coat is parted, other than for the white frill and ear tufts. Hair on legs, ears, feet, and face shall be white next to skin. Eye color—brilliant orange or deep copper. Leather—black.
Objections: gray topcoat; tabby markings; blue undercoat; white spots; black locket.

BLUE

Even blue, lighter shades preferred. One level tone without shading or markings from nose to tip of tail,

and sound to the roots. Undersides lighter. Type must not be sacrificed for lightness of color. Eyes—brilliant orange or deep copper. Leather blue or charcoal.
Objections: rusty or cream tinge; shadings or markings; light undercoat; drab, lifeless color.

BLUE CREAM

Only two colors, blue and cream, to be well broken into distinct patches, well defined. Tabby markings on legs or body a serious fault, as is brindling. Eyes—copper or deep orange.

BLUE CREAM AND WHITE

The head, back, sides, and tail shall be blue and cream in clearly defined and well-broken patches. The feet, legs, underside, and chest should be white, with some white on the face desirable. A white collar is desirable, but not essential. Spotting of one or both of the indicative colors (that is, blue and cream) on the flanks, legs, or feet should not constitute an objection on an otherwise outstanding specimen. Eye color should be a deep, brilliant copper. Markings should be symmetrical and pleasing to the eye.

BLUE SMOKE

Same as Black Smoke standard, except substitute blue for black, including leather.

BLUE TABBY*

Ground color icy blue-white, fawn overtones, permitted, with dense darker blue markings. Eye color—brilliant orange or deep copper. Nose leather—mauve with darker outline. Paw pads somewhat darker than nose leather.
Objections: cream spots; white chin.
Withhold wins for: white spots.

BROWN TABBY*

Ground color rich, tawny brown, with dense, clearly defined black markings. Eye color—brilliant orange or deep copper.
Objections: white chin area; silver tinge to ground color.

*See Tabby Pattern, page 74.

CALICO

Three colors—black, red, cream—to be well distributed, clearly patched on a white ground. There should be distinct, predominantly white areas on chest, face, legs, and paws. Belly all white; no other color permitted. Some white on face is desirable. Eyes—brilliant orange or deep copper.

Objections: blending of colors; brindling; white hairs in colored patches; tabby markings; black feet.

CAMEO SMOKE

Substitute red for black in the Black Smoke standard. Leather—pink. Eye color—copper or deep orange.

CAMEO TABBY*

Ground color of very pale ivory with well-defined red or deep beige markings. Leather—pink. Eye color—brilliant orange or deep copper.

CHINCHILLA
SILVER

Undercoat pure white; the coat on back, flanks, head, and tail being sufficiently tipped with black so as to give a sparkling silver appearance. Overall effect to be very light and ethereal. The legs may be very lightly shaded with the tipping, but chin, ear tufts, stomach, and chest may be pure white. Rims of eyes, lips, and nose to be outlined in black. Center of nose to be brick red. Eye color— green, brilliant blue-green shades preferred. Foot pads—black or charcoal.

Objections: obviously shaded face; barring; brown, blue, or cream tinge or dark spots on the body or dark tip to the tail; extensive black running up the heels.

Withhold wins for: yellow or hazel eyes in adults.

CREAM

One level shade of cream, neither beige nor light red nor orange, sound to the roots, undersides lighter. Lighter shades of coat preferred but soundness the criterion. Leather—pink. Eye color—brilliant orange or deep copper.

Objections: white lips and chin.

Withhold wins for: any dark or distinct tabby markings on legs or body, or shading.

*See Tabby Pattern, page 74.

CREAM TABBY* Ground color pale cream with dense dark cream markings. Leather—pink. Eye color—brilliant orange or deep copper.
Objections: reddish tinge; white chin area; blue spots.

RED Deep, rich, clear, brilliant red without shadings, markings, or ticking. Sound to the roots. Undersides lighter. Leather—pink. Eye color—brilliant orange or deep copper.
Objections: bars or markings in the coat.

RED TABBY* Ground color red with dense darker red markings. Leather—pink. Eye color—brilliant orange or deep copper.
Objections: ticking; white chin.

SHADED CAMEO Substitute red or reddish-beige for black in the Shaded Silver standard. Leather—pink. Eye color—copper or deep orange.

SHADED SILVER Pure, unmarked undercoat with jet black tipping shading gradually down the sides, face, and tail, from dark on the ridge to white on chin, chest, and stomach and under the tail; legs and face to have evenly distributed shading of the same tone and slightly lighter than the ridge; the general effect to be darker than a Chinchilla Silver but not so dark as to lose the sparkling effect characteristic of a Chinchilla Silver. Rims of eyes, lips, and nose to be outlined with black. Center of nose to be brick red. Footpads black or dark charcoal. Eye color—green; brilliant blue-green shades preferred.
Objections: barring; brown or blue tinge or dark spots on the body or dark tip to the tail.

SHELL CAMEO Substitute red or reddish-beige for black in the Chinchilla Silver standard. Leather—pink. Eye color—copper or deep orange.

SILVER TABBY* Ground color pale, clear silver, with broad, dense black markings. Rims of eyes, nose, and lips to be

*See Tabby Pattern, page 74.

outlined in black. Center of nose to be brick red. Pad leather—black or charcoal. Eye color—green.
Objections: brown or cream tinge; white on chin, chest, or stomach.

TORTIE SMOKE
Black, red, and cream outer coat with well-broken patches. Coat should be so heavily coated with color that the undercoat will not show until the coat is parted (except that there will be an overall haziness to the color which will give the coat a lighter appearance than that of the Tortoiseshell). Undercoat should blend from creamish white to white and this should also be apparent on legs, face, and head. Eye color should be brilliant orange or deep copper. In an otherwise faultless specimen, brindling should not be too heavily faulted.
Objections: body color having too much red, too much black, or not enough of the aforementioned colors; coat should have enough color that it is obviously a derivative of the Tortoiseshell.
Withhold wins for: solid face, legs, or tail; tabby markings; coat that appears to be more silver cream than tortie smoke.

TORTOISESHELL
Black, red, and cream in bright, clearly defined, and well-broken patches. Eye color—brilliant orange or deep copper. In otherwise outstanding specimens, brindling is not too heavily faulted.
Objections: body color too red, too black, blue tinge in coat.
Withhold wins for: solid color face, legs, or tail; white chin; tabby markings.

TORTOISESHELL AND WHITE
Head, back, sides, and tail should be black, red, and cream in clearly defined and well-broken patterns. The feet, legs, the whole underside, and halfway up the sides of the body preferably white. White should appear on the nose and halfway around the neck. In otherwise outstanding specimens, brindling is not to be too heavily faulted. Any other pattern tortoiseshell and white should be transferred to Household Pet if possible.
Withhold wins for: white spots in colored areas; tabby markings.

WHITE

Pure white. Dark spots are not to be considered a fault up to twelve months of age; these spots normally disappear during the maturing process. Leather—pink. Eye color—blue (any shade acceptable); deep copper or deep orange; one blue and one copper or orange. Deafness in blue-eyed whites is not to be considered a fault.
Objections: off-color tinge.

TABBY PATTERN

CLASSIC TABBY

Good contrast between the pale ground color and the deep, heavy markings. Head barred with frown marks extending between the ears and down the neck to meet the "butterfly" on the shoulder, which divides the head lines from the spine line. These spinals, or back markings, consist of a distinct, wide, dark center stripe with stripes of the ground color on either side, and these in turn are bordered by a second dark stripe, making three dark stripes down the back. The cheeks are barred with lines starting from the outer corners of the eye, giving the effect of spectacles. These lines follow the contour of the cheek and curve toward the back of the head. Over each shoulder are circular swirls of the dark color, centered at the base of the skull by the spinal lines. This combination gives the effect of the butterfly marking. Along each side are swirls and markings that outline an oval patch of the dark color surrounded by a whorl of the light color, making the bull's eye. Legs are evenly barred with the bracelets coming to meet the body markings. The tail is evenly barred and should always have a dark tip. Chest should have at least one complete unbroken necklace, preferably two. The underside of the body should have the characteristic "vest buttons," or rows of dark spots, in the color of the markings. These spots on Persians are only apparent when stomach fur is short; in full coat, these "vest buttons" will be diffused and will only be found when the stomach fur is combed down. The appearance when this is done is that of diffused patches of the dark coloring intermingled with the pale ground color. Judges should take into consideration that the tabby pattern can vary considerably and still fit the standard—such variations as width of spinal lines, single or double butterfly, number of necklaces, complete circular markings, or "bull's eye" or number of rings on tail. Ideally marked tabby is symmetrical.

Objections: white spots; blurred or indistinct markings; light tip on end of tail; ticking in the dark markings.

MACKEREL TABBY — Must conform to the specification for the respective colors of the Classic Tabby pattern. The color pattern differs in the design of the markings. Instead of swirls or circles, the Mackerel Tabby usually has one spinal line and vertical bands of the marking color on the sides. Frown marks, bracelets, necklaces, and tail rings are the same, but the "butterfly" is often delineated by thin lines instead of solid coloring. The Mackerel Tabby can have three distinct spinal lines, but they are very narrow and usually melt into what looks like one wide stripe. Good contrast must exist between the ground color and pattern.

Objections: broken side lines or side lines composed of rows of dots; brindling in ground color.

SPOTTED TABBY — Markings on the body to be spotted. May vary in size and shape with preference given to round, evenly distributed spots. Spots should not run together in a broken Mackerel pattern. A dorsal stripe runs the length of the body to the tip of the tail. The stripe is ideally composed of spots. The markings of the face and forehead shall be typical tabby markings; underside of the body to have "vest buttons." Legs and tail are barred. Nose leather pink rimmed with marking color.

TICKED TABBY — Body hairs to be ticked with various shades of marking color and ground color, with the outer tipping the darkest, and undercoat of ground color. Body to be free from noticeable spots, stripes, or blotches. Undersides and forelegs to be a tint to harmonize with the marking color. Tail, legs, and face will have tabby pencillings. Necklace tracings.

BALINESE, HIMALAYAN, SIAMESE

BLUE POINT

The body of a Blue Point should be an even bluish-white, shading gradually to a lighter color on the belly and chest. Points should be deeper grayish-blue, all points being as nearly the same shade as possible.
Objections: fawn or cream shadings.
Withhold wins for: clear pink on pads on the bottoms of feet.

CHOCOLATE POINT

The body should be an ivory color all over, without lilac or blue tones anywhere; shading, if any, to be in the color of the points. The points should be a warm, cinnamon, milk chocolate color, all points being as nearly the same shade as possible. Allowance should be made for incomplete mask, and so on, in kittens and young cats. The ears should not be darker than the other points. As a result of diluted pigmentation of the points, flesh tones show through at the tip of the nose leather, resulting in a burnt-rose tone, while the footpads have a tannish-pink color.
Withhold wins for: Lilac, Blue or Seal Point coloration; dark intensity of tone of footpads and nose leather as seen in the Seal Point.

LILAC POINT

The body color should be an even, glacial white color, without tan, brown, or blue tones anywhere. Shading, if any, in the color of the points which should be a very light silvery blue; there may be a slightly pink cast due to pigmentation of the points. The inner surface of the ear is a delicate peach blossom tone. Footpads range from coral-pink to translucent old lilac. Nose leather a translucent old lilac.
Withhold wins for: Chocolate, Blue, or Seal Point coloration; dark intensity of tone of footpads and nose leather as seen in the Blue Point.

SEAL POINT

The body color should be an even, pale fawn, shading gradually into a lighter color on the belly and chest. Points should be dense, deep seal brown, all

points being of the same shade. Leather dark brown, almost black.
Objections: black or gray shading.
Withhold wins for: pink pads.

HIMALAYANS ONLY

BLUE CREAM POINT
The two colors, blue and cream, to be well divided and broken into patches that are bright and well defined. Colors to be restricted to point areas and are not to be brindled. Body to be the same color as for the Blue Point. Shading, if any, to be of the same color as the points. It is desirable that the two colors be evident on all point areas.
Objections: tabby markings; colors brindled instead of patched; lack of two colors on points.

FLAME POINT
The body color should be a warm, even, creamy white, shading, if any, to a diluted orange-red, the same tone as the points. The points are to be a deep orange-red, the deeper the better. Since red or orange is a slowly developed, rather reduced color pigment, two years should be allowed for full point color intensity to develop. Kittens should have white body color with "hot" cream points. Footpads and nose leather—pink.
Objections: any pale tone (overall impression of point color to be "hot").
Withhold wins for: black or blue patches on body or point color; any sign of tortie pattern.

TORTIE POINT
The body color should be an even, creamy white to pale cream, the lighter the better, shading gradually into a lighter color on the belly and chest. Allowance to be made for slightly darker shading across shoulders and back in older cats. This darkening will not be as pronounced in the Tortie Point as in the Seal Point. Shading not to be confused with patching of red or cream on the body which is to be penalized. Mask, ears, legs, feet, and tail clearly defined in deep seal brown, with clear, bright patches of cream and/or red in the points only. Solid color masks are not desirable. Allowance to be made for

absence of red patching in kittens and young cats as
this color is slow to develop and appears with full
maturity. Wins are to be withheld for white toes or
feet, but cream or red patching is desirable. Nose
leather—seal brown; if a second color is present in
the mask, it may extend to the nose leather. Footpads to be patched; patching of red or cream on feet
may extend into pad.
Objections: uneven body color; shadings of off-stan-
dard color; dark spot on belly; tabby or ticked markings.
Withhold wins for: white toes or feet (as above).

AOV SHOW CLASS*

TORBIE   A tabby pattern combined with Tortoiseshell coloring. Split color on face. Patches of red on body, legs,
tail, and head.

EXPERIMENTAL (OR PROVISIONAL) BREEDS

BOMBAY

Head: Pleasingly round without flat planes, whether viewed
from the front or a side. The face should be full, with considerable breadth between the eyes, tapering slightly to a short, well-
developed muzzle. In profile there should be a visible nose-break.

Ears: Medium in size; set well apart on a rounded skull; alert;
tilting slightly forward; broad at the base, with slightly rounded
tips.

Eyes: Set far apart with a rounded aperture. The color ranges
from yellow to deep copper, the greater the depth and brilliance
the better. Green eyes are a fault just short of causing wins to be
withheld.

Body: Medium in size and muscular in development, neither

---

*The AOV (Any Other Variety) Show Class is for any cat of a breed recognized for
championship competition but of a color not recognized in that breed. *Any* color not
recognized for championship competition is eligible for show in the AOV class; colors
will be added as they are made available by breeders of that color.

compact nor rangy. Allowance is made for larger size in males. Legs should be in proportion to body and tail.

Tail: Straight and of medium length.

Color: The mature specimen should be black to the roots. Kitten coats should darken and become more sleek with age. The nose leather and paw pads are black.

Coat: Fine, short, and like satin in texture; very close-lying, with a patent leather sheen no other black cat possesses.

Condition: Perfect physical condition with excellent muscle tone.

CHARTREUX

Head and neck: The head is large and broad but not round. The nose is short and straight; a slight stop is permitted. The muzzle is narrow in relation to the head but is not pointed. The cheeks are well developed in the adult male. The neck is short, strong, and heavy set. The jaw is powerful, especially in the adult male at two to three years of age. The face has a sweet, smiling expression.

Ears: Small to medium, set high on the head, with slightly rounded tips. The inside furnishings cover one-half of the ear. There is an extremely fine coat on the outside of the ear.

Eyes: Large, round, expressive. The color range is from pale gold to orange, with the latter preferred. The eyes sometimes become lighter after females have kittened.

Body and tail: The body is large, well proportioned, and robust, but not gross. The shoulders are large and muscular. The chest is well developed, giving a solid, sturdy appearance. The tail is heavier at the base, tapering slightly to the top. Males are more massive than females.

Legs and feet: The legs are straight, finely boned, and comparatively short for the size of the body. The feet are small and round.

Color: Ranges from slate gray-blue to ash gray-blue. The nose coat is silver gray on blue leather. Lips are blue. Footpads are rose-taupe. Stripes or ghost markings are not permitted in adults but may be allowed in kittens. Tail rings may persist until nearly two years of age. No white is permitted.

Coat: Texture is dense and soft; there are silver highlights. The coat is less flat than that of the American Short Hair and may be longer. The female's coat may be silkier and not as thick as the male's.

Condition and balance: Excellent muscular condition, alert and leonine appearance. Calm, affectionate, and intelligent. Easily handled. Gentle voice but seldom used.

JAPANESE BOBTAIL

The Japanese Bobtail is a medium-sized cat with long, clean lines and bone structure; it is well muscled but straight and slender rather than massive in build. The unique set of its eyes, combined with high cheek bones and a long parallel nose, lend a distinctive Japanese cast to the face, especially in profile, quite different from the other Oriental breeds. Its short tail ideally should resemble a bunny tail with the hair fanning out to create a pom-pom, which effectively camouflages the underlying bone structure of the tail.

Head: Although the head appears long and finely chiseled, it forms almost a perfect equilateral triangle with gentle, curving lines, high cheek bones, and a noticeable whisker-break. The head is neither pointed nor blunt.

Ears: Large, upright, and expressive. The ears are set wide apart but at right angles to the head, rather than flaring outward. This gives the impression of being tilted forward in repose.

Eyes: Large; oval rather than round, but set wide apart and alert; set into the skull at a rather pronounced slant when viewed in profile. The eyeball shows a shallow curvature and should not bulge out beyond the cheekbone or the forehead.

Body and legs: The body is small to medium in females, slightly larger in males. The body is long and lean, but shapely. The legs, in keeping with the body type, are long, slender, and high. The hindlegs are longer than the forelegs but deeply angulated or bent. When the cat is standing relaxed, the torso remains nearly level, rather than rising in the rear. When the cat is standing, its forelegs and shoulders form two continuous straight lines, close together. Paws: oval. The cobby type is penalized.

Tail: The furthest extension of the tail bone from the body should be approximately two to three inches, even though the tail bone, if straightened out to its full length, might be four to five inches long. The tail is usually carried upright when the cat is relaxed. The hair on the tail is somewhat longer and thicker than the body hair and grows outward in all directions to create a pom-pom or bunny-tail effect which camouflages the underlying bone structure of the tail. The tail bone is usually strong and rigid rather than jointed (except at the base) and may be either straight or composed of one or several curves and angles. Withhold wins for: absent tail bone or tail extending too far.

Coat: Medium in length, soft and silky, but without a noticeable undercoat.

Color: The breed will be recognized in red, black, and white, and combinations thereof.

SCOTTISH FOLD

Head and neck: The head is broad between the ears. The cheeks are well developed. The face and nose are short.

Ears: Small and folded forward and down at the top of the ear pocket. Kittens may have a slight fold, but in the mature cat, a definite fold line should be visible.

Eyes and eye color: The eyes are round and well opened. The eye color relates to the coat color, as defined in the standard of the British Short Hair.

Body: Solid, well knit, and powerful. Compact and well balanced. The chest is full and broad.

Tail: Thick at the base and well set. Either short with a rounded extremity, or longer and tapering slightly.

Legs and paws: Legs of good substance and in proportion to the body. Paws neat and well rounded.

Coat color and markings: Short, fine, and close coat. Should resemble the coat of the British Short Hair. All colors and patterns.

SNOWSHOE CAT

Head: A modified, slightly rounded wedge, medium in width. The head is broader in the more developed studs. Cheek bones high. The nose has a slight break. Objections: extremely long head or muzzle; triangularly shaped head.

Ears: Large, alert, and pointed; broad at the base. The ears are set forward from the outside of the head, giving a continuing line from the head to the ears. Objections: extremely large or small round ears.

Eyes: Large and round, with a slant toward the ear. Deep vivid blue. Objections: small, oval, or severely slanted eyes.

Body type: Medium to large. The females are slightly smaller than the males, but should not be frail or dainty in appearance. The body should be well muscled, powerful, and heavily built. Long but not too extreme. The neck is medium in length, in proportion with the head and body. Objections: long, slender neck; body of extreme length; sleek, dainty, or Oriental in appearance.

Legs and feet: Solid with good length in proportion to the body. Feet well rounded. Objections: long, slender legs.

Tail: Length should be in proportion to the body, thick at the base and tapering slightly and gradually at the end. Objections: thin or whiplike tail; tail too long or too short.

Coat: Medium coarse texture; short, glossy, and close-lying. Objections: long, fluffy, or thick-texture coat.

Condition and balance: Cats should be hard and muscular, giving a general appearance of power and activity. When lifted, the cat should feel heavy. All physical aspects of the cat should complement each other to present a perfect picture.

Temperament: Should be very good natured; calm but alert.

Color: Should be even with a slightly darker shading across the shoulders, back, and top of hips. Shading into a lighter color on the chest and belly, and darkening, allowed in older cats. Kittens are generally lighter in color. The mask, ears, legs, and tail should be clearly defined, all the same shade. The mask covers the entire face and is connected to the ears by tracings. The front foot color is solid white with an even line around the ankle, both feet having the same amount of white. The back foot color is solid white extending up the leg to the top of the hock into a boot, with an even line around the top of the boot. The boots should be of an even height. The muzzle color consists of solid white making an even circle around it; the nose may be either white or point color. Withhold wins for: pure white spots on areas other than those described above; lack of white on muzzle or any foot; eye color other than blue. Objections: ticking or white hairs in the mask, ears, legs, and tail; uneven white on front or back feet; spots of seal in the white markings; white blaze.

SEAL POINT: The body is an even pale fawn to cream, warm in tone. The color shades gradually to a lighter hue on the stomach and chest. The points, except for the feet and muzzle, are a deep seal brown. The nose leather is pink if the nose is white and black if the nose is seal. The paw pads are pink or seal, or a combination of the two.

BLUE POINT: The body is an even, bluish white, shading gradually to a lighter color on the belly and chest. The points, except for the feet and muzzle, are a deep grayish-blue tone. The nose leather is pink if the nose is white and slate gray if the nose is point color. The paw pads are pink or gray or a combination of the two.

3. ACQUIRING A CAT

Ambrose Bierce defined the cat as "a soft, indestructible automaton provided by nature to be kicked when things go wrong in the domestic circle." If that is your idea of a cat, you shouldn't have one. On the other hand, if that were your philosophy, you wouldn't be reading this book, so it can safely be assumed that you do not agree with Bierce.

Not everyone should keep a cat. For example, it is not uncommon to hear a parent say a cat is wanted as a pet for the child. There's no harm in this—*if* the parents like cats and *if* they are prepared to take care of the cat. If they're getting the cat to teach the child a sense of responsibility by forcing the child to care for the cat, they are doing their child an injustice and committing an act of cruelty against the cat.

Cats require very little care, but they do require that minimum. If you are unprepared to give the cat that small part of your time and effort, you'd do better to get a stuffed doll or some other inanimate object to share your home with you. A cat may also be inadvisable for a person who suffers from allergic disorders. This is quite uncommon—the *Encyclopaedia Britannica* says that only 2 to 5 percent of the total population has allergies. But among those who do suffer from this nuisance, an allergy to cats is frequently found. This does not necessarily mean that the pleasure of a cat's company must be denied to such a person; it is possible to eliminate or diminish the allergy by desensitization. (The author of this book, in fact, was found to be allergic to cats years ago, and he now enjoys an untroubled life with two of them.)

BABIES AND CATS

Just what kind of a home is it that this cat is going to enter? Is it a home with a baby in it?

If you do have a baby, don't worry about those old wives' tales of cats that suck the breath from infants. This is an absolutely untrue, unjustified libel on cats, but it is incredible how widespread it is, even among people who should know better. In 1941 a survey among young men in the camps of the Civilian Conservation Corps disclosed that 34 percent were certain that cats did suck babies' breath. And today people are still troubled by this fantasy; every year several readers of my articles on pets write to me anxiously to say that they are about to have a baby and they're worried because they have a cat.

Dr. Morris Fishbein of the American Medical Association is authority for the statement that this is sheer superstition, undoubtedly spread by persons who are pathologically afraid of cats. Professor Bergen Evans of Northwestern University, after investigating the matter, reported in his entertaining book, *The Natural History of Nonsense,* that "there is nothing to support the belief."

Of course, if you have a baby and a cat in the same household, it is only prudent not to leave the cat alone in the room where the baby is sleeping. Cats almost always love babies and children in general, sometimes too much. The cat is happiest when it can cuddle up to the baby in its crib. But if it does lie down in the crib with the baby, it may unintentionally harm the infant by lying on it.

If you have a baby, don't hesitate to get a cat. You'll make a baby and a cat happy.

On the other hand, if you have small children you must use considerable caution, for children, without meaning harm, can be too enthusiastic and too careless in their handling of small animals. Instead of a very young kitten, it's probably best to get a young cat—say, about six months old—if you have children under the age of seven or thereabouts. Indeed, it is a fallacy that cats always land on their feet; many cats suffer severe back injuries when they are dropped by children. A bigger cat can take care of itself more easily with children about than a little kitten can.

AND THEN THERE ARE DOGS

But suppose you have a dog? Can you then bring a cat into the house, too?

The answer to that lies in the temperament of the dog and your relations with it. Despite the old simile about "fighting like cats and dogs," cats and dogs can get along beautifully together in the house. If you have a dog that's extremely jealous, you'll probably have trouble bringing a cat into the house, although it can be done even under those circumstances, in most cases, if you lavish an unusual amount of affection and attention on the dog to make up for the intrusion. If the dog isn't jealous, it's unlikely you'll have any problem.

One word of caution, however: Let matters take their own course. Don't try to force the cat and the dog to make friends. These things take time. Stand ready to protect either animal in case of trouble, but leave them alone until trouble develops (it probably won't). In a few days, after they've investigated each other at a distance, they'll begin to relax. Give them a month or two, and you may find them sleeping together.

One of my own dogs was purchased as a full-grown bitch. She was a confirmed cat hater and had even killed several cats in the neighborhood where her previous owners lived. When she first arrived at my home, she was greeted at the door by four cats, which were delighted to see another dog. They loved their own dogs and assumed that all dogs loved cats as much as their dogs did.

The new dog's hackles went up, but she didn't try to attack the cats. Four of them were too formidable for that, especially in a strange new home. She decided to think things over for a few days. In a week or two she was cleaning cats from stem to stern every morning, playing with them, sleeping with them.

Not that she gave up hating cats, mind you. She still hated all cats but her own. On a summer day she and her canine mate would stand on the screened-in porch, barking deadly threats at a cat across the street, while her own four cats sat beside her, apparently cheering her on.

WHAT KIND OF CAT?

With any such difficulties out of the way, we can assume that you do want a cat. Now you must decide what kind: Pedigreed or plain old alley? Longhair or shorthair? Male or female? Kitten or cat?

Between the pedigreed cat and the ordinary puss of uncertain ancestry there is not as much difference as one might suppose. You can be sure that either will give you affection, amusement, companionship, esthetic pleasure, and all the other innumerable benefits of life with a cat. I have had both, and I'd hate to have to choose between them.

It's true, of course, that with an ordinary cat you're buying a pig in a poke. You don't know anything about the cat's ancestry. Its color, structure, size, and temperament will all be matters for speculation until it grows up. This doesn't really matter terribly, as all of us who have had the privilege of sharing our lives with ordinary—as though *any* cat were ever ordinary!—cats can attest.

GETTING A CAT

How are you going to get this cat?

There are any number of different ways. You may open the door one day and there it will be, on your doorstep, just waiting for you. In a crowd of people, a cat may walk past a half-dozen people to rub against your legs and claim you as its own. A friend's cat may have kittens—helpless little things, all in need of homes. You may be accosted one day by a neighbor's child who holds his cat up to you and says, "My mother won't let me keep it."

If it doesn't just happen like that—a cat's adopting you, in a manner of speaking—you'll have to go looking for a cat. Many pet shops have unregistered cats at very low prices, usually between two and ten dollars; many pet shops give such kittens away free, on the assumption that anyone who gives a kitten a home will be a further customer for cat supplies.

Another place to get a cat is your local animal shelter. Taking a cat from an animal shelter can give you the extra satisfaction of knowing that you have saved one cat from the terrible mass slaughter that takes place every day. In New York City alone, nearly *one hundred thousand* cats must be destroyed every year; that's over two hundred and seventy cats a day! Animal shelters are only too happy to give away cats free in order to cut down this ghastly toll.

THE PEDIGREED CAT

If it's a pedigreed cat that you want, you'll have to take a little more care about finding a cat.

Your first problem is selecting the right breed. There is a breed, as Chapter 2 indicates, for every conceivable taste—a longhair for elegance, a Siamese for playfulness, blues for handsomeness, and so on. But if you choose a longhair, you must ask yourself whether you are prepared to give it the painstaking daily care that a longhair requires.

You will have to pay a fair price for a pedigreed cat, probably a little higher than you expected. But the price will have to cover all the breeder's costs, including purchase and care of the queen, perhaps stud fee, care of the queen in pregnancy, veterinary fees, care of the kittens after birth, inoculations, and so on. The costs of breeding good animals are much greater than most people suppose. Breeding cats is a hobby and the people who enjoy it are lucky if they break even on costs. Nobody's making a profit on cats—except the pet-shop owners.

If you want to get an idea of how prices range, drop into several pet shops and check the prices of the pure-bred kittens on display. You can assume that a cat breeder will charge 50 to 100 percent more than pet-shop prices. This is not, as you might incorrectly suspect, an attempt by the breeders to charge all the traffic will bear. The breeders charge more because their cats are better than those in pet shops—better bred, better nourished since birth, better cared for in every way.

This should be obvious. The pet-shop cats were purchased from breeders in the first place, but if they had been as good as the breeders wanted them to be, the breeders would have kept them and sold them themselves. Instead they sold them for next to nothing to a pet shop. (It can be assumed that the pet shop paid the breeder less than half the price that the pet shop charges for the kittens. That's the usual markup.)

The breeders keep the strongest, healthiest cats, the best specimens of their breed, to be sold at their own catteries. If you want to buy these cats—the finest, both show quality and pet quality— you must deal with the breeders. But how are you to locate them?

Many of the best breeders advertise at least once a week in the local newspapers, usually on the day when the newspaper's pet column or cat column—if it carries such features—appears.

Another way to find cat breeders is to attend a cat show in your area. About one hundred and twenty such shows are held throughout the country every year. At least one or two cat shows will be held in your city, or within a short automobile trip of it, in a year's time. These shows often are announced in the newspapers. They are also listed, months in advance, in *Cats Magazine*.

If you buy a pedigreed cat, there are two precautions that you must take:

1. Make sure that the breeder (or pet-shop dealer) explicitly agrees that the cat can be returned within a given period—say, forty-eight or seventy-two hours—if it does not pass a veterinarian's examination for health and soundness.

2. Insist that the cat's "papers" be transferred to you at the time you pay for the cat. The "papers" usually consist of one document—the registration certificate that attests to the fact that the cat's records, including its pedigree, have been kept by one or more of the seven stud-book organizations: American Cat Association, American Cat Fanciers' Association, Cat Fanciers' Association, Cat Fanciers' Federation, Crown Cat Fanciers Federation, National Cat Fanciers' Association, and United Cat Federation. In Canada, the appropriate organization is the Canadian Cat Association.

MALE OR FEMALE?

Now, whether you're getting a pedigreed cat or an unregistered pet, you are at the point where you must make another decision: Should you get a male or a female?

If all you want is a pet, it doesn't matter which you get. There is no substantial difference between males and females in temperament or in any other important quality. Both should be neutered before they're a year old. This question is discussed at greater length in Chapter 9.

If, however, you want to breed and exhibit cats, then you ought to buy a female, not a male. The chances are that you'll want to keep your cat in your home, and an adult male simply cannot be kept in the house unless it is castrated; the odor is not to be endured. A female, on the other hand, will prove difficult only when she is in heat.

This is as good a time as any to tell you how to distinguish between a male and a female cat. It's not as easy as you might think. The sex of a cat, unlike that of a dog or cow, is not readily identifiable. You must lift the cat's tail to find out. A male kitten's undeveloped sex organs look like a punctuation mark, the colon (:). The female kitten's look like an inverted exclamation mark (¡).

KITTEN OR CAT?

The next decision that you must make involves the age of the cat. Do you want a little kitten or should you get a grown cat instead?

This question, of course, will not concern you if you've adopted—or been adopted by—a stray. But you may wonder about it if you're setting out deliberately to procure a cat.

Generally, you'll be better off with a kitten. An adult has already formed its own habits and its way of life. There may be some adjustment difficulties until you and the cat agree upon a modus vivendi, especially if the cat was used to living with somebody else. But don't let this discourage you. Much depends on how you and the cat hit it off. If you take to each other, there won't be any problems at all. I've known many people who took home adult cats and had a wonderful life with them from the first day. It has even happened to me. A kitten, of course, is at a more malleable stage of life. It will grow up with the habits that you let it acquire. It will adjust itself to your way of life.

In general, it is best to choose a kitten that is nine or ten weeks

old, because by then the kitten is big enough and strong enough
to survive without its mother. You'd better not take a younger
kitten unless you're the kind of person who can take care of an
animal without any trouble. If the kitten is very young, you will
have to be a substitute mother for it, and there are a lot of unexpected jobs to do if you intend to fill that role. (See Chapter 6.)
Of course, the age of your children can be a factor, too, in your
choice of a cat, as the discussion earlier in this chapter pointed
out.

WHAT TO LOOK FOR

Now you're at the point of picking a cat. This is a moment when
you must really be on your toes.

If you're buying your cat from a breeder, his reputation stands
behind the kitten, so you've got a certain amount of insurance
against error. But 999 out of every 1,000 cats—that's a statistic
that I just made up—come from the litters of friends' cats, animal shelters, or other miscellaneous sources, and nothing will
protect you from an unhappy mistake in these cases except the
fine old rule of caveat emptor—"let the buyer beware."

Take a look at the litter as a whole before you begin looking at
individual kittens. Let's say there are six kittens. Five of them are
playing with the mock ferocity of young tigers. One sits sadly in
the corner, looking shy and lonely. Your heart goes out to it; this
kitten obviously needs a home and comforting. But don't give in
to the impulse. The kitten may be shy, but it's more likely that
it's staying out of things because it's sick. The lively, saucy,
friendly kitten is usually the safer choice.

Now it's time to begin looking at each kitten. Check each one
for health and then for soundness.

If there are bare spots anywhere in the coat, the kitten may
have ringworm. Beware of scales on the eyelids or running eyes.
Look into the ears; if they don't look clean, the kitten may have
mites. The nose should not be running, although it can be wet
and cold, of course. Lift up the tail and look carefully around
the vent for any signs of diarrhea; the fur of the back legs may
also give a clue to this.

Now consider the cat's condition. Does it weigh as much and is it as big as you would expect a kitten to be at that age? (Remember that a Siamese, say, is not going to weigh as much as a longhair at the same age.) Shake some keys in the air behind the kitten and see if it whips its heads around; that's one rough test of the cat's hearing. See if the kitten blinks its eyes when the light is cut off suddenly.

SEEING A VETERINARIAN

These precautions are enough when you're acquiring the kitten, but you should take it immediately to a veterinarian (see Chapter 6 on choosing a vet). A vet can detect trouble signs that you'd never notice. I say *immediately* because the longer you have the kitten, the harder it will be for you to return it, no matter how sick or malformed it may be. Tell the veterinarian that you have just obtained the cat and you want a thorough examination for health and soundness.

While you've got the kitten at the veterinarian's office, ask the doctor to start it on its immunization program. The veterinarian probably will want to vaccinate the kitten against panleukopenia (also called feline distemper, feline enteritis, cat plague, and any number of other names) and rabies. Some veterinarians also like to give shots against feline rhinotracheitis and feline pneumonitis. When it comes to vaccines, it's best to go along with your veterinarian's recommendations.

The veterinarian is also the person with whom to discuss any special problems the kitten may have with regard to feeding or general care, subjects that will be discussed in later chapters.

ASK QUESTIONS

Before you take the kitten from the person who had it, talk to him at some length about the manner in which the kitten has been cared for up to now. This is of particular importance if you have not been used to caring for young animals. You can use all the information, advice, and help you can get.

Find out—and write down, for you'll forget it otherwise—what the kitten is accustomed to eating, and at what times. Be sure that the information includes quantities, too.

Has the kitten been housebroken in its toilet habits? If it has been, was it trained to go outdoors or in a sanitary pan in the house?

All these things are important, because you cannot change a kitten's way of doing things overnight without upsetting it terribly. In the beginning, you should imitate as closely as possible the care it has been receiving, and gradually, over the next few days, begin changing those things which seem to require change.

CARRYING THE CAT

It's unlikely that you'll have a carrying case when you go to pick up your cat, but take a big, thick bath towel with you to wrap around the cat. The towel serves two purposes: it protects you and it comforts the cat. You may need protection because the cat is likely to be frightened, and frightened cats tend to claw frantically. After all, the cat has never seen you before. All it knows is that a stranger has picked it up and is taking it, perhaps in a car, through a bewildering, new area of unfamiliar sights and sounds and smells. But the cat can't claw you in its panic if you've wrapped it well in the towel and keep a firm grip on it. Unable to escape, the cat will then want to hide from the fearsome world. Cats love to hide their faces under those circumstances. The towel offers it that hiding place.

As soon as possible, however, you should buy a carrying case. Every pet shop carries cat cases. Some are made of basketweave, others are solid-sided boxes with air holes at each end and a handle at the top. A carrying case is invaluable when you have to take a cat to the veterinarian or to a boarding cattery or on a trip.

EQUIPMENT

The carrying case is not the only equipment you'll need. Let's see what else there is.

House training will be discussed in the next section. The equipment you'll need for this will be a sanitary pan of plastic, aluminum, or enamel-coated metal; a bag of litter to put in the pan; and a little sieve-shovel for sifting the solid matter out of the pan every day. All these articles are available in your pet shop.

Although most cats will pick their own beds, you'll probably want to provide one at the start. If the new cat is a kitten, a bed is essential. You can buy one at the pet shop or fix your own. A box makes an excellent bed (especially if you can cover half the box so the cat can feel that it is sleeping in a cave). The bed should not be placed on the floor, but on a chest or trunk, so that it will be out of the way of drafts. How long the cat sleeps in its bed depends on you. If you permit it, the cat's almost certain to share your bed with you after it settles down in your house.

The bedding should help the cat conserve its body heat. The best bed is newspaper with a blanket laid on top of it. The blanket should not be neat and flat, but pushed roughly into the bed box, so that the cat can wriggle around and get the blanket up around itself. The blanket will need frequent laundering, of course, and if the cat has gotten itself wet, you can assume the blanket will get wet, too. Don't let the cat sleep on a wet blanket.

A brush and a comb for grooming the cat are also necessities. The kind of brush will depend to some extent on the hair length of the coat. The bristles should be firm, but not set so close together that they cannot get down through the fur. Some all-plastic pet brushes are available now, which work very well. The comb is used for working mats out of the hair, so a relatively open-toothed comb, which your pet shop carries, is necessary.

Nail clippers are essential. Clippers of the kind used for human fingernails are perfect.

A collar is indicated, preferably with an identification tag attached to it giving your name, address, and telephone number. Innumerable cats are strangled to death by their collars, so be careful about the kind of collar you buy. It should be one that will expand and release the cat if the collar gets caught on a nail or the limb of a tree. One excellent safety collar has one side of elastic material that will stretch to let the cat escape if it gets caught.

If you live in the city or the suburbs, and you want to take the cat outdoors, which you should from time to time in good weather, you'll need a round leather collar and a leash to fasten to it. Light leashes especially made for cats can be found in pet shops. You may also want to buy one of the special harnesses made for walking cats; they are better than a collar for this purpose.

HOUSEBREAKING

Nothing could be easier than training a cat, even a kitten, to use a sanitary pan. Cats are naturally clean animals. Three and a half centuries ago Edward Topsell, the first English zoologist, said of the cat, "Her nature is to hide her own dung or excrement, for she knoweth that the favor and presence thereof will drive away her sport, the little mouse being able by that stool to smell the presence of her mortal foe." Whether that is the reason why the cat buries its waste no one knows, but certainly the cat's instinct is to do its business where it can bury it.

The sanitary pan—or "cat box," as most cat owners call it—should be put in one place and kept there. Under the sink in the bathroom is one of the most convenient places for most households. The cat should be taken to the box, which has been filled with clean litter. Put the cat in the box so it can tell that this is a place where unpleasant things can be buried. If you have a kitten, take its forepaws in your hands and gently dig a hole in the litter with them to give the kitten the idea.

Then keep your eye on the cat. You'll be able to guess when it needs to use the box; the look of discomfort and uneasiness is usually quite clear. When the cat looks as though it might need the box, take it there again.

You must expect one or two mistakes on the part of the cat. As soon as you find such a mishap, hold the cat close to it—*do not* touch its nose to it!—and give it a light slap while scolding it. Then take it to the box and keep it there for a few moments. Some cats are easier to train than others. I have never had a cat that made more than two mistakes before learning what the box was for. On the other hand, I have brought into my home kittens, only six weeks old, that never made a single mistake.

Once the cat is housebroken, you need not worry about its hygienic habits except for two problems.

The first is a fireplace. Unfortunately, the ashes in a fireplace strike many cats as an excellent place to hide their dirt. From a cat's point of view, there is a certain logic to this. But it can be an unpleasant practice from the owner's point of view. The best way to handle this problem is to punish the cat, but also to keep the fireplace as clear of ashes as possible when no fire is lit. It may also help to put a fireplace screen before the fire pit so that the cat just can't get in.

The second problem may puzzle you. Your cat, let us say, is and has been housebroken perfectly. You've been able to trust it for months. Suddenly it begins to disgrace itself. This sort of thing can be quite a shock to the complacent cat owner. There can be two explanations. One is that the cat is suffering from cystitis (see Chapter 8), in which case you should take it to the veterinarian for treatment. Before doing so, however, investigate the second possibility: maybe you yourself are at fault. You may have caused the problem by neglecting to take proper care of the cat box. If the litter needs changing or sifting, the cat may refuse to use it. If the need continues, and you do nothing about it, the cat may take the law into its own hands and demonstrate forcefully to you its desire for a clean box.

The cat box should be sifted once a day. The litter should be changed as often as necessary. No set time can be stated, for the condition of the litter is affected by many factors: the kind of litter that is used, the number of cats using the box, and the kind of weather you've been having. No one litter seems best for all cats; some litters will cover the odor of one cat best, others will be better for another cat. The weather comes into play because several rainy days, during which the litter never dries, will make the cat box objectionable.

One last word about this matter of housebreaking: Some people train their cats to use a toilet, which is convenient. It's a nice trick, if you want to take the trouble.

It takes about a month to train a cat to use the toilet. You must begin with a cat that is trained to use a sanitary pan. Encourage the cat to jump up on the seat by putting the pan there. You must secure the pan so it won't slip when the cat jumps in or out. Cut a slit two inches wide down the length of the pan, in the middle. Put litter around the side of the slit or fashion a stall which will force the cat to poise itself over the slit. When it is used to doing its business under those circumstances, take the pan away and substitute a platform, with a two-inch slit down the middle of it. Eventually, it you wish, you can remove the platform and the cat will continue to use the toilet, balancing itself on the sides of the seat.

THE ESSENTIAL REQUIREMENT

By now it must seem to you that a cat is a great deal of trouble. It isn't.

In practice, preparing for a cat is as simple as it sounds complex. It is much easier, for example, than bringing a dog into your home. As a dog breeder, I know—I've had to adjust to both animals.

If I have given the impression that the cat needs to be treated like a delicate flower, I've misled you. It is extremely hardy, ingenious, and resilient. But all cats have intricate psychological systems, and kittens have the special vulnerability of all young life.

Try to put yourself in the cat's or the kitten's place. You are wrenched from the place that has been familiar to you, carried by a strange human in a frightening vehicle through unknown streets to a new house. It can be a shattering experience.

The cat needs not only care, but love and understanding, too. A soothing tone of voice, the stroke of a comforting hand on a furry little head, a warm lap to lie on—these are the things that can ease the strain on a cat during its first few days in your house.

Don't try to grab the cat or make sudden moves toward it. You'll only frighten the little thing. Don't use a loud voice or permit loud noises until the cat is settled down with you and you've adjusted to each other. If you have children, keep them away from the cat for a day or two. If you have a dog or another cat, don't try to force them to make friends with the newcomer; you'll just get everyone upset and annoyed.

If you use patience, understanding, care, and love, your cat will very quickly be a part of the household. Then you will know what Mark Twain meant when he wrote, "A house without a cat, and a well-fed, well-petted, and properly revered cat, may be a perfect house, perhaps, but how can it prove its title?"

4. THE NATURE
OF THE CAT

Cats and people have a good deal more in common than their mutual preferences for warmth, dry places, good food, and soft beds. In fact, cats have too much in common with people for their own good, for the similarities are so marked that the cat is considered one of the best substitutes for man in laboratory experiments. (This use of the cat, happily, is limited by the intractable character of the cat when it is subjected to something it doesn't like.)

Think of the cat's body, then think of your own, and you will find the two have a great deal in common. Both humans and cats are mammals. Both have a four-chambered heart and the same circulatory systems to carry the blood on its circuit through the body. Both have noses, windpipes, and paired lungs for breathing. Both have the same internal organs: stomach, pancreas, liver, kidneys, small intestine, large intestine. Each has a brain and a central nervous system. The bone structures of both are quite similar; run down the names of the cat's bones and see how familiar they sound—occiput, cranium, vertebrae, ribs, sacrum, ilium, fibula, tibia, tarsus, metatarsus, humerus, radius, ulna, carpus, metacarpus, and so on.

It should be obvious that there are marked differences between the body of a man and the body of a cat, despite the similarities. Have you tried touching your tongue to your back lately?

There are more important differences, of course; for example, the tolerance of a cat to drugs compared to that of a human. The cat can contract feline distemper, to which you are immune (and so is your dog, by the way, for this is different from canine distemper); you can get the mumps, but the cat can't. All of this, one must add hastily, is stated on the basis of present knowledge.

In Chapter 8 we'll go into the question of disease more fully, but at this point it might be illuminating to run down a list of some of the ills to which the cat is a prey and see how many are familiar names of human maladies: anemia, bronchitis, cancer, cirrhosis of the liver, dandruff, diabetes, eczema, encephalitis, food poisoning, heart disease, hernia, jaundice, obesity, pleurisy, ringworm, shock, tooth decay, uremia, virus infections.

Nevertheless, the cat is a different creature from man—and also from a dog. Zoologists consider the dog, in Dr. Edwin H. Colbert's words, "structurally primitive," in contrast with the cat, which is "highly evolved." A knowledge of this sophisticated organism, with its peculiarities, may help you better to enjoy life with your cat. So let us see what kind of a creature this *Felis catus* is.

SKIN AND HAIR

The hair that has almost vanished from most of the human body still covers the cat thickly. All cats have fur, even the so-called hairless cat of Mexico, New Mexico, and Uruguay, which has a fine, almost imperceptible covering. The fur grows everywhere on the cat's body except for four places: the nose, the pads of the feet, the anus, and the nipples.

It is worth considering, for a moment, how the hair grows and how the skin nurtures it. The skin, as in man, consists of two layers, the outer, called the *epidermis,* and the inner, the *dermis.* The epidermis, also known as the cuticle or scarfskin, is made up in turn of four layers. The deepest of these is the level at which regeneration takes place, where new skin is produced constantly.

The skin is not an absolute barrier, even when it is unpunctured. Although it is waterproof, it does permit the absorption of some oils and drugs. This is an important point to remember: I have seen a kitten paralyzed—only temporarily, fortunately—by chemical baths it was given to cure a purely external skin condition. The drug had been absorbed through the skin, and its effect was toxic.

The hair grows out of follicles, or sacs, which are buried in the skin. Attached to the follicles are tiny erector muscles. You have a few such muscles yourself at the back of your neck; that's why you can "feel your hair stand on end" when you're frightened. The cat's body is covered with such muscles. When it is frightened or angry, it seems as though almost every hair on its body stands erect. Even the fur on the tail stands out so that it looks as though the slim tail has suddenly been turned into a fox's full brush. It has been theorized that this phenomenon is a gift of nature to the cat in the form of a psychological weapon with which to frighten its enemies. With all its fur fluffed up and its back arched, a small cat, spitting and growling, can look like a most formidable foe.

The skin also contains the sweat glands. There are sweat glands in the pads of the cat's feet but it's doubtful how much these glands have to do with regulating the temperature of the body. Together with the sweat glands in the skin, however, they help in the elimination of impurities.

More common than the sweat glands are the sebaceous glands of the skin. Most of these glands open into the hair follicles. Their secretion, a substance called *sebum,* an oily, semiliquid material which solidifies when it is exposed to air, coats the hair as it grows up and through and out of the skin. Around the follicles are also other cells, called *melanoblasts,* which are believed to produce melanins, the substances of which pigment is composed. Granules of pigment are deposited in the follicles as the hair grows, and the color of the coat reflects the activities of these cells in the skin.

One of the most remarkable qualities of the cat's skin is its speed in regeneration and its ability, as the cat's first line of resistance, to fight off infection caused by a wound.

THE SKELETON

Man may be roughly fifteen times the size of the cat, but he has fewer bones. To be precise, the cat has 230 bones in its skeleton, while man has only 206. Their distribution is different, too. The cat has thirteen ribs; man has twelve. Both have several cervical vertebrae. The cat has thirteen thoracic vertebrae, one more than man, and seven lumbar vertebrae, two more than man. But man has five sacral vertebrae, compared with the cat's three. When it comes to the coccygeal vertebrae—the tail—there is, as you might suppose, a considerable difference between cat and man. Man usually has four or five of these vestigial tailbones, while the cat's tailbones can range from none (in the Manx) to twenty-eight; most cats have between eighteen and twenty-three.

Nevertheless, if you stood the skeleton of a cat on its back legs so that it was erect, like a man, you'd find almost a bone-for-bone identity with man. Many of the bones have been modified in the cat to adapt to its special needs, but they are still essentially the same bones. These modifications can cause important distinctions between cat and man. To get back to the question that arose earlier, why *can't* you touch your tongue to your back like a cat, assuming, of course, that you wanted to do it?

There are two basic reasons for the cat's incredible flexibility of body. First, the shoulder joint is free and relatively open, permitting the cat to turn its foreleg in almost any direction without undue strain. Second, the clavicle (collarbone) is very small in comparison with man's; many cats have no clavicle at all.

All the bones are manipulated by more than five hundred voluntary skeletal muscles, which can twist the cat into some amazing shapes when it so desires. One of the few useful physiological features which the cat does not possess—and man does—is the thumb. You can feel the cat's equivalent of the thumb on the inside of the leg near the point where it meets the foot. The claw is there, but the bone that would be the thumb has never properly developed.

The feet and claws of a cat deserve some attention. One notable fact is that the cat walks on its toes. The part of the foot which includes the palm, instep, heel, and ankle in man forms the lowest part of the leg in the cat.

Polydactylism—extra toes—is frequently encountered in the cat, because it is a hereditary trait carried by a dominant gene. Usually it takes the form of six toes on each front foot, but sometimes the cat will have seven toes on the front feet, six on the hind feet.

The claws are, as everyone who has ever played with a cat

knows full well, retractile; that is, the cat can withdraw them into their sheaths or slip them out at will. Usually the claws are sheathed when the cat walks, unless it is a slippery surface.

There is still another unusual aspect of the cat's skeleton and moving structure. The cat does not run like the dog or the horse or most other animals. When those other animals walk or run, the left front leg moves when the left hindleg moves. The cat, however, moves the front and back legs on the other side. Only two other animals move like this—the camel and the giraffe.

THE NERVOUS SYSTEM

The brain and central nervous system of the cat are very much like the dog's, but somewhat different from man's. In all three, the brain is divided into the cerebrum, the front part, and the cerebellum, the lower part.

The cerebrum, which is the seat of conscious, deliberate, rational actions, is smaller in the cat and the dog than in man. This does not mean that the cat is not intelligent—on the contrary, it is a highly rational creature.

The cerebellum, which is the seat of instinct, unconscious memory, and reflex actions, is as highly developed in cats as in dogs. Scratch your cat on its back just in front of its tail, and it will automatically arch its tail and lift its hindquarters; this involuntary action is directed by the cerebellum. Many veterinarians, when they are anesthetizing a cat, will test the level of the cat's consciousness and its sensitivity by tugging gently on the hair that grows between the pads on the bottom of the foot. If the cat pulls up its foot instantly in a reflex action, the cerebellum is still functioning and deep anesthesia has not yet been achieved.

The nervous system is designed to make the cat one of the most alert and perceptive animals on earth. For example, the *vibrissae,* the stiff whiskers growing out from the sides of the muzzle, are sensory organs. They have very acute nerves at their root, which transmit messages to the brain. Thus the cat, blindfolded in tests, can put its front feet firmly on a table if only its whiskers have touched the table's edge. The whiskers are important to the cat in getting about at night, as we shall see (below) when we begin considering the cat's eyes.

THE DIGESTIVE SYSTEM

The cat's organs of digestion are very much the same as man's: mouth, esophagus, stomach, duodenum, small intestine, large intestine, rectum. But the processes that take place in those organs differ a good deal from the activities that take place in the human digestive system.

The difference begins in the mouth, where digestion starts. It is far more important to man than to the cat, for food remains in the man's mouth longer. A cat tears off a piece of meat, chews it very briefly, and swallows it. The salivary juices have only a little time to work on the food. The salivary juices in a cat's mouth also differ from those in a man's. There is a good deal of *ptyalin,* an enzyme which helps to break down starches into blood sugar, in the human mouth, but scarcely any in the cat's. This means that starches are relatively untouched by the digestive process in the cat until they reach the small intestine—and food doesn't remain there very long.

The stomach juices in the cat are a great deal stronger than those in a human stomach. They are so strong, in fact, that in an hour they can break down hard bone to a soft, pliable state like cartilage. This does not mean that it's all right to feed bones to your cat. It isn't.

The cat's stomach is surprisingly sensitive, which is good for the cat. If the cat eats a mouse, it will retain the nutritive parts of the rodent and regurgitate the hair, bones, and nails. It will also regurgitate most foods that it has difficulty digesting.

One curse of man's digestive tract also bedevils the cat—ulcers. The cat can, and not infrequently does, develop ulcers in the stomach, duodenum, or small intestine, which may be considered another proof of what an intelligent, highly developed animal it is.

THE MOUTH AND TEETH

The cat has thirty teeth as an adult, while the human has thirty-two. The teeth bear the same names as those given to human teeth: incisors (the shearing teeth at the front), canines (the fangs), premolars, and molars.

The kitten's full set of teeth looks like this:

Upper jaw: six incisors, two canines, six molars
Lower jaw: six incisors, two canines, four molars

The adult cat's full set is arranged as follows:

Upper jaw: six incisors, two canines, six premolars, two molars
Lower jaw: six incisors, two canines, four premolars, two molars

The teething process in kittens and the problems involved are discussed in Chapter 6. Dental problems in the adult cat are dealt with in Chapter 7.

Cleft lips and cleft palates occur occasionally in cats. Sometimes surgery can remedy the condition, but it is usually better to let the kitten be put to sleep.

Lacking the sphincter muscle of the mouth which the human possesses, the cat can use its lips only to keep food and liquids in its mouth. Fortunately for us, it can't make faces with its lips.

The tongue's upper surface is a rasping tool. It is covered with minute hooks of four different shapes. With this rough tongue, the cat is admirably equipped to lick every last trace of meat off a bone and to brush its coat spotlessly clean. (Thanks to its flexible body, as we have seen, the cat can reach with its tongue all of its body except the back of the neck and the small area between the shoulder blades.) The tongue is also used as a spoon with which to lap up liquids.

As the owners of some cats know, the tongue may also be used to express affection. One of the cats that shares my home with me "kisses" with her rough, little tongue very frequently.

THE EYES, EARS, AND NOSE

The eyes of the cat are so spectacular that they have lent themselves to gems, folklore, and demonology.

Superficially the eyes are very much like man's. There are a couple of minor differences, however. One is the nictitating membrane, the "third eyelid," in the lower part of the eye. This helps to protect the eye. It may also be a diagnostic aid to the veterinarian, for it sometimes will partly cover the iris if the cat is suffering from an intestinal disorder. (Nobody knows why.) Another obvious difference is the iridescent layer of cells, called the *tapetum lucidum,* on the retina. These cells reflect light, which is why a cat's eyes shine at night.

The eyes not uncommonly are unmatched in color. What the cat sees through those eyes has been a matter of dispute until recently. The great majority of scientists held that cats are color-blind, and that they live in a gray world. But recently it has been discovered that their retinas contain rods and cones, which are essential to color vision. This discovery has led to experiments which tend to confirm that cats, unlike dogs, do see colors.

One of the hardiest myths about the cat is the belief that it can see in the dark. If by "dark" we mean total darkness, there is no truth to this. It is true, however, that the cat does see much better at night than man does. After all, the cat is basically a nocturnal animal. Visual purple in the epithelial rods of the retina is said to be the reason for the cat's excellent night vision. The cat can even see ultraviolet rays and other light invisible to us.

To compensate for its night vision, perhaps, the cat has been denied day vision on a par with ours. It sees better at dusk than at noon on a bright, sunny day. The ability of the cat's pupil to contract and expand in order to accommodate the amount of light available explains why the eye looks different every time we see it. In darkness, the pupil is at its widest to admit every possible bit of illumination. In bright sunlight, it is narrowed to a thin slit to cut down on the light pouring into the eye. It is an old folk belief, all over the world, that one can tell the time of day by the shape of the cat's pupil. You can test this yourself and see the falsity of it.

The ear of the cat is extremely sensitive to sound. Cats can distinguish even between the sounds of several motors of the same make, if one of them is in a car belonging to the cat's owner. Like dogs, cats can hear many sounds that are inaudible to the human ear. Research has indicated that the cat may be able to hear sounds that are even beyond the range of a dog's ear. The dog's range is believed to be close to twenty-five thousand cycles a second, compared with fifteen thousand for the human.

Like many breeds of dog, the cat has a naturally erect ear that helps to catch sound in the same way that a parabola microphone does.

Inside the cat's ear, however, is something quite different from the interior of the dog's ear. What that difference is, nobody has yet been able to discover. But we know it exists. For the cat, unlike man and the dog, is highly resistant to motion sickness, that is, car sickness or seasickness. Motion sickness is intimately associated with the sense of balance; this, in turn, is dependent on the membranous labyrinth found in the internal ear. When the labyrinth is removed surgically from both ears, a dog is no longer liable to motion sickness. Why is the cat virtually immune to motion sickness, although it has the labyrinth intact? At this moment, no one knows.

The nose, cold and moist in a healthy cat (unless the cat has been sleeping), is the smallest part of the cat's olfactory system. The internal organs of scent are much larger than one might expect for such a small animal. The size of those organs, in fact, tells us that the cat, myths to the contrary, has a very keen sense of smell. All the other animals with sensitive noses have large internal scent organs.

From a considerable distance a cat can distinguish by scent the sex of another cat. This causes a good deal of confusion when a whole cat catches the scent of a neutered cat. It just doesn't smell right. This may explain why neutered and whole cats almost inevitably fight when they are loose and encounter each other.

Most of the odors we dislike the cat dislikes, too, for it is not a carrion eater, as the dog is. On the other hand, cats are very fond of perfume, hand lotion, and eau de Cologne.

The delight of cats with catnip is well known. If you grow catnip in your backyard, you can expect to have the neighborhood cats visiting you often. Diluted oil of catnip has been used with considerable success as a lure of bobcats and pumas. A small glass jar with the solution in it, capped by a perforated lid, will still draw the wild cats six to ten months after it has been buried in the ground with only the cap exposed, according to Stanley P. Young of the Fish and Wildlife Service of the United States Department of the Interior. How the catnip affects the cat internally is still a matter of conjecture. But give the cat a few leaves of catnip, and it will behave in a weird and wonderful fashion—

purring, growling, rolling on its back, play-fighting, rubbing itself against the mint, and carrying on generally in what can only
be described as an orgiastic manner. It is almost certain that
catnip—or cat mint, as it is also called—excites the cat sexually. It
is also believed to have a soothing effect on its nervous system.
(Those two effects of catnip might seem to be contradictory, but
that's what the scientists say.)

There are other scents pleasing to the cat. Among them are
valerian, lavender, violet, patchouli, wallflower, bean, some
roses, and silver vine.

THE VOICE

No animal on earth except man is as capable of expressing itself
as the cat. The basic element in its voice is the vocal cords. These
are the superior (false) vocal cords and the inferior (true) vocal
cords.

The way in which the cords are used by the cat is still not understood. It has been theorized that the cat's various calls are
produced by the true vocal cords. On the other hand, the mech-
anism by which purring occurs is more puzzling. Some investiga-
tors believe that the purr is produced by the false vocal cords.
Others think the purr is created by vibrations in the wall of an
important blood vessel in the chest, with the sound then being
transmitted through the air passages. Neither explanation would
provide a basis for understanding why only the members of the
cat family purr.

There are many different purring sounds that every cat can
make. One purr means contentment, affection. Another purr,
harsher and deeper, means pain. There are many messages in
purrs.

All cats purr, although the purring of some is inaudible. However, even with those cats one can feel the vibration by touching
the cat's throat. Sometimes a cat that has been purring audibly
becomes silent and, conversely, a cat that has been purring inau-
dibly suddenly begins to fill the room with sound.

Kittens begin to purr when they are about a week old. From
then on they're likely to purr whenever they want to express
their state of mind. Some cats will even purr when they are in a

light sleep. The ultimate expression of happiness on the part of many cats is to purr deeply and drool a few drops of saliva at the same time. Young cats purr in a monotone, but older cats usually purr on two and sometimes even three notes.

The cat's calls are more varied than its purrs. Many persons have found, upon study, that the cat has more than thirty different calls, and some have counted as many as one hundred. There is the meow of greeting to the humans, a different meow of hunger, a welcome meow that sounds like a chirp, a meow of threat to another cat, and so on. The growls are almost as varied. And there are spitting sounds, hisses, and screams. There is the caterwauling of the mating time and the caterwauling that is simply a serenade to the moon.

The cat even has physical means of expressing its feelings. Its tail is the most eloquent. Gently waving, it tells of the cat's quiet pleasure. Whipping from side to side, it expresses annoyance. Held out stiffly behind, it indicates the threat of imminent attack. When the cat holds its tail vertically in the air, possibly with a crook at the very tip, it is expressing a benign sense that all's well with the world.

The paws are often used to express love. This is the meaning of the "kneading" action that sometimes puzzles new cat owners. The cat stands on its owner's lap or even on a bed or a pile of clothes and works its fore paws with great determination, as though it were kneading bread dough. It looks a little as though the cat were playing an imaginary piano. This is an infallible sign that the cat is happy and bursting with affection. I believe that the action is a carry over from infancy, for the kitten, when nursing, employs the same kneading motion on both sides of the teat.

Each cat has its own language. One must listen to its voice and watch its expressive tail to interpret what it is saying.

INTELLIGENCE

Webster's New World Dictionary defines "intelligence" in these terms:

> 1. The ability to learn or understand from experience; ability to acquire and retain knowledge; mental ability.

THE NATURE OF THE CAT

2. The ability to respond quickly and successfully to a new situation; use of the faculty of reason in solving problems, directing conduct, etc., effectively.

3. In psychology, measured success in using these abilities to perform certain tasks.

The cat meets every one of these criteria superbly. No one who has ever played a teasing game with a cat, watched a cat figuring out how to open a cupboard, or had a cat patiently make clear that its litter box needed changing could ever doubt how powerful is its reasoning power.

The question of whether cats are more intelligent than dogs has often led to hot disputes between dog and cat fanciers. Cat lovers, as one might expect, insist that their pets are smarter (and more affectionate in their own way) than dogs, and they have a supporter in Dr. James B. Allison, who dealt with cats for years as director of the Bureau of Biological Research at Rutgers University. He pointed, for example, to the cats' cleverness in discovering how to open cages closed with a hasp and bolt. By lifting the bolt on its chain out of the hasp, the cats could open the door of their cages and escape. This clearly took a high degree of reasoning.

Some people judge animals on the basis of their ability to learn tricks. Cats can learn tricks, but it is much more difficult to teach a cat to do tricks than to train a dog. Does this indicate less intelligence? I don't think so. A cat is quick to learn anything that concerns its own welfare. It doesn't learn tricks as easily as a dog simply because it is not as docile or as eager to please. It is too independent and self-reliant for that.

But cats do learn what interests them. In Long Beach, California, there was a firehouse cat that was the first to slide down the pole when the bells began to clang. Other cats have learned, without being taught, how to ring doorbells to gain admittance or to bang knockers. Most cat owners have seen their own pets trying to open a door by grabbing the doorknob, which surely shows that the cat has reasoned out the connection between the doorknob and the opening and closing of the door. Ida Mellen has written of a cat in a family with one blind member. If the cat wanted to go into the house while any other member of the family was on the porch, it simply went to the door and waited. But if only the blind person was on the porch, the cat would jump on him to let him know what it wanted.

LONGEVITY

Cats live longer, on the average, than dogs. The typical lifespan of the cat used to be about twelve to fourteen years. But the advances in veterinary medicine have had the same effect on the life expectancy of the cat that human medical progress has had on man. Today the typical cat, properly cared for, probably has a life expectancy of about seventeen years or more, but this is affected by many factors. Diet is important, as is health care; trips should be made to the veterinarian whenever any serious illness appears.

The most important question of all in determining how long a cat will live is whether it is permitted to roam freely or is confined to the house. A cat that roams at will usually has a much shorter life than its indoor friends. Sooner or later the law of averages in this automobile age catches up with it. That is the reason so many people train their cats to use a litter box rather than let them out to relieve themselves. Today, one rarely hears about putting the cat out at night.

Some amazing records for longevity have been established by well-cared-for cats. A Los Angeles cat was well into its thirty-fourth year when it died. A South African cat lived to the age of thirty-one, and so did at least one California cat and another in Canada. A Connecticut cat lived to be twenty-eight. There have been a goodly number of cats who have lived within a year or two of that mark. (Several of my own cats have lived to their late teens and been healthy and spry in their late years.)

It is impossible to compare the cat's lifespan with man's. One proposed comparison held that a cat of one year was the equivalent of a child of three years and four months. But a year-old cat is an adult animal; it has probably already reproduced, if it is a stray, and it is certainly able to take care of itself. A three-year-old child, on the other hand, is still a helpless infant.

5. NUTRITION AND FEEDING

A great deal of nonsense is spoken and written about cats, and this is true above all in the area of nutrition and feeding. We are told that all cats love milk; that they should never be fed starch or vegetables; that fat is bad for them; that bones do them no harm. Perhaps the silliest thing that is said about the cat is that it will, given the opportunity, instinctively choose a balanced and sensible diet. It won't. Most cats will choose sugar, white bread, spaghetti sauce, or some other unlikely treat, often preferring such delicacies to fresh red meat.

Yet meat is the basic food of the cat, which is a carnivore. Its natural prey includes many small animals, such as the rabbit, which are herbivorous. In eating these animals, the cat consumes everything: muscle meat, internal organs, the half-digested vegetable contents of the digestive system. In this way the cat's overall nutritional requirements are met.

But the cat that is not feral develops tastes for foods unavailable to cats that have to kill their own game. It is the responsibility of the owner to see that the cat gets the proper kind of diet, a balanced diet that will meet all of its needs.

For many years that was easier said than done, for comparatively little research had been carried out on the nutritional requirements of the cat, compared with the enormous amount of information available on the dog. In the early 1960s, however, an increasing number of scientists began to take an interest in this area of research. The Committee on Animal Nutrition, National Academy of Sciences–National Research Council, periodically publishes a report entitled *Nutrient Requirements of Laboratory*

Animals. This chapter is based, to a large extent, on that publication and on an excellent article by Jane Heenan which appeared in *Consumer,* a publication of the Food and Drug Administration, summing up the current knowledge of nutritional needs of cats and dogs. I have made use of additional information provided by Drs. Patricia P. Scott, A. Carvalho da Silva, and Marny A. Lloyd-Jacob in *The UFAW Handbook on the Care and Management of Laboratory Animals,* published by the Universities Federation for Animal Welfare of Great Britain and distributed in the United States by the Animal Welfare Institute. I have also consulted research reports in American veterinary journals.

PROTEINS, FATS, CARBOHYDRATES

Man requires five major elements in his food: proteins, fats, carbohydrates, minerals, and vitamins. The cat needs all of these with the possible exception of carbohydrates. The need for carbohydrates has not been demonstrated, which does not mean that the need doesn't exist; it just means that we don't know. In case such a need does exist, it may be just as well to provide some carbohydrates in your cat's diet, in addition to proteins and fats.

Proteins exist in a number of forms. Each kind of protein is a combination of several of the many amino acids. When proteins are taken in through the digestive system, they are broken down into their constituent amino acids, which are then reassembled in the form of new protein. Surplus amino acids are burned as energy.

Fats are broken down in the body into fatty acids and glycogen. The body then transforms glycogen into glucose, a body fuel. The fatty acids are changed into body fats. (Generally the same course is taken by carbohydrates in man, but in a more roundabout way.)

"Most cat nutritionists favor high-fat, high-protein diets for cats," government researchers found. "Purified diets containing twenty-five to thirty per cent fat and thirty-four to forty per cent protein were commonly used. These high-fat rations appear to be more palatable than low-fat diets."

The cat's requirements of proteins and fats are much higher than those of the dog. Over 30 percent of the diet must be protein, for example, if a kitten is to grow properly; the best results are obtained when the protein content reaches 40 percent. Cat-show exhibitors should be especially interested in one finding reported in England: cats which were "maintained for three months exclusively on lean beef muscle had an extremely good appearance and especially soft fur." On the other hand, a high-fat diet apparently enables the cat to absorb vitamin A more efficiently than it can with a low-fat intake. "This suggests that many low-fat commercial cat foods may supply inadequate vitamin A," according to the researchers. Cats maintained on the high-fat diet were found to accumulate a small amount of fat around the liver, unlike cats fed low-fat diets. Whether the liver fat is harmful has not been determined.

MINERALS

All animals need minerals—calcium and phosphorus to build teeth and bones; iron, copper, and cobalt to produce healthy blood; other elements for the development and maintenance of all the nerves, muscles, and organs of the body. The exact amounts of these minerals needed by the cat have not been determined. Until we know otherwise, it must be assumed that the cat needs reasonable quantities of the minerals, in roughly the same proportion, say, as man and the dog.

The effect of mineral deficiencies has been studied. It was found that kittens fed only raw or cooked heart—a diet particularly deficient in calcium and iodine—showed undesirable effects after seven weeks. These effects included nervousness, inability to coordinate, and finally paralysis of the hindlegs. The bones softened and then collapsed, causing the paralysis. The thyroid was affected and so were the kidneys. When calcium was added to heart in the diet of kittens, the bones did not soften and the thyroid was not affected as it had been. Adding iodine strengthened the thyroid and delayed the weakening of the bones.

A unique problem in considering the cat's mineral needs is the unusual susceptibility of the cat to kidney and bladder stones. There has often been speculation that high-mineral diets might be a factor in this. But several nutritionists were unable to cause urinary stones in kittens even with diets containing as much as 30 percent minerals.

VITAMINS

Vitamins are accessory organic substances that are needed for metabolism. They are essential to life and growth. The cat's needs for these vitamins are not necessarily the same as man's.

Vitamin A: The human body manufactures this vitamin mostly from carotene, but the cat does not, at least not in important quantities. Cats whose diet is deficient in vitamin A lose their appetites and become emaciated. Some show weakness of the hind-legs with signs of stiffness. There are scaly changes in the tissues of several of the organs. The lungs and eyes often become inflamed. The teeth are affected adversely. The hearing and the nervous system are impaired. Acute deficiencies of vitamin A usually result in death.

Fat in the diet helps the cat to utilize fat-soluble vitamin A, so it is important that there be enough fat in the cat's food.

Niacin: This is the anti-pellagra factor in the vitamin B complex. A lack of it in cats results in a feline disease resembling pellagra. The cat suffers diarrhea, emaciation, and death. Often a respiratory disease precedes death. Of forty-five cats used in one experiment, not one lived more than twenty days on a diet without niacin.

Folic acid: This is another vitamin B complex factor. Absence of this vitamin from the cat's body causes anemia and a sharp drop in white corpuscles.

Choline: Also lumped in the B complex, this vitamin is important to cats. The lack of it causes weight loss and fatty livers.

Thiamine (B_1): A cat whose diet provides an insufficient amount of thiamine may suffer from loss of appetite, vomiting, inability to coordinate, abnormal reflexes, convulsions, and heart disorders. One team of researchers found that cats fed raw carp or herring ultimately displayed a thiamine deficiency, but cats fed raw perch, catfish, and butterfish did not.

Riboflavin (B_2): Cats suffering from the lack of this vitamin lose their appetites, fade away to skin and bones, and finally die. The hair, particularly around the head, sometimes falls out. Cataracts have been observed in chronically deficient cats. Impaired nerve function, digestive disturbance, anemia, sore mouth, poor litters, and inadequate nursing of kittens have also been reported as results of riboflavin deficiencies.

If the cat's diet is high in carbohydrates, its need for riboflavin is slightly lessened. The reason for this, it appears, is that more riboflavin is manufactured in the cat's intestines when the intake of carbohydrates is high.

Pyridoxine (B₆): The deficiency of this vitamin in cats is characterized by stunted growth, emaciation, convulsions (the nervous system is affected), anemia, kidney disease, and deposits of iron in the liver.

Ascorbic acid (C): The need for vitamin C in cats has not been established.

Vitamin D: Rickets, as one might suppose, is the result of a lack of vitamin D in cats, just as in man. However, rickets is quite uncommon in kittens; when it does appear, it usually afflicts kittens born in winter, kept in the dark most of the time, or born to dams whose diets lacked vitamin D. This vitamin, which is essential to the utilization of calcium and phosphorus in forming teeth and bones, is especially needed by the pregnant queen and the growing kitten. The requirement of vitamin D for cats over a year and a half old, however, is believed to be quite low. This cautionary note must be added: There is a real hazard of making the cat sick by overdosing it with vitamin D.

Vitamin E: One effect of an insufficient supply of vitamin E may be steatitis. This disease is most likely to occur in cats which have been consuming a diet high in polyunsaturated fatty acids, particularly from marine fish oils. Steatitis is not only an extremely painful disease in cats; it may also be fatal. (See a discussion of this in the section on commercial foods later in this chapter.) Vitamin E deficiency also can cause lost litters, sickly kittens, and a drop in the red blood cells.

Vitamin K: The need of the cat for this vitamin has not been determined.

Pantothenic acid: Loss of weight and fatty livers are among the ill effects that follow upon an inadequate supply of this vitamin.

CALORIES AND ENERGY

A kitten's caloric requirements are, proportionately, a great deal higher than an adult cat's. The kitten must burn up enormous amounts of energy just producing all the cells that enable it to grow. On top of that, kittens usually play harder than grown-up, sensible cats. It has been noted that a growing cat consumes about 80 calories per pound of body weight every day. Around the time that kittens are weaned, they need about 125 calories a day per pound of body weight. This drops off as the kitten grows. By the time it is thirty weeks old—about seven or eight months—the kitten needs only about 65 calories per pound of body weight per day.

The adult cat's caloric requirements depend on the kind of life it leads, just as with humans. They also depend on the weather, to some extent, particularly with cats that are permitted out of the house to roam. From the time it is a year old, the cat that goes out for its exercise, chases rabbits, is chased by dogs, and climbs into trees (for firemen to rescue) needs 40 to 45 calories per pound of body weight every day.

Dr. Mark L. Morris, a well-known specialist in animal nutrition, has found that temperature changes, on the average, affect the amount of food consumption by 46 percent. Outdoor cats tend to eat a good deal more heavily at the onset of cold weather in the fall and gain extra weight. However, the food consumption tapers off even though the weather remains cold. The reverse of this process takes place in the spring.

The sedentary cat—and that includes most pet cats, living wholly in apartments or houses, sleeping a considerable portion of the day, playing only briefly, exercising hardly at all—needs substantially fewer calories, in the neighborhood of 30 calories a day per pound of body weight.

Obesity is less common in cats than in dogs, and far less than in man. The average female cat's weight is between six and ten pounds; the average male's, eight to fifteen. (There are authentic records of cats that have weighed as much as thirty-five pounds.) Obviously, the simplest way to bring down a cat's weight is to cut down its food supply. Unlike its master or mistress, the cat can't sneak fattening treats that aren't on its diet, so a weight-reducing diet almost always is effective. If your cat is sedentary and weighs fifteen pounds, and you want to get its weight down to about ten pounds, figure the number of calories it would require to sustain itself at the ten-pound level and make that the daily ration. It may also be helpful to add vitamin B complex as a supplement to the diet.

A note of caution: Before putting your cat on a reducing diet, consult with your veterinarian and carefully observe your cat's eating habits. Its obesity could be the result of a glandular imbalance. One of my own cats eats very little but weighs more than twice as much as another of my cats that is a big eater.

COOKED OR UNCOOKED?

There are few arguments concerning cat care that can arouse greater passions on the part of some fanciers than the question of whether the cat's food should be cooked or uncooked.

There are some foods, of course, that everyone agrees must be cooked—pork, for one, because the muscle worms that cause trichinosis in man can also kill the cat. It's generally agreed that fish should be cooked, too. But after that, the arguments begin.

The National Research Council's survey of technical knowledge about cat nutrition examined two studies of the comparative values of cooked and uncooked foods. The survey summarized the reports of these experiments: "Consistently better growth, development, reproduction, and lactation were obtained when raw meat and milk were fed to cats than when they received cooked meat and milk." Moreover, once the "deficiency state" resulting from the cooked diet "was produced in kittens, it could not be reversed. When deficient adult cats were returned to a raw diet, normal animals were not produced for several generations."

Now, these results must be viewed with a great deal of caution. The diet itself—meat and milk—was something less than ideal. How would those cats have managed on a good canned cat food or dog food? Would vitamin-mineral supplements have had any material effect on the results? Until those questions are answered, it is best to consider this whole matter of cooking like this: If you are feeding your cat fresh meat, let it be raw. If you are feeding the cat a canned (which means cooked) food or some other precooked food, make sure it meets all the nutritional requirements listed above.

MEAT

Beef: Excellent. The best for the cat is muscle meat. Feed it in small chunks or ground. Once a week the muscle meat may be varied with organ meats: "lights" (lungs), heart, tripe, kidneys, or liver. Some veterinarians insist the liver should be cooked.

Horsemeat: Good, but fat must be added, for horsemeat is much too lean.

Veal: Many cats prefer this to beef. Either the muscle meat or the organs will do nicely.

Lamb: It is too expensive to serve your cat the chops, unless you are an unusually generous master or mistress, but the kidneys are very good and they are a convenient size for purchasing. Cut up in one-inch cubes, lamb kidneys are an almost sure-fire cure for a jaded feline appetite.

Pork: Trimmed of fat, ground, and well cooked, pork may make a pleasant change of diet for the cat.

FISH AND CHICKEN

Fish once a week is a treat and it's good for the cat. It must be cooked, preferably steamed to retain as many of the nutrients as possible. And it must be carefully boned. Even canned fish that's labeled "boneless" sometimes has wicked little spears in it, so be careful. Shellfish are perfectly acceptable, too, but an extravagance; the cat will appreciate mackerel just as much.

Chicken is good for the cat and most cats love it. (Turkey, too.) Be sure it's cooked, however, and that there are no bones to catch in the cat's throat. One more caution: do *not* let the cat have the skin of the chicken or the turkey. The skin is not easily digestible and may irritate the cat's digestive system.

OTHER FOODS

Milk: A great many cats cannot tolerate milk and some of those that can keep it down can't stand the sight of it. One effect that milk has on many cats is cathartic. When milk is given to a cat, it should always be lukewarm.

Cheese: Occasional servings of cream cheese and cottage cheese are approved by many veterinarians. My own cats love all kinds of cheese, but they don't get them for dinner.

Eggs: Ideally, the cat should get the yolk of a one-minute boiled egg twice a week or more often. It can be mixed with milk or with the cat's other food. Many cats will also tolerate raw egg yolk. But *raw egg white should never be fed to cats, because it destroys biotin, an essential nutrient.*

Vegetables: Green vegetables, in small quantities, are good for the cat. They can be cooked or raw. If you want to give the cat a treat, get some oat seeds and plant them in a flower box in a sunny corner of the kitchen. The cat will be delighted at the opportunity to eat the green, growing grass. But it won't keep the cat away from your philodendrons, unfortunately.

Potatoes: It has long been an article of faith with many cat lovers that no cat should ever be fed any starch, particularly potatoes. The theory was that the cat couldn't digest starch. It can be digested, however, provided it is broken in texture before it is ingested. This means the potatoes should be cooked and mashed. Cooked, mashed potatoes were an important part of one of the experimental diets cited by the National Research Council.

Water: The cat needs water to drink. Some owners who give their cats milk think water is unnecessary. They're wrong; milk is a food and is not a substitute for water. A dish of clean, fresh water should be on the floor, available to the cat, at all times.

COMMERCIAL CAT FOODS

There is a great variety of cat food available in pet shops, supermarkets, and—in the form of special-diet preparations—veterinarians' offices. Today pet foods outsell baby foods in grocery stores throughout the country. Most of this merchandise is of excellent quality (which doesn't necessarily mean it's the best thing for your cat*) and it is carefully prepared in order to give your cat most of the substances it needs in its diet.

---

* In the September 1972 issue, *Consumer Reports* carried an article on cat-food tests conducted by Consumers Union. It found only five of twenty-two brands tested "Acceptable." Some of the cat foods fed to the test kittens were so lacking in essential nutrients, apparently, that some kittens died during the experiments, although precautions had been taken to prevent such deaths. Post-mortem examination of the kittens that died showed the cause of death, in each instance, to be malnutrition. Any cat owner would be well advised to read that issue of *Consumer Reports.*

Can you simply open a can of cat food, give it to your pet, and know that it is getting the nutrients it needs? The National Research Council survey answered that question with these words: "Much of the commercial cat food is nutritionally inadequate and must be supplemented with other foods." It will be noted that *all* commercial cat foods are not lumped in the "inadequate" category; it can be assumed that some prepared foods are properly nutritious.

The cat owner should study carefully the labels on available foods, which list ingredients and an analysis of the contents. The ingredients and the analysis should be compared with the requirements listed in this chapter. In general, the cat owner is well advised to alternate a carefully chosen canned food, for cats or for dogs, with fresh meat.

The dry-food question: One of the continuing controversies in the area of pet nutrition concerns the relative merits of dry versus canned foods. Dry foods offer a certain convenience to pet owners, but there is a still unresolved question as to whether the usually higher ash content of dry foods (often about 8 to 10 percent, as opposed to percentages as low as 3 percent for canned foods—read the labels) plays a part in causing cystitis, a very common malady of cats. On this issue of dry versus canned, the FDA's *Consumer* magazine article said: "For cats, canned food is traditionally preferred—by both owner and cat. One reason that has been offered is that cats have always chosen to obtain most of their water supply from the food they eat and have, therefore, never been known as 'heavy drinkers.' Some scientists suspect cats may do better on moist food, although this has not been conclusively proved." (Like most generalizations, that statement about cats not being heavy drinkers of water should be taken with a good deal of skepticism. I have had cats that drank more than my dogs.)

The canned fish problem: Another unresolved conflict exists among scientists regarding the dangers of canned fish as the exclusive element in a cat's diet. Until this matter is resolved to everyone's satisfaction, cat owners ought to exercise extreme caution in feeding canned fish to their pets. This is particularly important because several cat foods make a point of advertising that they are all fish.

There have been six reports from research teams that cats fed exclusively or almost exclusively on canned cat food consisting entirely of fish contracted a disease called *steatitis*. In most—but not all—of these cases, the fish was red meat tuna. (Because other fish packs were involved, however, the findings ought to be applied to any all-fish cat foods.)

Steatitis is an agonizingly painful disease. The fatty layer just under the skin becomes inflamed; the cat displays "exquisite tenderness," as *The Merck Veterinary Manual* puts it, "manifested by resentment" when it is touched on the back or the abdomen. The animal loses its agility; it is reluctant to move at all. The cat becomes feverish and loses its appetite. As the disease progresses, the lightest touch is enough to make the cat cry out with pain. The disease often ends in death.

Why canned all-fish cat food causes steatitis is still not definitely known. When the association of the food with the disease was first observed, it was believed that absence of vitamin E from the diet was responsible. Almost all the companies packing all-fish cat foods quickly enriched the food with alphatocopherol, one of four forms of vitamin E, and slapped "added vitamin E" labels on the cans. But a team of researchers at Angell Memorial Animal Hospital in Boston then reported on eight more cases of steatitis traceable to canned all-fish cat food, and four of these had been fed from cans labeled "added vitamin E."

It seemed that the addition of vitamin E was not the answer—at least, not the entire answer—to the problem. Then Danish scientists, studying the same disease in minks, came to the conclusion that "yellow fat," as steatitis is sometimes called, "is primarily due to the contents of marine fat in the feed." They decided that "the most satisfactory method of preventing 'yellow fat' . . . is control of the fat composition in feeds, so that the content of marine fat does not exceed three to four per cent."

The picture is still unclear, for a new report from an American source says that cats in its experiments were completely protected against steatitis by the addition of vitamin E to a fish diet.

As an additional complication, Dr. Morris, in his manual on *Nutrition and Diet in Small Animal Medicine,* warns: "The possibility of alphatocopherol containing a toxic factor for cats should be considered. In the preparation of experimental rations for cats, we added excessive amounts of alphatocopherol to the diet. This substance was very unpalatable to cats and the animals would actually starve unless alphatocopherol was removed or added at a much reduced level."

This raises some question as to whether *enough* vitamin E can be added to canned fish to protect the cat.

The only conclusion that can be stated at this time is this: If your cat likes canned all-fish cat food, feed it only such food if it is labeled "added vitamin E." Give the cat this food only once a week. The rest of the time feed it foods that do not include fish.

SUPPLEMENTS

Everything that has been said in this chapter up to this point should make clear that it is not as simple as it might at first appear to ensure your cat a balanced diet with the proper intake of vitamins and minerals. This problem becomes more acute when the cat is sick, pregnant, lactating, or growing.

Nevertheless, some authorities believe it is unnecessary to add extra vitamins or minerals to the diet. They meet disagreement from other experts who think vitamin-mineral supplements make good sense. I'm inclined to agree with the latter group. There is a very slight danger of overdosing the cat, but this is so remote as to be unimportant in our considerations. On the other hand, a vitamin-mineral supplement is a kind of insurance that your cat is getting a sufficient amount of these two essential kinds of nutrients.

However, it is necessary to be cautious about the vitamin-mineral supplement that is used. One of the supplements most popular with pet owners, for example, provides a seriously inadequate supply of pantothenic acid. The formulas should be compared with the table of nutrients on page 126.

Vitamin-mineral supplements for cats come in many forms: drops, capsules, pills, powders, and small pellets designed to be highly palatable to animals. Supplements intended for use by humans can be used, if you prefer.

KITTEN FEEDING

The feeding of kittens under the age of five weeks will be discussed in Chapter 6. Here the subject under consideration will be the kitten from weaning to adulthood.

About the time the kitten is five or six weeks old, it can begin to get its first food as a supplement to the milk it obtains nursing. This early food can be a prepared cereal for human babies or a preparation devised especially for kittens. The latter is preferable; it is much higher in protein than pablum for babies (30 percent as against 15 percent). This is an important point, for kittens grow at a much faster rate than human babies, and so they need a bigger proportion of tissue-building protein. Whichever kind of cereal is used, it should be moistened with warmed milk or with evaporated milk diluted with water.

If the kitten has difficulty taking this food from a spoon at first, stick your finger in the cereal and then let the kitten suck it off your finger as though it were a nipple. Feed this to the kitten three or four times a day, and let it continue to nurse in between.

After a week or two, it's time for the next step in weaning. Now strained meats of the kind prepared for human babies should be added to the diet. These should be warmed, of course—everything fed to the kitten should be warmed.

Scraped meats are added to the diet next, then twice-ground lean meat, finally boneless canned fish, finely broken up. The meals can then look something like this:

Morning: Warmed milk with a barely cooked egg yolk and baby cereal mixed into it. Vitamin-mineral drops.
Forenoon: Strained baby meats mixed with baby cereal.
Noon: Scraped or doubly chopped raw lean meat.
Afternoon: Warmed milk and egg yolk again.
Evening: Baby strained meats or doubly chopped raw lean meat.
Night: Baby strained meats or doubly chopped raw lean meat.

The meals should be cut down to four a day as soon as the kitten begins to show a diminished interest in the frequent feedings. As the baby teeth appear, more solid food can be added: meat softened and cut into tiny cubes, fish carefully boned and mashed, and so on.

In the fourth month, the meals can be reduced to three. After the fourth month, two meals a day should be sufficient.

The average kitten weighs slightly more than three ounces at birth. It can be expected to gain about an ounce every three days until it is seven weeks old; it then weighs about twenty ounces. In the next month it will probably gain another ten ounces. The weight will gradually increase month by month—by ten ounces, then by eleven ounces, by twelve ounces, and so on. The top of the growth curve is reached in the ninth month. Then the monthly gain in weight begins to fall off very gradually for the next five months.

ADULT FEEDING

Many cat owners feed their full-grown pets twice a day. There is nothing wrong in this, but it is unnecessary. Barring unusual conditions, one meal a day is sufficient for almost all cats.

About four to seven ounces of food a day will sustain the average cat very well. In the adult cat the stomach will hold four and a half ounces of food or more. At one feeding the cat can take in quite enough food to keep it comfortably occupied for the next twenty-four hours.

It is a good idea to serve the food in a bowl on the floor with a generous supply of paper under the dish, because cats love to drag morsels of food out of their dish onto the floor, for no reason that I've ever been able to determine.

The food should be put down for the cat at about the same time every day, for cats are creatures of habit and essentially conservative. If the cat hasn't eaten its food within a reasonable time—say, half an hour—and shows no interest in it, take it up. *Never leave food out for the cat!* When food is left out for the cat, it attracts insects, dries out so that it completely unappetizing, and simply bores the poor cat, who gets sick of the sight of it.

Whether the cat needs variety in its food is something that nobody really knows. On general principles, there seems to be no harm in giving the cat a change of dish for a day or two now and then.

Sometimes a cat is a fussy eater. Usually this is because it has not been fed in the proper manner in the past—most often because its food has been left out for it all day. Feeding the cat by hand for a day or two or petting it while it eats may induce it to eat properly, especially if its food is set out for it only for a short time each day. If that doesn't start the cat eating, a meal of diced lamb kidneys will usually stimulate the most listless appetite.

If the cat absolutely refuses to eat anything but food which is not good for it, its proper diet should be set out for it every day nevertheless. When the cat refuses to eat, the food should be taken up. This should be done until the cat eats. The process can be quite a strain on the owner's nerves, for the cat may very well starve itself for a week before surrendering, but surrender it will, in time.

In persistent or recurring cases of inappetence, it is wise to consult your veterinarian. Judicious prescription of vitamins sometimes can help with such problems.

Special diets: There are several companies which manufacture special formulas of canned foods for cats with dietary problems. These foods are available only on prescription from a veterinarian. If he recommends such a food, follow his advice.

Snacks and tidbits: If a cat has been eating its meals properly, there is no reason why it should be denied snacks from time to time. Little treats, specially prepared to be palatable to cats, are available in pet shops and supermarkets. They are the best tidbits your cat can eat.

Other snacks do no harm. My cats all love cheese, for example, and they're all hearty eaters. So, when I have cheese, they have cheese—tiny pieces, of course. They also like a little cake, cookies, bread, meat, chili (terrible thing to give a cat!), curried rice (ditto), and so on.

THE LAST WORD

Remember, above all, that your cat is not the best judge of what it should eat. The National Research Council survey summed it up this way: "Some foods of high acceptability were found to be nutritionally inadequate when used over extended periods."

DAILY FEEDING SCHEDULE

AGE	FROM 5 TO 9 WEEKS	FROM 9 WEEKS TO 4 MONTHS	FROM 4 MONTHS TO 1 YEAR	OVER 1 YEAR
Number of feedings	4	3	2	1 or 2

SATISFACTORY LEVELS OF NUTRIENTS TO MEET THE NUTRITIONAL REQUIREMENTS OF THE GROWING CAT

NUTRIENT	PER POUND OF DIET [1]
Total proteins	4.6 ounces
Minerals	Required
Vitamins	
Vitamin A	Required
Vitamin D	Required
Vitamin E (international units)	(34) [2]
Vitamin K	— [3]
Thiamine	4 milligrams
Riboflavin	(4)
Vitamin B_6	4 milligrams
Niacin	40 milligrams
Pantothenic acid	(5)
Biotin	—
Folic acid	Not required
Choline	—
Vitamin B_{12}	—
Inositol	—

[1] The values that are *not* in parentheses are estimated from various adequate rations, hence are probably in excess of the actual requirement.

The values in parentheses are tentative estimates of the minimal requirements and contain no margins of safety.

[2] Not satisfactory if excessive dietary source of polyunsaturated fatty acids is fed.

[3] No information is available on a qualitative requirement.

6. THE KITTEN

Even cat haters often like kittens. It would be a cold heart indeed that could resist one of these fluffy, playful, pretty, coy, silly, and utterly charming little creatures.

Sometimes kittens are too attractive for their own good. A person who doesn't like cats may be so taken by a kitten that he'll take it into his home, only to abandon it when it grows into a cat.

Presumably, a person capable of this kind of callousness would not be reading this book, however, so it can be taken for granted that your kitten will grow into a cat. How healthy, happy, and congenial a cat may depend to a considerable extent on the care you give it as a kitten.

Regardless of its age, the kitten's first and most urgent need is for love. It's a baby which has just left its warm mother and its brothers and sisters. It has probably been enclosed in a box or a carrying case for the first, frightening time in its young life. Chances are that it has had its first automobile ride. It is suddenly in the midst of strange, new surroundings.

You can't set the kitten down and then walk off and leave it to its own devices. What the kitten needs at this stage is a warm lap, caressing hands, and soft, reassuring voices. Then, as it begins to show an interest in its surroundings, it can be introduced to all the humans in the house. It can be permitted to explore its new home.

If the kitten's had a long, as well as an exciting, day, it may prefer, as most babies would, to go to sleep instead. It may be so worn out that it will sleep for the better part of a day or two. There's nothing to worry about if it does sleep that long, unless the kitten shows signs of illness.

A REMINDER

In Chapter 3 many of the initial problems that a cat presents to its new owners were discussed, including introductions to babies and to dogs, equipment, examination by a veterinarian, and sleeping accommodations. If you've forgotten what was said there, it might be a good idea to glance over that chapter again and refresh your memory.

CHOOSING A VETERINARIAN

Even before you acquire your kitten—if that's possible—it's well to decide on the veterinarian to whom you're going to take the cat.

If you haven't had a pet before, you may be in for a surprise. The old-time "horse doctor" is a thing of the past. Today's veterinarian is a professionally educated physician, surgeon, dentist, psychiatrist, gynecologist, obstetrician, allergist, orthopedist, ophthalmologist, endocrinologist, neurologist, and pathologist, all in one. No general practitioner in human medicine must be skilled in so many areas and specialties of medical science. To prepare for this mission, the veterinarian must undergo training that closely resembles that of the doctor of medicine.

Nevertheless, in veterinary as in human medicine, the expertise of doctors varies a good deal. Not all men and women will be equally talented, equally intelligent, equally devoted to their responsibilities. The average veterinarian will be a person to whom you can gratefully and confidently entrust the care of your pet. But if you want to find a superior veterinarian, or if you want to avoid one of the few inferior vets, then you'll have to give some thought to the matter.

One good way to find out about vets is to talk to some of the people who are their clients: cat owners, dog owners, and breeders of cats and dogs. The breeders are likely to be better informed than the usual pet owner. However, there's a good chance that you'll get contradictory opinions, so you will have to exercise your own judgment on what you hear.

On your first visit to the veterinarian's office, you'll be able to form your own opinion. Don't pay too much attention to the doctor's manner of dealing with you; it's the cat who's the patient, not you. Some excellent veterinarians are very brusque with their human clients but very gentle and compassionate with their four-legged patients, and that's what counts. If the veterinarian is somewhat curt and disinclined to listen to your stories about the cute things that kitten does, remember that the doctor is a busy person with other patients waiting. If the vet's manner with you is short and rather distant, it's probably because a lifetime of watching people neglect their animals by failing to follow veterinary advice has left this doctor more than a little disillusioned about human beings.

Watch closely how the doctor handles the animal patients. The good vet may sometimes appear very firm with animals, but he or she never *needlessly* inflicts pain. (Of course, sometimes pain must be inflicted—remember some of your visits to the dentist?) The veterinarian's confidence should be apparent. At the same time, the doctor should admit it when the case presented to him or her is puzzling and difficult to diagnose and treat. The good vet should be relaxed in the examination of the animal. I tend—perhaps unfairly—to have some doubt about a vet who shows fear of a dog or a cat.

The examining room, operating room, and equipment are good clues to the veterinarian's ability and attitude to the profession. Obviously, a vet with a practice in a low-income neighborhood is likely to have a less impressive office than a Park Avenue vet. But both should have examining rooms that are clean, neat, and professional in appearance.

While you are watching the vet, remember that the doctor is undoubtedly forming an opinion of you, too. Vets tend to put pet owners into two groups: those who take care of their pets by following instructions, no matter how much inconvenience or effort may be involved; and those who expect the vet to perform miracles, who neglect the pet until its problems are advanced and complicated, but won't do as the vet suggests because it's too much trouble.

You have the right to expect the vet to explain your pet's problems fully in language you can understand. Your vet has the right to expect your cooperation.

On your visit to the vet for the first time, explain that you've just acquired a kitten (or cat) and that you want it thoroughly examined. The doctor will check its eyes, its hearing, its teeth, its bone structure, its general health and development. And the vet can give you sound advice on the care of the cat.

Don't expect the vet to judge the merits of the cat, if it is a purebred. Only a cat-show judge or an experienced breeder is qualified to make such judgments. The fine points of cat judging are not taught in schools of veterinary medicine.

FORMULA FOR THE NURSING KITTEN

It's best to get a kitten that's at least eight weeks old and already weaned or ready to be weaned. But if, by some unfortunate circumstance, you find yourself suddenly saddled with all the responsibilities that a mother cat normally has, you'd better be prepared for your maternal role.

If you're lucky—and you probably won't be—you may be able to find a mother cat in the neighborhood who's still nursing her young. It's far more likely that you'll have to prepare the milk yourself.

The problem will be to approximate cat's milk for the nursing kitten. This may require more thought than you might suppose. For the nutritional needs of the cat, as we have seen, are quite different from those of other animals and of humans.

Let's take a look at the composition of various milks:

	CAT	DOG	COW	HUMAN	GOAT	SHEEP
Water	82.0%	75.1%	87.0%	87.4%	86.8%	84.0%
Protein	7.0	8.4	3.4	1.3	3.7	5.0
Sugar	5.0	3.2	4.9	7.0	4.6	4.0
Fat	5.0	9.8	3.8	3.5	4.0	4.0
Ash	0.6	0.7	0.7	0.2	0.8	0.9

A study of these percentages indicates several facts. Obviously, cow's milk will not be an adequate substitute for cat's milk; the protein content is far too low. For the same reason, a formula that might be used in preparing a human baby's bottle won't give a kitten the nutrient values it needs.

The only other milk that is close to cat's milk is that of the dog, which is higher in protein, fat, and ash, although it is lower in water (which need not trouble us unduly) and in sugar. This is one formula for foster feeding of *puppies:*

1 cup of whole homogenized vitamin D milk
1 egg yolk
1 teaspoon lime water
1 teaspoon of dextrose

Adapting this for *kittens,* we might increase the dextrose to two teaspoons. Then it should be perfectly suitable for the orphaned kitten.

There are also commercial preparations for cat's and dog's milk that are acceptable and convenient, but a trifle expensive.

The formula should be fed to the kitten at body temperature. In the cat, this means 101.5 degrees Fahrenheit (38.6 degrees Celsius). Testing it on the wrist, as parents do with a baby's bottle, is an easy way to check the temperature.

The bottle and nipples should be sterilized, of course, for kittens are as susceptible to germs as babies are. The nipples may give some slight difficulty in the first week. Those for human babies may be too big. In that case, a doll's bottle and nipples, which are smaller, may prove helpful. As a last resort, try an old, clean handkerchief, twisted to a point, dipped in milk and then inserted in the kitten's mouth. This never fails.

A kitten can take about seven c.c.s (cubic centimeters) of formula, or a little more, five times a day. A teaspoon, for comparative purposes, is about four c.c.s. One sign that the kitten has had enough milk at a feeding is the bubbles of milk that appear at its mouth. If it stops sucking, it might be full, lazy, or forgetful—you'll have to decide which.

When the kitten is through feeding, jiggle it gently, and pat it on the back to burp it. Then take a soft, synthetic sponge, moistened with lukewarm water, and rub its abdomen and the area around its anus. Rub the abdomen gently but repeatedly, and always toward the hindquarters. This is what the mother cat does with her tongue after the kittens have nursed. They are unable to urinate and defecate by themselves; she must help them, and in her absence this task is yours.

It is well to do this away from the kitten's bed, to avoid soiling it. After the massaging, when the kitten has eliminated its wastes, it is necessary to clean away carefully all urine and feces from its body. After a week or two this sort of thing will no longer be necessary. It will be apparent when the kitten is able to carry out these functions on its own.

The entire procedure—warming formula, feeding kitten, burping, massaging, and cleaning—should be performed approximately every two hours during the kitten's first week. If the prescribed method is followed, and the kitten is basically healthy, it should survive, although you may not.

At the beginning of the second week, you can begin giving the kitten a little more at each feeding, and the feedings can then be three hours apart. You'll really enjoy that extra hour.

EYES AND TEETH

At first the kitten won't be able to see. Between the eighth and the twelfth days its eyes will open. But it will be another day or two before it can coordinate its muscles and nerves and optic mechanisms in such a way as actually to see. And until it is nearly a month old it should not be exposed to strong, direct sunlight or to an unshaded electric light bulb.

Often the eyelids will begin to stick together a day or two after the eyes have opened. This is caused simply by the normal secretion from the eyes. Moisten a piece of cotton with warm water and rub it gently along the eye from the nose outward. As the crystallized secretion begins to soften, the cotton can be moved up and down across the eyelids until they are ready to separate. Then the eyes should be dried with sterile cotton. Your veterinarian can recommend an ophthalmic solution that should clear up the condition quickly.

The teeth, too, do not become operative at once. They are in the kitten's jaw, but buried under the gums. The kitten begins to cut its deciduous (milk or "baby") teeth at about eleven days. By the fourth or fifth week all twenty-six of these are in place. As in human children, these teeth are later pushed out of the gum to make way for the adult teeth. This process can begin as early as the fourth month or as late as the seventh; the usual time is about the sixth month.

The teething process, as all parents know, can be a trying

period. The kitten often works up a mild fever at this time. It may appear to have some difficulty in eating.

Occasionally the milk teeth show some stubbornness about dropping out, and the adult teeth may begin to grow in beside them. For this reason, the owner should examine the kitten's mouth every few days while it's teething. At the first sign of trouble, the kitten should be taken to the veterinarian, who can remove the obstinate baby teeth, thus permitting the adult teeth to move into their proper places.

If the kitten undergoes a painful teething, its appetite may drop off. Your vet can suggest a nontoxic local anesthetic that can be applied to the gums to ease the pain and thus make eating more inviting. At this crucial stage in the kitten's development, you cannot permit its intake of food to fall off, for now, especially, it needs vitamins, tissue-building protein, and bone-building minerals if it is to have sound teeth and bones.

There is one other—fortunately rare—problem that can occur in the teething kitten: fits. If this should occur, try to get the kitten into a darkened room, but don't try to control it or touch it; you'll only risk a bite, for no good reason. Instead, telephone your vet immediately. (The fit could also be caused by worms. This possibility will be discussed later in this chapter.)

BATHING

A healthy, happy kitten keeps itself clean, but it should be encouraged and assisted by regular brushing on your part. Not that the kitten will be grateful for your brushing it. On the contrary, although the kitten probably will enjoy the brushing while it is going on, it will be certain that you have dirtied its fur. As soon as you're through brushing, the kitten will begin cleaning itself.

Unless you specifically receive a recommendation to the contrary from your vet, *do not bathe your kitten!* Bathing should be a last resort, employed only in dire emergency. If the kitten falls into a filthy or foul-smelling mess, of course, a bath is unavoidable. In that event, put a drop of mineral oil in each of the kitten's eyes and put a daub of cotton in each ear, to protect those delicate organs from the soap. Your pet shop or druggist may stock shampoos especially prepared for cats. If not, use as mild a shampoo as possible, such as those sold for babies. Rinse and dry the kitten thoroughly and keep it out of drafts.

CLAWS

Unless the claws are clipped, they will grow too long and begin to curve into wicked little hooks. But clipping a kitten's or cat's nails takes a little thought and care. It is really a two-man job, although one very agile person can manage it alone. Have another person hold the cat from the back, with the person's arms about the cat's midsection. While the front claws are being trimmed, the hindlegs should be held, so the cat can't strike out with the hind claws. The front paws are restrained while the hind claws are being trimmed.

Have at hand a pair of fingernail clippers. Take the paw in hand and put pressure from two fingers on the top and bottom of the paw, thus forcing the claws out of their sheaths. Your light should be strong enough to shine through the claw. Look at it carefully; you will see a pink area in the middle. This is the quick; *you must be careful not to cut into it.* The cat's quick is as sensitive to pain as the quick under your nails. Cut the claw back close to the quick.

If you should, by some mischance, cut into the quick, you'll find that the bleeding does not stop quickly, for it is fed by a vein. The best way to stop the bleeding is by dabbing the bleeding claw with a piece of cotton dipped in Monsel's solution. Incidentally, a small bottle of Monsel's solution should be kept in the house for just such emergencies. (Men will find it is better than a styptic pencil for stopping the bleeding when they've cut themselves shaving.) Monsel's solution, known under its technical designation as ferric subsulphate solution, can be obtained from your pharmacist.

Clipping the cat's nails will prevent scratches on your hands and cut down on damage to furniture and rugs. A scratching post also will help with this problem, especially if you get the kitten early and train it to use the post. Scratching posts are made in horizontal and vertical forms; the latter are the better. The post is usually a piece of wood covered with bark or catnip-impregnated fabric. One excellent scratching post, which cats love, is made of cork.

DECLAWING

If a kitten or a cat becomes really destructive toward furniture, and a few problem cats do, there is one drastic remedy available: declawing. The entire claws are removed surgically, roots and all, so that they never grow again. The operation is performed under anesthesia.

Declawing, the technical term for which is *onychectomy,* is a controversial procedure. It is so hotly disputed that two very respected leaders in the cat fancy have offered a reward for the "arrest and conviction" of anyone who has been responsible for declawing a cat. Declawing, of course, is *not* against the law. But these people believe sincerely that it should be outlawed.

I disagree. I have had cats declawed, and they have enjoyed full, happy, and secure lives without their claws, just as though they had them. Many people who love cats with a passion but fear the damage that cats can do to furniture and rugs go through life without cats for that reason. Occasionally a cat will be taken to a vet to be put to sleep because it has been guilty of so much damage with its claws. Declawing solves this problem.

Of course, declawing creates certain problems and imposes new responsibilities on the owner. A declawed cat can defend itself, but not as well as a cat with claws; it can climb trees if the customary procedure of only removing the front claws is followed, but it can't climb with the ease of an untouched cat; it can still capture its prey, sometimes just as well as the cat with claws. Because its abilities are diminished to some extent, however, the declawed cat must expect special care from its owner. I do not believe that a declawed cat should be permitted out to roam at will. There is no question that the hazards to its life are greater. Otherwise, the declawed cat enjoys life every bit as much as it did before its operation.

Declawing should not be resorted to until every attempt has been made to correct the cat's objectionable habits by training. This means that the cat will usually be nearly full-grown before being declawed.

The cat displays surprisingly few signs of discomfort after the operation. For twenty-four hours, sterile dressings are maintained on the paws. But very quickly the cat is walking, despite the recent surgery, with no indication of sensitivity. In time, the paws harden a good deal, apparently as a result of the declawing. The cat uses them more often then as hands. My cat can make tight, formidable little fists out of her declawed paws, and she slugs with those fists like a prizefighter, as the other cats have learned to their sorrow.

When you are considering whether to have your cat declawed, you should bear in mind that declawed cats are barred from cat shows. So, if you think you may want to show your cat, don't have it declawed.

WINDOW SITTING

One difficulty experienced by declawed cats—and cats with claws as well—has to do with windowsills. When a cat jumps to a windowsill, it extends its claws to grab the surface better. A declawed cat has a harder time stopping its skid across the sill.

This is a real hazard to an apartment cat. Hundreds of cats are killed every year in New York City alone in falls from apartment windowsills. We always assume that the cat's judgment of distance and ability to stop is well-nigh perfect. It isn't. If the sill is smooth, and most sills are, the cat—claws or no—may slide right off the sill, to plummet to the concrete below. If there is a fire escape, the cat often will try to jump to the railing. It will succeed, too, forty-nine out of fifty times. The fiftieth time the cat proves that it has only one life, not nine, as it misjudges the distance, goes off balance, teeters briefly, and then plunges into space.

Don't trust your cat's judgment in such matters. Keep screens on your windows and don't let the cat out on the fire escape. If the cat leans against the screen and causes it to bulge, a narrow strip of wood can be nailed across the frame.

INOCULATIONS

Two of the diseases commonly encountered in kittens— pneumonitis and feline distemper—can usually be warded off by vaccines. Both diseases will be discussed at some length in Chapter 8. Here it is enough to say that kittens are especially vulnerable to these diseases.

A serum that offers protection against feline distemper for about two weeks is available, and this may be worth considering if the kitten is about to be exposed to cats that may be carrying the disease.

There are vaccines against both feline distemper and pneumonitis. The inoculations are usually made when the kitten is about three months old. The distemper vaccine is given in two injections two weeks apart.

Many vets feel that these vaccines have not yet been developed to a sufficiently satisfactory point to warrant their use. They feel the protection is still inadequate. On the other hand, an unvaccinated kitten is exposed to disease every time you bring another cat into the house. In this perplexing situation, the best course to follow is that prescribed by your own vet.

One inoculation which most vets favor these days guards cats against feline viral rhinotracheitis.

WORMING

Parasitism in the kitten usually concerns us most in respect to worms. Cats are involuntary hosts to several forms of worm: eye worms, heart worms, muscle worms, hookworms, roundworms, and tapeworms.

Eye worms: These parasites, designated *Thelazia californiensis,* are uncommon. When they are found, it is usually in the Pacific Coast states. The worms are found, not only in the cat, but also in man, the dog, the coyote, the deer, the sheep, and the black bear. Tiny, threadlike worms of the Nematodes order, they can be seen moving across the cat's eye. As many as six have been found in a single eye.

Your vet can remove them with forceps after administering a tranquilizer and a local anesthetic to the cat.

Heart worms: These parasites are more common in dogs than in cats, but our feline pets are sometimes unwilling hosts to them. Their technical name is *Dirofilaria immitis.* The mosquito is the intermediate host. It acquires the active embryos when it sucks blood from a dog or cat, shelters the changeling worms as they grow into larvae, and then injects them back into the dog or cat in the process of sucking more blood. The embryonic worms circulate in the blood, but when the larvae get back into the body of the dog or cat, they head for the muscle and fatty tissues, there to grow until they are ready to make their way through the blood system to the heart, where they reach maturity.

The symptoms of heart-worm infection are coughing, labored breathing, and collapse when the animal exercises. A typical feline victim, cited in one of the professional journals, collapsed early one morning and was hospitalized in shock and evident pain. Its body temperature was well below normal at 97 degrees Fahrenheit. The cat responded to stimulants but three hours later it collapsed again and died. An autopsy uncovered one male and four female worms in the right ventricle of the heart.

Drugs are available against heart worms. However, different drugs must be used to kill the adult worm and the embryos, called *microfilariae*. Usually the drug that kills the adult worms is administered one month before the drug designed to kill the embryos. In some cases, the vet may prefer to remove the worms surgically.

Muscle worms: Trichinosis, a parasitic disease which exists in man, is also caused in the cat by the worm called *Trichinella spiralis*. At various stages in their development, these worms inhabit almost every kind of tissue in the body. When they finally reach their destination, the muscle fibers, they encyst. The cat, like man, usually becomes infested with these worms if it eats uncooked, or undercooked, pork in which the worms are encysted.

The symptoms appear in three stages: first, for about a week there may be diarrhea, slight fever, mild abdominal pain, sometimes nausea and vomiting; second, for two or three weeks there may be loss of appetite, muscular pains, labored breathing, and low fever; third, the period of encystation, muscular stiffness, nerve disorders, lung trouble.

The best way to fight trichinosis is not to let your cat get it in the first place—not to feed it pork that hasn't been cooked long enough (thirty minutes) at a high enough temperature (212 degrees Fahrenheit). The vet can make your cat more comfortable if it becomes infested, but he can't destroy the worms without cooking the cat, which the cat might regard as a rather extreme measure.

Hookworms: Three kinds of hookworm are found in the cat; their technical names are *Ancylostoma caninum, Ancylostoma braziliense,* and *Uncinaria stenocephala.*

Infested animals appear anemic and, in severe cases, produce black, tarry stools. There are sometimes respiratory difficulties.

These worms can be destroyed by biochemicals administered by your veterinarian. It is important to have him treat hookworm disease, because it can cause death.

Roundworms: Also called ascarids, these parasites are very common in kittens and puppies. In fact, the babies can acquire the worms while they are still in the mother cat's womb.

The symptoms include failure to grow at a normal rate, engage in normal activity, or display good condition. The coat may be dull, the body pot-bellied. There may be signs of digestive difficulties. The kitten may vomit, and the vomitus and the feces may be found, upon microscopic examination, to harbor the roundworms.

There are a number of new drugs which are highly effective against roundworms.

Tapeworms: There are at least eight different cestodes, or tapeworms, that infest the cat. The worm segments are sometimes seen in the stool.

The symptoms include general unthriftiness, an attitude of sickness, irritability, capricious appetite, ruffled coat, colic, mild diarrhea, emaciation, and sometimes fits.

Effective drugs are available to the veterinarian for treating tapeworm infestation. A major problem, however, is the prevention of reinfestation.

This list includes only the most common worms that infest cats. It does not, by any means, exhaust the list of internal parasites to which the cat is prey. For example, there are also flukes and stomach worms.

My purpose in listing these worms is to emphasize the variety of parasites in the cat. Each of these worms is quite different from the rest; each requires a different kind of treatment. *No one but a veterinarian is competent to identify and treat the offending parasite!*

Pet shops, drugstores, and even supermarkets offer commercial "worm medicines" for sale. These patent medicines should never be used, for the following reasons:

1. A patent medicine is able to kill only one kind of worm. You may give your cat a medicine intended to kill roundworms when your cat is actually infested with hookworms. Only a vet can prescribe the right worm-killer for the right worm.

2. Many vermifuges, as worm-purge chemicals are called, must be very strong if they are to be effective; they can be dangerous to the cat unless their use is supervised by a vet. A commercial vermifuge is likely to be too weak to be effective. If it is strong enough to do the job, it's dangerous to the cat's health.

3. Any vermifuge is, basically, a kind of poison. Before the cat is subjected to the shock of a worming, its general health and stamina must be assayed. For example, a cat with a heart murmur may have more difficulty withstanding a vermifuge than in carrying the extra burden of the parasites.

When a kitten is about a month old, its stool should be examined microscopically for worms by a vet. If the kitten is older when you get it, ask the vet to make such an examination the first time he sees the cat. After that, the cat should be checked from time to time when it's at the vet's office, and certainly whenever it displays any of the symptoms of worm infestation.

LEASH AND COLLAR

Some cats love to go out for walks, just as dogs do. And all cats that are confined permanently indoors like to get outdoors once in a while to enjoy the sun, the fresh air, and a nibble or two of grass. But first they must be trained to a collar (or harness) and leash. And the time for that training is when the cat is still a kitten.

Start indoors. Just put the collar or the harness on the kitten, without the leash, and then let the kitten get used to it. If it struggles to pull the collar off, try to distract its attention by playing with it.

Do this for a few minutes one day, a few more minutes the next day, and so on, gradually lengthening the time, until the kitten is accustomed to the feel of the collar about its neck.

Then attach the leash to the collar, and gradually, as with the collar, let the leash become a familiar thing to the kitten. Only when the kitten is at home with the leash and collar should you begin to guide it by gently pulling on the leash.

It takes patience—a great deal of patience—but it's worth it.

TOYS AND BONES

Cats love to play games all their lives, and they are the most inventive and imaginative of animals. Left to their own devices, they can conjure up a mouse in a rumpled bed, transform a length of string into a sinister viper, pursue a bottle cap across the floor as though it were a fleeing mouse.

There are many good toys available in pet shops. Many of them are filled with catnip, which always delights a cat (well, almost always). The toy should not have any sharp or small parts, like buttons, which the kitten could swallow, to its ultimate discomfort. Rubber balls are good—but they should be too big for the cat to swallow.

Sometimes your own ingenuity will provide the best toys. Every cat is happiest when it has a shoe box or a paper bag to climb in and out of. A crumpled-up piece of newspaper is always fun.

There are some things that cats should never be permitted to play with—pins, buttons, short lengths of string that could be swallowed and cause trouble inside the cat, rubber bands, beads, decorations, breakable glass objects, and the like. If the cat has swallowed this sort of thing and, in the case of string or stringed objects, it has been only partway eliminated, don't yield to the temptation to pull it out. There may be a hook or a knot on the string, so the danger of tearing delicate tissues must be considered. Let your veterinarian handle the problem.

Some cats like bones for playing and gnawing. This is quite all right, if the bones are the proper kind. The *only* bones the cat should ever be permitted to have are the large beef bones—the heavy leg bones or the big knuckle ends, whole or cut into sections. These cannot splinter in the cat's mouth, nor can the specially processed bones sold in pet shops and pet-supply sections of supermarkets.

No other bones should ever be given to your cat, regardless of whatever nonsense to the contrary you may hear or read. There are those who like to argue that a cat in the feral stage eats small rodents and fish, bones and all, so nature must protect it from the harm that bones could do. This mystical exaltation of nature is rather absurd, of course; nature doesn't protect cats from larger predators, viruses, and many other hazards. Every vet has had experience in removing bone splinters that have cut into palates or throats or stomachs. For example, the *Journal of the American Veterinary Medical Association,* in 1960, reported the case of a nine-month-old male that had become suddenly depressed, vomited, refused to eat, and had a temperature of 105 degrees Fahrenheit. It was believed to be suffering from feline distemper, but an X-ray disclosed a curious chain of objects in the pharynx. Under anesthesia, the spinal column of a fish was removed from the upper part of the throat.

CAR SICKNESS

For some reason as yet not understood by science, cats hardly ever suffer from car sickness. A cat may show abnormal fear in a car—by foaming, for example—but this is not from car sickness. If your cat is one of those rarities that do suffer from this malady, your veterinarian can prescribe medication to prevent or control the condition.

7. THE ADULT CAT

In 1607 Edward Topsell, the early English zoologist, offered his advice on how to keep a house cat. "Those which will keep their cats within doors, and from hunting birds abroad," he wrote, "must cut off their ears, for they cannot endure to have drops of rain distill into them, and therefore keep themselves in harbor."

Fortunately, this drastic method for curbing the cat's wanderlust has gone out of fashion since Topsell's day. Nowadays the question is not: Indoors or out? It is, rather: City or country?

It is true, of course, that cats, unlike dogs, are not required to be licensed in most communities (although a few places have ordinances that force cats to be licensed and belled). Thus a city pet can legally be permitted to roam at will.

Some city dwellers prefer to give their cats the freedom of the streets rather than keep sanitary pans for them indoors. I once had a neighbor who lived in a first-floor apartment. She kept a length of carpeting hanging out a rear window. Her cat would climb down on the carpet until it could drop to the ground. Then it would go about its business. When it was ready to return home, the cat would leap up, catch hold of the carpeting, and climb up in through the window.

Usually city pets are kept indoors all the time. The cats that roam free have a much shorter life expectancy because of automobile traffic, poison, cat stealers, feline plagues, and infections from rodents.

In the suburbs, it's often a toss-up whether a cat should be kept indoors or permitted to roam. Uncastrated males must be permitted out because of their objectionable scent. Many people like to let their cats enjoy the sport of hunting. To make matters more convenient for the cat's master, a tiny cat's door can be cut into the back door so the cat can go in and out at will. A ready-made cat's door for this purpose is on the market now.

In addition to the city hazards, however, suburban and country cats face the danger of being hunted by cat haters. Cat owners usually are unaware that the cat does not enjoy the kind of legal protection that guards the dog against trigger-happy hunters. Almost every state has a provision like this. In New York, for example, the state conservation law, Section 205, reads:

> Any person over the age of twenty-one years possessing a hunting license may, and game protectors and other peace officers shall, humanely destroy cats at large found hunting or killing any bird protected by law, or with a dead bird of any species protected by law in its possession, and no action for damages shall lie for such killing.

This is an absurd and unfair law. Who is to say whether a cat creeping along the ground is hunting a "bird protected by law" or a mouse? If a cat comes upon a dead bird lying on the ground and stops to sniff at it, is the bird then to be presumed "in its possession"? In effect, this law provides for an open season on cats the year round.

This attitude has been upheld by the Supreme Court of Oklahoma, which exonerated a chicken breeder who had killed a cat outside his backyard. But in Canada the courts have held that, although there may be some circumstances under which a cat may properly be killed, it is not justifiable to kill the cat simply because it is trespassing on one's property, even if it is hunting game.

Such legal discrimination against cats also is evident in the larceny statutes. In most states the law classes the stealing of a dog as larceny, but makes no mention of the theft of a cat. In the common law, however, any pet is a thing of value and its theft is therefore larceny.

Cats deserve at least as much, if not more, protection from the law than dogs, for cats are abducted for use in laboratory experiments on an even greater scale than dogs. Indeed, the traffic in dogs and cats for laboratories is on a scale undreamed-of by most people.

In 1960 a Wisconsin company sent out an announcement to Midwestern high school students. The announcement, addressed to "any groups or classes of high school students wishing to raise money now," offered fifty cents each for "all the cats you can collect for cash." The company planned to kill the cats, embalm them, and send them to school laboratories. "You will be surprised just how easy it is to collect 150–300 cats," said the announcement. The company was surprised, almost immediately, by the protests from cat lovers who had been alerted by *Cats Magazine*. In the face of this reaction, the company withdrew its offer, but not before "some schools had collected and sold us cats," a company spokesman conceded.

OTHER LEGAL CONSIDERATIONS

Is a cat owner responsible for the acts of his pet? Does he have any recourse in law if another person, or an animal belonging to another person, does injury to the cat?

These are questions which occasionally puzzle cat owners. It is important that they be aware of their responsibilities and rights.

The courts generally recognize the propensities of the cat. Let us assume that your cat invades your neighbor's house, sees a parrot sitting on its perch, pounces upon it, kills it, and carries it off. This sort of thing is likely to strain relations between you and your neighbor—or, at the very least, to moderate your neighbor's enthusiasm for your cat—but such a misfortune will not subject you to a lawsuit. A Pennsylvania court and a British appellate court have both held that cats cannot be kept under the same restraint and discipline as dogs; therefore, their owners cannot be held responsible for their acts while roaming.

On the other hand, if your neighbor should catch the cat trespassing and kill it, there's nothing much you can do about that. The cat's depredations, in that case, have made it fair prey.

Cat bites and scratches can be another problem. There is, for example, the case of the woman who is bitten and clawed by a household pet. She may, or may not, recover damages from the cat's owner. In such a case, a Connecticut court has held, the victim must prove that the cat was known to be vicious and aggressive, and that the cat's owner, knowing this, did nothing to restrain the cat. But if the cat is just an ordinary one, with no special delight in attacking humans, or if the owner had no reason to believe otherwise, then the victim cannot hope to win a damage suit.

In Massachusetts a woman who owned a dog broke up a fight it was having with a cat. After the animals had been separated, the woman took the cat's paw in her hand and promptly got herself bitten and scratched, as any cat owner might have predicted. The court held that the woman had been negligent, even though she'd grabbed the cat's paw because she was afraid the cat might go at the dog again.

If a cat is wrongfully injured by a person or an animal belonging to another person, the cat's owner has the right to recover damages, providing that the injury was the result of a willful act of negligence on the part of the person. If the cat's owner has been guilty of contributory negligence, however, the right to recovery does not apply in some jurisdictions.

HUNTING AND TROPHIES

As the courts have recognized, hunting is basic to a cat's nature. The cat doesn't hunt because it is hungry, although many people mistakenly think so. (It is a pity how many cats are starved because humans think the animals will hunt better in that condition.) There is even a good deal of evidence that a hungry cat isn't as good a hunter as a well-fed cat: its reflexes aren't as fast, its sight may be impaired by malnutrition, its strength is sapped by the lack of nourishment. The sleek cat with the contented stomach is in much better shape to use all its patience, wit, agility, and strength in the hunt.

In ancient Egypt cats were trained to hunt as retrievers, and even to recover game from the water, for some cats—not many—enjoy swimming. Today I know of no cats that hunt with their masters.

As a solitary hunter, however, the cat is well-nigh unbeatable. Its killing of birds, rabbits, rats, mice, shrews, and snakes helps to maintain the balance of nature. There is even reason to believe that the cat is all that stands between man and the plague. The cat should not be discouraged by a squeamish owner from the pursuit of its natural prey. It is merely fulfilling its role in nature's great cycle. Besides, the cat owner must be realistic about his own limitations; nothing he can do will make the cat change its favorable attitude toward hunting.

One of the most distressing aspects of the cat's hunting instinct is the cat's pride. Many cats insist on bringing their dead prey home as trophies to be presented proudly to their humans. This is sometimes a little too much for humans to stomach. A white cat of my acquaintance used to bring home at least one trophy— usually a rat or a field mouse, but occasionally a rabbit, squirrel, or bird—every day. One day, while the mistress of the house was having a cocktail party, the cat slipped into the house through an open window, trophy in mouth, and proceeded to put it down on the floor beside the hors d'oeuvre table. It created quite a stir.

BIRDS

The cat is fascinated by birds and will stalk its feathered prey whenever it can. Nevertheless, it is possible to keep both cats and birds. At an animal talent agency I've seen birds walking unconcernedly along the floor in front of cats who couldn't have been more disinterested. To achieve this state of affairs requires constant vigilance, a suspicious mind (as to the cat's motives at any given moment), and the ability to discipline a cat. With sufficient discipline, the cat can be made to learn that the bird is not to be considered food for more than thought.

For this sort of discipline, a water pistol is very useful. Keep the pistol filled and sit within range of the bird cage. Every time the cat approaches the cage or shows an interest in the bird, shoot some water at the cat. It's remarkable how chastened a cat can become when hit suddenly by a jet of water out of nowhere.

Bird lovers usually assume that cats outdoors spend all their time hunting birds. It has been shown, however, that this is not the case. At least two studies have been made, in Wisconsin and Oklahoma, of the stomach contents of cats killed while roving. In Wisconsin, of fifty cats examined, seven had been pets, thirty-nine had been hunters without established abodes, and two had been feral. In Oklahoma all the cats subject to the post-mortem examination were feral. The Wisconsin cats' last meals were classed like this: meadow mice, twenty-six cats; deer mice, eight cats; house mice, three cats; unidentified mice, nine cats; Norway rats, seven cats; rabbits, three cats; short-tailed shrew, one cat; chicken heads and feet (apparently stolen from human garbage), three cats; grasshoppers, three cats; crickets, one cat; June bugs, one cat; human food remnants, twenty-one cats. One cat had swallowed a heavy cord and another a piece of cloth. Only six of the fifty cats had fed on birds. Of these birds, three were unidentified small birds. Two were English sparrows, and one was a pigeon. The Oklahoma cats had similar tastes. Fifty-five percent had eaten rodents; 12½ percent, insects; 2 percent, reptiles; 26½ percent, human food. Only 4 percent had enjoyed a bird as the last meal.

Obviously, cats kill fewer birds than hunters do in duck and pheasant season. Moreover, a few cats each year are killed by birds, usually by the great horned owl, although eagles also carry off cats. (The cat is also prey to the dog, the fox, the coyote, and the lynx.) Nevertheless, bird lovers from time to time raise a great hue and cry about cats. In a few communities they have even succeeded in enacting laws requiring that all cats be collared, belled, and leashed.

ADLAI STEVENSON'S VETO

When Adlai E. Stevenson was governor of Illinois, the legislature of that state passed a cat-control measure. The governor vetoed the bill. His veto message has become a classic:

> I cannot agree that it should be the declared public policy of Illinois that a cat visiting a neighbor's yard or crossing the highway is a public nuisance. It is the nature of cats to do a certain amount of unescorted roaming. Many live with their owners in apartments or other restricted premises, and I doubt if we want to make their every brief foray an opportunity for a small game hunt by zealous citizens—with traps or otherwise.
>
> I am afraid this bill could only create discord, recrimination, and enmity.
>
> Also consider the owner's dilemma: to escort a cat abroad on a leash is against the nature of a cat, and to permit it to venture forth

for exercise unattended into a night of new dangers is against the nature of the owner.

Moreover, cats perform useful service, particularly in rural areas, in combatting rodents—work they necessarily perform alone and without regard for property lines.

We are all interested in protecting certain varieties of bird. That cats destroy some birds, I well know, but I believe this legislation would further but little the worthy cause to which its proponents give such unselfish effort. The problem of cat versus bird is as old as time. If we attempt to resolve it by legislation, who knows but what we may be called upon to take sides as well in the age-old problems of dog versus cat, bird versus bird, or even bird versus worm.

In my opinion, the State of Illinois and its local governing bodies already have enough to do without trying to control feline delinquency.

CAT FIGHTS

There are few things in this world so noisy, wild, fierce, and thoroughly frightful as an out-and-out cat fight, as distinguished from a cat skirmish of the sort that occurs frequently without any serious results. Most cat fights are between unaltered adult males or between a whole cat and a neutered cat.

The owner's impulse is to plunge into the fray and separate the two cats, but this is most unwise. The two animals are so excited that they are virtually incapable of recognizing a human identity. Every fiber of their bodies is keyed to the fight. They will lash out at anything that hinders their attempts to defend themselves and attack their foes. In this momentary kind of madness, the cat will even unwittingly attack its own master. The human who tries to separate two fighting cats, therefore, is almost certain to be badly bitten and clawed for his trouble.

There are two ways to separate fighting cats. The first is to throw water on them. A bucket of water flung on a couple of fighting cats has an immediate, sobering effect on them.

The other method is to fling a heavy blanket or some other kind of cloth over the cats. Once they are entangled in the folds they will tend to separate of their own accord.

Regardless of which method is employed, the cat owner

should be careful not to pick up his cat immediately after the fight, because the cat is still likely to strike out instinctively. It is better to wait a few moments, murmuring comfortingly to the cat until it shows that it has calmed down enough to be handled.

HABITS—GOOD AND BAD

Whatever your own politics may be, there is one fact of life that you'd better be prepared to admit to yourself: The cat is a confirmed conservative. It is even a diehard.

The cat demands an ordered existence. Except in its sex life, the cat is no Bohemian. It likes to have its meals at the same time and place every day. It likes to have the same place to sleep and the furniture in the same place every day. You may, if you wish, live your own carefree, helter-skelter life, but one day the cat will pack its things and go off to find some humans who know that calendars and clocks and decorators' schemes are not to be trifled with.

Without training, the cat will learn to recognize the sound of your footstep or your car, and you'll find the cat waiting for you whenever you return home. It also has a time sense, and it will know and expect a break in routine on weekends.

But there are other habits that require training. If you want to keep the cat off the tables or other furniture, you can train it to respect those areas, but it's not easily done. It's long-drawn-out and often discouraging. You must keep after the cat constantly when it tries the forbidden.

Often a cat will develop a taste for your house plants. The best thing to do if that happens is to put the plants in a room from which the cat can be barred. A taste for house plants can be dangerous for the cat, as some plants can be poisonous. A Brooklyn veterinarian, Dr. Bernard Wasserman, in a report published in the *Journal of the American Veterinary Medical Association,* described a cat that died after eating the leaves of a house plant later identified as sheep laurel, *Kalmia angustifolia.*

Some cats develop a habit of chewing electrical cords. This problem is discussed in the next chapter.

Sometimes a cat's bad habits are created by its owner. A cat that scratches in playing usually does so because its owner started out playing the teasing game of wiggling his finger in front of the cat and then snatching it away. The cat, not unnaturally, grabs with its claws in an effort to catch the finger. This sort of game should be played with a piece of string or a pencil, not with your finger. There is no reason why a cat owner's hand should be constantly scratched.

TRICKS

It is generally believed that cats cannot be taught to do tricks. That is not true. It is true, however, that cats are far more difficult to teach than dogs—not because they are less intelligent, but because they are too sensible to think that sort of thing is really worthwhile.

Therefore, to teach a cat tricks you must make it worth the cat's while. If you want the cat to come on call, call it when it is close to you and immediately give it a treat as a reward. Do this a few times and the cat will soon realize that when you call its name there's a treat worth coming for. The same can be done with whistling.

If the cat does what you want it to do, exactly right, praise it and reward it. If it is not quite right, say, "No, No," and make it do the trick again. Reward the cat only when it has done the trick perfectly and praise it over and over again.

Train the cat for only about five minutes at a time, with a rest of at least a half-hour between training sessions. Never train the cat if its attention is wandering to other things.

If owners are patient enough, cats can be taught to shake hands, lie down and roll over, come on command, stay indoors, jump through a hoop, retrieve, talk, sit up and beg, sit in a designated place, and wave goodbye.

GROOMING

The comb and brush to be used in grooming the cat have been discussed in Chapter 3. A somewhat unorthodox addition to that equipment is your vacuum cleaner. Many cats love to be vacuumed; their exhibition of pleasure is nothing less than orgiastic. It's an unusual way to rid the cat of dead hair.

Whether the cat is long-haired or short-haired, it should be brushed frequently—if possible, every day. This need is particularly urgent in the case of long-haired cats, as one might expect. The longhair's coat should be brushed and combed carefully down to the skin, and any mats should be eliminated. A mat is a mass of hairs stuck together as though with glue. It is most often found on the underside or on the back legs of longhairs. A twig, a thistle, or a piece of leaf may be the initial factor in the development of the mat. If the coat is neglected, the time will come when the cat will be forced to endure a rather painful and unhappy session with a brush.

A longhair's coat should first be brushed against the normal lie of the hair and later in the direction that the coat lies. The brush should be worked against the coat in short, controlled strokes, taking a very small section of coat at a time. As hair collects in the brush and comb, clean them out and then resume brushing and combing. The comb is used after the brushing has been completed.

If no amount of brushing removes a mat, it may be possible to break it up by moistening it to soften it, then breaking it up with the blunt—*not* the sharp—end of a knitting needle. In unusually stubborn cases, which are almost always the result of neglect on the part of the owner, it may be necessary to cut the mat out with scissors.

When the grooming of a long-haired cat has been completed, you may still have reason to believe that there is dirt in the coat. If that is so, don't bathe the cat. Instead, have your pet dealer or veterinarian recommend a safe dry bath powder for the cat. Apply the powder as directed by the label, being careful to remove all the powder afterward.

Short-haired cats present much less of a problem in grooming. The brushing and combing is quite simple. A hound's glove, available in most pet shops, is sometimes a handy additional tool.

FLEAS, TICKS, LICE

When you are grooming the cat, you should also keep your eyes open for any signs of certain external parasites, such as fleas, ticks, and lice. These minute creatures can cause discomfort, suffering, crippling, and even death.

Fleas: Some cats never catch fleas, but most cats do. Why some apparently are immune is still a matter of speculation.

There are several varieties of flea which afflict the cat. These fleas will also trouble humans if there are no cats about, although they prefer cats. The fleas like dogs about as well as cats—a popularity desired by neither quadruped. The cat flea, *Ctenocephalides felis,* is more common than the dog flea, *Ctenocephalides canis,* although their indiscriminate habits make the names of both these fleas somewhat misleading.

The flea is a small, wingless (it hops), blood-sucking parasite. Its eggs develop on the ground, in the cat's bedding, or in crevices in the floor, so that even while you're getting rid of the fleas *on* your cat, new fleas may be maturing in your cat's environment.

For this reason, many persons prefer a remedial powder instead of the sprays and baths made for this purpose. The cat will shake the powder to the floor and into its bed, and thus kill many of the developing fleas as well as those already on its body.

No powder, spray, or bath using DDT, Rothane (TDE), lindane, benzene hexachloride (BHC), toxaphene, or malathion should ever be applied to a cat. These are all highly poisonous to cats. Some anti-flea preparations which are safe for use on dogs cannot be used on cats, because cats clean themselves so thoroughly with their tongues that they will ingest the powder, spray, or bath and poison themselves. Use only preparations specifically developed for cats.

On the cat, fleas will be found most often around the head, the ear, the back of the neck, the rump, and the tail.

Often the flea bites will cause a serious skin irritation. It is best to let your veterinarian manage the treatment of this condition. There are a number of soothing treatments that he can apply.

Ticks: Until recently, ticks were mostly found in the Midwestern, Western, and Southern states. Now they have extended their territory to cover almost all of our country. They are exasperating, pernicious, and persistent pests. They can be dangerous to cat, dog, and man. There are many varieties of this blood-sucking insect, and unfortunately all of them are perfectly happy to make a home on a cat.

The tick has a fearsome mouth and jaws, and with these it bites deeply into the skin of its host, so deeply that almost all of its head may be buried in the cat's skin as the tick's belly swells with the blood it is sucking. If you succumb to temptation and tug at the tick, all you'll get is the body. The head and jaws will remain buried in the cat, to fester and cause a serious infection.

The correct way to remove a tick is to soak a small piece of cotton or a Q-Tip in ether or alcohol and then press it against the insect until it releases its grip and can be lifted away intact. But the tick is still not dead. The best way to dispose of it, after it has been removed from the cat, is to burn it.

In massive infestations of ticks, your veterinarian may prefer to give the cat a tick dip. This is all right for the vet, but you should not attempt it, for the cat is susceptible to poisoning by some of the substances commonly used in animal dips.

Lice: There are two types of lice, the biters and the bloodsuckers. It is the biter that usually attacks the cat.

Lice can kill a cat rather quickly. Moreover, lice on a mother cat will quickly migrate from her to her kittens and will almost surely kill them. Even when the lice are killed, the nits (louse eggs) remain on the hair as a continuing menace. This is, clearly, a parasite difficult to destroy.

If you suspect the presence of lice on your cat—frequent scratching should attract your attention to the problem—the best thing to do is to take the cat to the vet and let him prescribe the chemical to be used and the method of treatment.

HAIR BALLS

Regular grooming will help to cut down on the development of hair balls, a curious phenomenon in the cat.

Hair balls result from the cat's habit of licking its coat frequently every day. This hair collects in the stomach. From time to time, perhaps every other month, the cat regurgitates the hair in a cylindrical, feltlike roll.

If the hair ball escapes from the stomach into the intestine, the pylorus (the exit valve from the stomach) prevents the cat from vomiting the hair ball. Then the cat is in trouble; it stops eating. At this point it should be taken to a veterinarian, and surgery may be necessary.

Preparations are available in pet shops for encouraging the

elimination of hair balls. These products usually consist of petro-leum jelly flavored to be especially palatable to the cat. The jelly is applied to the nose or paws, and the animal promptly licks it off. In the cat's stomach, the jelly acts as a lubricant.

The same use can be made of plain petroleum jelly, although the cat won't like it as well. Mineral oil, which is sometimes rec-ommended for this purpose, should be used only with the great-est caution. If mineral oil is not properly dropped into the cat's mouth, it may go into the windpipe and ultimately the lungs, in-stead of the esophagus and then the stomach.

The natural function of the hair ball has been a matter for speculation. Hawks and owls, it has been pointed out, disgorge the indigestible parts of their prey in pellets with bones inside and fur and feathers outside. When cats are permitted to roam and hunt freely, Dr. W. R. McCuistion argues, their hair balls often are found to contain small animal teeth, claws, beaks, bones, scales, burrs, and other rough material. The purpose of the hair ball may be to protect the cat's insides from the sharp bits of material it swallows and then must regurgitate.

TRAVELING

Although they rarely suffer from motion sickness, most cats are not good travelers. Occasionally one will meet a cat that loves to ride in a car, but such is the exception, not the rule. Most cats are much too conservative to enjoy being uprooted and carted off on some uncomfortable journey to a place that's really not better than home. So if you *must* travel with a cat, take precau-tions. A cat loose in a car is likely to get frightened easily, and it's quite a feat to drive a car while trying to capture and pacify a cat that's climbing about one's head. To avoid this predicament, make sure the cat is in a carrying case. You can open the case a little from time to time, of course, to pet the cat, and it will hear the soothing sounds of your voice even when the case is closed. If the case fastens with a bolt and hasp, it's best to use a padlock instead of the bolt for your journey, because cats can be devil-ishly clever at opening supposedly secure cages and cases.

If you're traveling by car, you must remember the cat's sani-tary requirements. If you're going by train or plane, you may be permitted to keep the case with you at your seat, but many air-lines and railroads won't allow this. Be sure to check on their rules ahead of time.

Since cats don't enjoy traveling, it may be well to ask your veterinarian for a tranquilizer to give to the cat before starting out.

Your vet is also the best source of information about boarding facilities if you must travel but cannot take your cat—or do not want to. Follow the vet's advice in this, for boarding facilities can be reservoirs of disease, and your vet is best equipped to know which places are the safest.

MOVING

It follows that a cat which doesn't enjoy travel will not enjoy moving to a new house. This problem is easily handled, however. Put the cat in its carrying case before the movers begin taking the furniture out of the house. Then release the cat in the new house in one closed room which contains some furniture to which the cat is accustomed. After the rest of the furniture is moved in, the cat can be let out to wander through the rest of the house, exploring. If the cat continues to show distress in its new home, try smearing butter on its paws and leg. The cat will be so distracted by its need to lick them clean of the awful stuff that it will forget all about its unhappiness over the move.

8. FIRST AID AND HEALTH CARE

Before you begin ordering the cat to stick out its tongue and say, "Ahhhh!" let me explain that it is not the intention or function of this book to transform the cat owner into a Doctor of Veterinary Medicine. Nor into a hypochondriac.

In this chapter, however, you will find information on home nursing of the sick cat, what to do in emergencies, and—most important of all—the symptoms that warn you of serious illness that requires the professional attention of a veterinarian.

The cat is subject to a remarkable range of serious illnesses, and disease usually rages within the cat's body for some time before it is detected. Unlike illness in man, diagnosis for the cat is frustrated by the animal's inability to express its pain or discomfort in plain words. But the cat does communicate to the observant cat owner, and in this chapter you will learn how to interpret the feline language of health and sickness.

The cat, because of its curiosity, agility, and courage, has the knack of getting into more difficulties than anyone but an overworked humane society rescue worker could ever imagine. So you must learn how to take care of the cat after accidents and odd—that's just the word for them—and assorted mishaps.

FIRST-AID SUPPLIES

Before trouble strikes, the prudent cat owner will lay in those supplies which are most likely to be needed in an emergency.

Some of these are supplies which one might keep on hand for the humans in the family, but a few may be unexpected. The cat's first-aid kit should include the following:

A rectal thermometer: This can be either an instrument intended for veterinary use or one intended for measuring human temperatures.

Aspirin: These tablets should be the "baby" aspirin, available at any pharmacy. Each tablet provides 1¼ grains of aspirin, which makes each pill one-fourth the strength of the five-grain tablet usually taken by adult humans. Aspirin eases pain, reduces temperature.

Milk of magnesia: Liquid or tablets. A laxative.

Kaopectate: A liquid preparation which helps to control diarrhea, in cats as well as in humans.

Peroxide: This should be the 3 percent solution which is a drugstore standard. Useful as an antiseptic and for inducing vomiting.

Gauze bandage rolls: These should be either the two-inch or the three-inch rolls which are standard items in any drugstore. They are just right for making bandage pads, compresses, bandages, and tourniquets.

Sterile cotton: Besides its frequent use as a cushioning element under bandages, this is also handy for removing ticks, cleaning ears, and many other uses.

Adhesive tape: An absolute necessity.

Rubbing alcohol: This is necessary for removing ticks, cleaning the thermometer, and so on.

Vaseline: This—or any other brand of petroleum jelly—should be used to lubricate the thermometer before inserting it into the cat's rectum. (Be careful that the petroleum jelly you use is not carbolated, for that can poison a cat.)

Yellow mercuric oxide ophthalmic ointment: This is excellent first aid to relieve minor eye irritations and to protect the eyes when soap or chemicals must be applied near the eyes.

Universal Antidote: This can be made up by your druggist. It is composed of two parts of activated charcoal, one part of light magnesium oxide, one part of kaolin, and one part of tannic acid.

No medication containing phenol (carbolic acid) should be administered to a cat. It is believed to be toxic to cats.

TEMPERATURE

The normal body temperature of the adult cat averages 101.5 degrees Fahrenheit, but a degree below or above that is within the normal range. (If you have a Celsius thermometer, the equivalent temperature is 38.6 degrees.)

If the cat's temperature is not normal, don't panic. Many factors besides illness can affect temperature, for example, age, sex, season, time of day, environmental temperature, exercise, eating, digestion, and drinking of water. Kittens usually run temperatures about a degree higher than adult cats. The difference is even greater in diseased cats: a kitten with an infection may have a very high temperature, but an old cat's temperature may be normal, or close to normal, even when it is seriously diseased.

Cats love heat and sunlight, and on a hot summer day a cat may stretch out in the sun for a snooze. For this reason many cat owners underestimate the effect of environmental temperatures on the cat. Cats *do* become overheated on occasion. Scientists have found that 90 degrees is the critical temperature. When the temperature of the surrounding air hits 90 degrees, the temperature of the cat's body begins to go up. Before the body temperature rises, the rate of breathing increases and the cat begins to pant. Panting is a cooling device: it causes the increased evaporation of water from the tongue and mouth. When it is hot the cat will appear to clean its coat much more often than it usually does. Actually, this is a wonderful, instinctive reaction to the heat; the cat is spreading saliva on its coat because the evaporation of the saliva helps to lower the body temperature. In very hot weather, in fact, the salivary flow in the cat is greater than it is at more comfortable temperatures.

Heat becomes dangerous to the cat when the temperature of the air hits 105 degrees Fahrenheit and the relative humidity rises above 65 percent. If those conditions persist for any length of time, the cat is likely to collapse with heat exhaustion and can die. (See page 163.)

Clearly, the cat's temperature is an extremely important indicator of its general well-being. Whenever you have reason to believe that the cat is sick, you should take its temperature before telephoning the veterinarian, unless the cat is so excited that you cannot manage to do the job. With most cats it's not difficult to take its temperature single-handedly. Plump the cat down on your lap, coat the bulb end of the thermometer with Vaseline, and insert it about half an inch into the cat's rectum. The thermometer should be kept in the cat for three minutes. If the cat is on your lap, you can keep its head in the crook of your left elbow, and murmur soothingly to it all the time. Your right hand will be occupied in keeping the thermometer inside the cat.

Remember that a sick or injured cat is governed to a very large extent by its instincts, rather than its conscious mind. The most gentle of cats may very well scratch or bite its beloved master or mistress when it is handled at such times. Accept this fact and conduct yourself accordingly, and both you and the cat will profit in the end.

HOW TO RESTRAIN A CAT

Because of its excellent natural endowments, a cat seems to have the strength of ten animals—especially if you're trying to restrain it. But there are many circumstances in which it is necessary to restrain the cat in order to help it.

There are three problem areas to be controlled: the forelegs, the hindlegs, and the teeth. Many an unfortunate cat owner—or veterinarian—has restrained the legs but forgotten the teeth, to his or her subsequent regret.

The method of restraint depends on the area of the cat's body that must be treated. If you want to apply medicine, say, to any part of the cat's head or neck, wrap the rest of its body in a thick towel.

If the area to be treated is elsewhere on the body, two persons are needed to restrain the cat. One holds the cat's head with one hand and its forelegs with the other hand; the other person holds the hindlegs and administers the medication.

GIVING MEDICINE

It's not at all difficult to give a cat medicine in pill or liquid form—once you get the hang of it.

Every effort should be made to get pills down the throat, not merely into the mouth. If the pill is in the mouth, the cat may bite into it, and the medication often tastes bitter or even nauseating. To administer a pill, set the cat on your lap or on a table, facing your right. Take the cat's entire head in your left hand, with the middle finger against one corner of the cat's mouth and the thumb against the other corner. Tip the cat's head back until its nose points to the ceiling. With the pill in your right hand, *gently* force the cat's lower jaw down with that hand, while exerting pressure on both corners of the mouth. Drop the pill at the back of the tongue, where it touches the palate, and close the mouth.

Liquid medication requires a plastic, beak-tipped medicine dropper. Don't use a glass dropper: it could break in the cat's mouth. Great care must be taken in administering liquid medicine to a cat. If the liquid goes down the windpipe instead of the esophagus, there may be serious consequences. The best way to give liquid medicine to a cat is the lip-pocket method. The preparation for this is the same as that described above for pills, except that the head is not tilted back. With the head level, take the loose skin at one corner of the mouth—where the upper and lower jaws meet—and lift it away from the teeth. You will find that this forms a loose sort of pouch. Empty the medicine dropper's contents into the pouch and then let the skin go back to its natural position, but hold the cat's mouth shut for a moment.

It has happened on rare occasions that a medicine dropper falls into the cat's mouth in the midst of these exertions. If it does, turn the cat upside down immediately, with its hindquarters up in the air and its head hanging down, and shake it vigorously. The medicine dropper usually will drop out at once.

BANDAGES

Rare is the cat owner who can apply a bandage that will remain in place on the cat. Veterinarians are able to perform minor miracles of bandaging, however. My own vet applies a bandage so skillfully that the cat isn't troubled by it at all, but cleans it in the firm conviction that the bandage is a part of its coat.

If the cat does fuss about a bandage, try smearing some butter on the cat's legs. The cat will be so busy cleaning the butter from its coat that it will forget all about the hated bandage.

ACCIDENTS

When an accident of some kind has befallen your cat, it's up to you to keep calm and use your wits. If you panic and fail to think clearly, you will fail your pet when it needs you most. Don't try to do everything at once. Take the time to think out what you're going to do. The few seconds you spend on thinking about the problem cannot cost the cat its life, but they might save it.

Keep the cat as quiet as possible. It should be kept lying down, if necessary under restraint.

Check for wounds and bleeding. If there is a heavy flow of blood from a wound, apply a pressure bandage—a heavy pad of absorbent material covered with gauze or other cloth and held in place by adhesive tape. It may be unconventional, but a sanitary napkin of the type manufactured for women is ideal for this purpose.

If there is no profuse external bleeding, examine the cat's gums. If they are white or very light pink, there's a possibility that the cat is bleeding internally.

Keep the cat as warm as possible. It should have a blanket or heavy towel under it and another over it. Lift the cat as little as possible; in fact, any movement of the cat is undesirable.

Call the vet and *calmly* describe the accident, the apparent injuries, and the cat's overall appearance. Omit nothing; the vet isn't a mind reader.

Usually the vet will ask you to bring the cat to the office. If so, you must move the cat as quietly and carefully as possible. Wrap a blanket, towel, or coat around it to immobilize it and keep it warm; slip one hand under its head and neck and the other under its hindquarters. As you lift the cat, try to keep it level.

One of the most baffling and dangerous of all physiological phenomena is shock. Scientists still do not understand its cause and function. Shock occurs after, and as a result of, severe stress, such as serious accidents, heart trouble, massive hemorrhage, burns, overwhelming infections, blockage of the alimentary tract, anemia, dehydration, poisoning, and electrical contact. (See page 166 for treating electrical shock.)

Shock can be fatal, so it is important to know its symptoms: a lack of interest in everything, prostration, a lowered temperature, shallow and rapid breathing, thirst, vomiting, and diarrhea. Keep the cat warm. Stroke it and act as reassuringly as possible toward it. But these are only first-aid measures. In any serious case of shock, the services of a veterinarian are needed urgently. The vet can take vigorous steps to counteract the shock, including blood transfusions, corticosteroid injections, and oxygen therapy.

HEAT STROKE

Extremely high air temperature, high relative humidity, and inadequate ventilation are the usual causes of heat stroke. As indicated above in the section on temperature, a cat cannot long withstand a temperature of 105 degrees Fahrenheit and relative humidity over 65 percent.

When heat stroke occurs, it is quite sudden. There is very little time in which to act to save the cat's life. Its breathing abruptly becomes deep and rapid, like that of a long-distance runner gulping air after a race. The cat collapses, often with a staring expression in the eyes. Sometimes there is vomiting. The body temperature soars as high as 110 degrees Fahrenheit.

First aid must be applied as quickly as possible. The aim is to bring down the cat's temperature. Immersion in cold water or application of liberal amounts of cold water to the cat's body is recommended. Ice packs applied to the head are helpful, too. It's wise to check the cat's temperature with the rectal thermometer every five minutes because it is undesirable to bring the temperature down too fast.

CUTS

Broken glass, tacks, nails, barbed wire, jagged metal edges on cans, and many other hazards can cause serious cuts. Usually the cuts are not lethal.

First aid for cuts requires trimming of the hair around the cut. This is especially important when the injured cat is a longhair.

Then the cut should be cleaned gently. A mild soap and water lather can be used or, better still, the germicidal soap pHisoHex, available (on prescription) in all pharmacies. It is advisable to follow with a second cleansing, this time using peroxide solution. Be sure to dry the cut thoroughly with a sterile material after cleansing.

An extensive cut should be painted with Isodine and covered with a bandage, and then the cat should be taken to the veterinarian, so that the wound can be sutured. A deep cut can be adequately cleaned out only by the vet.

If a cut in the foot bleeds excessively—and this is not uncommon—it may be necessary to apply a tourniquet. A handkerchief will do. Tie it loosely around the leg, either above or below the ankle, and tighten it by twisting a pencil between loop and leg. Release the pressure briefly every five or ten minutes.

BITES

First aid for bites is essentially the same as for cuts. It is even more important, however, that the cat receive the prompt attention of a veterinarian, for the puncture wounds inflicted by other cats, dogs, rats, squirrels, and the like often are deep. If the wound is not thoroughly cleansed in its entire depth, abscesses are likely to develop.

The possibility of serious infection is greater in bites than in cuts, of course. Even if the animal that bit your cat is not rabid (rabies will be discussed later in this chapter), it may very well be carrying dangerous germs in its mouth.

Puncture wounds of the type inflicted by fangs often close up so completely that they pass unnoticed by the cat's owner. Your first indication that something is wrong may be the swelling that signifies the presence of an abscess. This means that the skin has healed over the wound, sealing it off from the air and trapping the germs inside. The veterinarian can open the abscess, clean it out, and treat the cat with antibiotics and other medications.

Rodent ulcers are often assumed to be caused by rat bites; hence their name. In fact, no one really knows what causes these nasty lesions. The first appearance is on the lip, where a thickened, protruding ulcer appears, sometimes with eczema. Some veterinarians suspect that the ulcer may originate in an allergic condition, which is then irritated by the rough surface of the cat's tongue. Other lesions appear elsewhere in and around the mouth, and often the sores are spread, apparently by licking, to other parts of the body, such as the inner surface of the thigh. Some rodent ulcers become malignant and must be removed surgically. Your veterinarian can treat most other rodent ulcers with gentian violet, protective ointments, radiation, or drugs injected into the abdominal cavity. But be patient with the vet's efforts, for rodent ulcers are unpredictable in their response to medication, and only trial and error will disclose the best treatment for your particular cat.

DROWNING

Not all cats hate immersion in water, although all do hate to get just their paws wet. Some enjoy swimming; others fall into water accidentally. Sometimes a cat may nearly drown before it can be fished out of the water; then it needs artificial respiration.

Hold the cat up by its hindlegs and let the water drain out of its mouth. Then put the cat on the ground and sit beside it. Make sure that the cat's tongue is pulled to the side of the mouth. Then begin the alternating imposition and relaxation of pressure on the cat's chest.

Put your whole hand on the cat's side behind the shoulder, press firmly but gently (don't break the rib cage), then let up. Press again, let up. Press again, let up. Press for two or three seconds, let up for two or three seconds, press for two or three seconds, and so on. Maintain that rhythm as long as there is a heartbeat. In most cases the cat will respond after ten or twenty minutes and begin to breathe again by itself, shallowly at first, then with increasing depth and strength.

When the cat is breathing by itself, keep it warm and quiet, for it is almost certain to be suffering from some degree of shock as a result of its experience.

ELECTRIC SHOCK

When a cat suffers electric shock, it is usually because it has chewed through an electric cord. Some cats insist on chewing electric cords. Covering the cord with cayenne pepper or some other substance that the cat hates may help; on the other hand, you may merely give your cat a taste for cayenne pepper. There are also commercial preparations available in pet shops which are supposed to make cats avoid cords; these are effective with some cats. If nothing else works, you can always cover the cord with a spiral plastic intended for telephone cords. No cat can chew through *that*.

Another cause of electric shock in cats is an inadequately protected electric appliance. This is a threat to the humans in the family, too, but the hazard to the cat is greater because its curiosity may lead it to inspect the appliance more closely than humans do. Some appliances are especially dangerous to cats. Most electric blankets, for example, are sold with the warning that no weight should be laid on the blanket, but cats love to sleep on their masters' beds. Moreover, cats like to paw at the blanket with a kind of kneading movement. If they do this to an electric blanket or a heating pad, there is great danger that they may pierce the outer covering and come in contact with a current-bearing wire.

Death from electric shock because of chewing electric cords or touching an unprotected electric appliance is rare in cats, but it happens. More often the cat is shocked, burned, and frightened.

If the cat appears to be unable to let go of the electric contact, *don't* grab the cat. Instead, take a thick piece of dry cloth and seize the wire; then jerk the wire out of the cat's mouth. Be careful in approaching the cat as long as it is in contact with the electricity, for it is not unusual for an animal to urinate involuntarily during an electric shock, and you may be in serious trouble if you are standing in a puddle of urine while handling the electric wire.

After the cat has been freed from the electric contact, administer artificial respiration and treat as for shock (see page 162). Telephone your veterinarian as quickly as possible. The vet may be needed to inject a stimulant for the heart and respiration.

BURNS

Heat, friction, electricity, or corrosive chemicals can cause burns. A cat can be scalded by steam or hot water, most commonly in kitchen accidents. Second-degree burns (blistering) are rarely found in cats, though burns of greater severity are as likely to occur in cat as in man.

Any bad burn should be treated by a veterinarian. The cat owner's care until the vet can take charge must be the administration of first aid. Any step that is taken to help the cat in this emergency must be based on the realization that a burned cat is almost certainly suffering from shock as well. So the first problem is to keep the cat quiet, warm, and restrained.

First aid begins with cleaning the burned area as much as possible. The hair should be trimmed away from the edges of the burn. Tannic acid should be applied; the most convenient form may be weak, cold tea. A weak solution of baking soda is an acceptable substitute. The whole burned area should be covered with white petrolatum. (Do *not* use carbolated petroleum jelly or any phenol compound.)

A "baby" aspirin tablet (1¼ grains) will help to bring the temperature down and keep the cat calm.

FRACTURES

Broken bones used to mean a death warrant for cats years ago. But veterinary surgery has progressed as dramatically as human surgery in recent decades. Even fractured spines are sometimes repaired today, although a cat that has suffered a fracture of that severity probably is better off if it is put to sleep. Most fractures, however, can be handled very well by your veterinarian.

Your principal concern must be to get the cat to the vet as promptly as possible so that he can reduce the fracture. The fractured bone should be immobilized, if possible by a splint. Any rigid, straight object—a foot of broomstick, a ruler, and so on—can be used as a splint. The broken bone should be tied to the splint above and below the fracture. Then the entire limb should be wrapped in a bandage with the splint until the cat can be rushed to the vet.

If the ribs are broken, the cat should be kept lying down, with the broken ribs up, until the vet can attend it. If the vet cannot come to your house, ease the cat onto a blanket, lift the blanket cautiously and slide a board under it, and then transport the cat on the blanket to the animal hospital.

Cats often suffer fractured tails because they fail to whisk their tails out of the way of doors in time. A broken tail is painful and it often mends with a kink in it, but it is usually not a dangerous fracture.

Dislocation of the jaw, which is technically a fracture, is common in the cat. Often it results from the cat's being struck by a car or having a door swing shut on its face. Your vet can wire the upper and lower jaws into place and in about three weeks the cat will be as good as new. For the first few days of that period only liquid food can be fed to the cat; after that, until the three weeks are up, the cat will have to be fed foods softened with water, bouillon, and so on.

As in human surgery, fractures in the long bones often are repaired with the use of metal pins.

Many times what appears to be a fracture turns out to be a sprain. Usually it's best to have a veterinarian examine the area to make sure whether a fracture or a sprain has occurred. If it is a sprain, an ice bag should be applied to the swollen area and a "baby" aspirin should be given to the cat.

FOREIGN OBJECTS

Curiosity, hunger, and activity can result in all manner of trouble for cats, including foreign bodies in the mouth, the alimentary tract, the skin, and the feet. Usually the cat first shows signs of its trouble by pawing at its mouth or face, coughing, drooling, licking, and gnawing at its skin or feet. The cat may be unable to defecate and may emit pitiful little cries of pain.

A twig or a small bone may be caught in the mouth or throat; a round, hollow bone may have slipped over some teeth; a needle or a fishhook may be imbedded in the skin or palate; a piece of broken glass may have been driven into a paw—the possibilities are almost infinite.

At such a time, keep calm and examine the cat carefully, especially in the area in which it appears to be affected. If you can find the foreign object and remove it, do so, regardless of where or what it is. If you can't find it or can't remove it, rush the cat to a veterinarian.

If both ends of a bone are stuck in the flesh, it is necessary to be extremely careful to avoid tearing the flesh while removing the bone. If the offender is a fish bone, it can be cut for easier removal; a scissors will do, but only scissors with rounded ends.

A very common foreign body that causes problems in the cat is a rubber band—not only internally, by swallowing, but externally, as a result of unthinkingly cruel acts by children. Veterinarians often have found rubber bands wrapped tightly around the base of the tail, a foot, a leg, or even a penis. The rubber band digs deeply into the skin. After a time, the skin may even grow over the rubber band, and the only sign of the foreign object is a white, hairless ring on the skin. If the rubber band has been in place for a long time, it may be necessary to have it removed by a vet.

Any foreign object is likely to make the cat nervous and excited, so it is wise to restrain the cat before attempting to help it.

FITS

Excitement, ear mites, poison, disease, and other factors can cause convulsions. Kittens are most prone to fits which have no permanent significance. A kitten may rush about in an apparent panic for perhaps a minute, then lie down calmly on its belly, fully conscious. Often the kitten never suffers a second fit.

There are two other types of fits that are more serious. In one, the cat remains conscious but becomes rigid, falls to the ground with its legs kicking, and cries out in pain. In the other, the cat cries shrilly as it rushes about as though mad, sometimes frothing at the mouth, often running into furniture or other objects in its path. Even after it falls it may thrash about as though it were still running. Frequently the cat loses consciousness.

The best policy is to leave a cat alone while it is having a fit. If it is possible to handle the cat—being careful to avoid being bitten—it's desirable to move it into a dark room. Let the convulsion run its course. Then keep the cat in the dark room, keep it quiet, and apply a cold pack to the head. A quarter-grain or half-grain Phenobarbital may be helpful in calming the cat. If you don't have Phenobarbital, aspirin can be used as a substitute.

Remember that the fit is a symptom of an underlying problem that only your veterinarian can diagnose. As soon as possible after the convulsion, the cat should be taken to the vet for an examination.

POISONING

Despite the fears of owners, cat poisoning is, fortunately, rare. When it does occur, it is more often accidental than malicious. Frequently what appears to be poisoning is illness. For example, a dozen stray cats will suddenly die on one city block. The neighborhood always assumes this is due to poisoning, but it is more likely that the cats were swept away by feline distemper, also known as cat plague.

When cats are poisoned, it is usually because they have eaten insects that were dying from insecticides, or gnawed on painted wood, or eaten a rodent killed by rat poison, or chewed the leaves of poisonous plants. And then there are the rare occasions when psychotic cat haters put out poisoned meat or fish for cats.

The symptoms of poisoning are similar to those of several illnesses; they include pain, vomiting, diarrhea, panting, trembling, fits, slimy mouth, coma.

The most important rule in treating poisoned cats is speed. You must work quickly to fight the poison before it can do its damage inside the cat.

An emetic is the vital first step. You must make the cat vomit the poison. Here are some emetics that can be used:

Salt water: Two tablespoons of salt to a half-pint of warm water. Dosage: two or three tablespoonfuls.

Hydrogen peroxide and water: Mix one part of hydrogen peroxide with one part of water. Dosage: one teaspoonful to one tablespoonful, depending on the size and age of the cat.

Mustard water: Mix a teaspoon of powdered mustard with a quarter of a glass of warm water.

No emetic should be administered when the cat has swallowed a corrosive acid or a caustic alkali. Vomiting those substances would only burn the mouth and throat more. Neutralizing acids or alkalis should be taken to treat this problem safely.

If the cat has swallowed an acid, neutralize it by administering milk of magnesia or a solution of four teaspoons of baking soda to a glass of water.

If the cat has swallowed an alkali (lye, for example), neutralize it by administering vinegar or lemon juice.

Whether an acid or an alkali is involved, the cat should be given milk, raw egg white, or olive oil after the neutralizing agent.

If you do not know what kind of poison has been swallowed, the Universal Antidote (see page 158) can be administered. You should keep a supply of this dark-gray powder in your medicine cabinet for emergencies (it can be used if humans have swallowed poison, too). When it is needed, the formula is dissolved in warm water in the proportion of four heaping teaspoons of Universal Antidote to one glass of water.

A makeshift and not entirely satisfactory substitute for the Universal Antidote can be put together in a jiffy. For the charcoal, substitute charred, crumbled toast; for the tannic acid, strong tea; for the magnesium oxide, milk of magnesia. Don't worry about a substitute for the kaolin: there isn't any. Mix them in these proportions: two parts of toast, one part of tea, one part of milk of magnesia.

If you are certain what poison the cat swallowed, tell your veterinarian on the telephone. *And then—provided the vet approves—* administer the antidote. It's more likely that the vet will want you to rush the cat to the office.

These are some of the most common poisons:

ANTU: rat poison used by some exterminators. First aid: induce vomiting.

Arsenic: insecticide. First aid: induce vomiting, then give milk of magnesia and follow it with strong tea.

Cyanide: fumigant. Kills so quickly that nothing can be done to save the victim, in most cases.

Malathion (and other pyrophosphates): agricultural sprays and insecticides. First aid: ineffective. Rush cat to vet for injection of antidote.

Sodium fluoracetate (1080): rat poison. Induce vomiting, then rush cat to the vet.

Squill: rat poison. This poison is a violent emetic, so nothing should be done to stimulate additional vomiting. First aid: keep cat warm and quiet, give it two or three tablespoons of mineral oil, followed by three tablespoons of Kaopectate.

Strychnine: the most common rat poison. First aid: *in early cases* an emetic should be given, and after the cat has vomited, it should be fed four to ten tablespoons of strong tea; *in late cases* or during convulsions this should not be done—instead, the cat should be moved gently but quickly to the vet's office.

Warfarin: a supposedly nontoxic rat poison which can be dangerous in a very large dose or in repeated doses. First aid: ineffective; rush cat to the vet.

For those cat owners who may be worried about the possibility of their cats' eating poisonous plants, these are the American plants dangerous to cats: water hemlock, cocklebur, buttercup, corn cockle, nightshade, nettle, bladder pod, rattlebush, crotalaria, jimson weed, laurel, common oleander, castor bean, locoweed, poison vetch, choke cherry, and arrow grass. It is well to avoid these plants in or around the house if you want to keep a cat.

ANAL GLANDS

Sometimes you may notice that your cat is dragging its hindquarters along the ground. Most people believe this is an indication of worm infestation, but they are wrong. This action means that the cat is suffering from an anal gland problem. Another sign of this difficulty is the cat's biting frequently at the base of its tail.

The anal glands are two small sacs which are located one on each side of the anus and which empty into the anus. A yellowish, oily, foul smelling musk is secreted into these sacs. The function of the anal glands, as the sacs are usually called, is still not understood. One theory has it that the sacs are intended to lubricate the rectum and thus facilitate the passage of bones, pebbles, and other things. Another theory holds that the anal glands are fundamentally vestigial musk glands like those of a skunk. As a matter of fact, a skunk's musk glands are located in the same place as a cat's (or dog's) anal glands and the secretion is similar, except for the intensity of the odor.

Whatever the function of the anal glands, they can sometimes pose a problem for the cat owner. The anal glands may become impacted or infected; an abscess may even develop. When this sort of difficulty is suspected, the cat owner should try to express the anal glands or take the cat to a veterinarian to have this done. If you want to try it yourself, well and good—but let the vet show you how to do it the first time. If you do it wrong, you'll exasperate the cat and disgust yourself, for this is an uncommonly unpleasant job. This is the way you do it: With the cat on a table, facing your left, take its tail in your left hand firmly and lift it. Holding a good-sized piece of cotton over the anus, press firmly with your fingers simultaneously on both sides of the anal opening. (The cotton is necessary because the secretion spurts out when the sacs are expressed.)

CONSTIPATION AND DIARRHEA

Constipation can be a very serious matter in the cat because of the constant accumulation of hair in the alimentary tract. If this hair and fecal matter become impacted, the consequence can be more than distressing. To avoid constipation in the cat, every third or fourth day give it mineral oil, uncarbolated petroleum jelly, or one of the preparations especially prepared for this purpose and sold in most pet shops (most cats love the latter). It is helpful, too, to give the cat some roughage in its diet—spinach, lettuce, or perhaps grass or green oat shoots grown in a pot or window box.

Diarrhea usually can be stopped with Kaopectate, followed by a dose of olive oil to soothe the inflamed digestive tract. If that doesn't work, take the cat at once to the veterinarian, for the diarrhea may be a symptom of more serious trouble. If the diarrhea recurs, the diet may be at fault; it may be necessary to give the cat a different type of food.

EARS

Despite its open, erect ear, the cat has a tendency toward ear problems. These include mite infestation, infection of the outer ear, tumors and inflammatory polyps, and blood tumors. These can all become serious disorders, and even in their initial stages they can cause considerable difficulty. Ear mites, for example, are the most common cause of fits in cats.

Ear ailments require the skill of the veterinarian. Attempts at home treatment are likely to end in disaster. The most important duty for the cat owner is to learn to recognize the symptoms of ear ailments. These include the cat's shaking its head, pawing at its ear frequently, or rubbing its ear against furniture. A foul smell from the ear and a black or gray accumulation of matter inside the ear are indications of trouble. Abnormal growths sometimes can be seen. Blood tumors sometimes cause the ear to become hot and sensitive and, in certain cases, to swell.

TEETH

Decay is less common in a cat's mouth than in man's. The enamel is thicker, the salivary juices are less damaging, the shape of the teeth discourages the retention of food particles, and the diet is usually better.

Nevertheless, decay and other problems do exist. Teeth are broken. Roots become infected; abscesses sometimes occur. Tartar accumulates. Gums are pushed back and become flaccid.

A good diet will help to keep your cat's teeth in good condition. Small, hard biscuits or pellets made for cats or dogs are good for the teeth, too. Chewy kidneys, muscle meats, and other flesh that provide some resistance to the teeth and gums are all beneficial.

Occasionally—about once a year—a veterinarian should remove the tartar from your cat's teeth. In the intervals, it is not necessary to brush the teeth.

Bad breath, drooling, pawing at the mouth, shaking the head, or pale-colored gums are all clues to possible trouble in your cat's mouth. Only a veterinarian is competent to deal with these matters. The vet may remove teeth under anesthetic or administer drugs to treat infections. Often vitamins may be prescribed for gum conditions.

EYES

The eyes of many cats exude a small amount of matter from time to time. This eye fluid, which dries and cakes on the muzzle near the corner of the eye, should be gently cleared away with a facial tissue.

If any hairs around the eye have a tendency to curl into the eye, they should be trimmed away.

Serious injury to the eye requires a veterinarian's care, of course, but minor irritations can be treated by washing the sore eye with a piece of cotton which has been soaked in warm water. The ophthalmic ointment listed for your first-aid kit can then be applied.

BONES

Excepting fractures, most bone problems occur in kittens rather than adult cats. However, hip dysplasia has occasionally been found in some adult cats. It should be emphasized that this condition is rare in cats, although it is not uncommon in dogs.

Hip dysplasia is a malformation of the ball and socket joint of the hip, which may result in a minor maladjustment or a complete dislocation. Often the socket is flattened, inadequately cupped to hold the ball at the end of the thigh bone.

The lameness which is a symptom of this condition may appear while the cat is still a young kitten or at any age thereafter. In a mild case there is often no outward sign of trouble at all, and the cat probably never will need treatment. An Alabama veterinarian has reported discovering hip dysplasia in a family of cats after X-raying one cat because it appeared to have a pelvic fracture.

Cats suffering from hip dysplasia should never be bred, for this is a congenital disorder that is transmitted genetically as an irregular dominant characteristic.

SKIN

Skin disorders are common in cats, especially in those permitted to roam. Stray cats, when first adopted, are usually found to be suffering from some skin ailment, most often ringworm. For that reason, a newly acquired cat should be examined by a veterinarian as soon as possible.

Ringworm: This malady is misnamed, for ringworm has nothing whatever to do with any worm; it is caused by a fungus. Although most ringworm cases look alike to the lay eye—little, round, sore, hairless patches on the skin—there are many varieties of ringworm. There are several species, grouped in two genera, that afflict the cat, but the fungus most often found in the cat is a species called *Microsporum canis.* This, too, is grossly misnamed; most authorities now believe that the cat, rather than the dog, is "the major reservoir" and "the natural host" of this fungus.

Most forms of ringworm—and especially that caused by *Microsporum canis*—are extremely contagious. One cat can spread the disorder to other cats, dogs, and other domestic animals, and even to man. One stray cat was the unwitting cause of an outbreak of ringworm in my own household that affected all the cats and dogs and the humans, too. (We kept the cat, cured all the cases of ringworm, and received so much pleasure from the culprit that it more than paid us, a hundred times over, for the inconvenience it caused us.)

The first sign of ringworm is the appearance of small, scabby circles on the skin on any part of the body, but most often on the ears, face, neck, and tail. The cat should be taken to a veterinarian as soon as scabby circles appear on these areas.

The veterinarian probably will want to examine the cat under a Wood's light, an ultraviolet lamp. Many forms of ringworm, but not all, will fluoresce in this light. So will certain other things, such as mineral oil, petrolatum, and a number of skin medications. (It is curious that ringworm in calves sometimes clears up spontaneously when the animals are turned out to pasture in the sunshine, with its ultraviolet rays, or when they are otherwise exposed to ultraviolet. Never try home treatment of cats in this manner.)

Until recently ringworm was one of the worst curses of cat life. Today, thanks to griseofulvin, an antibiotic discovered in 1939 but not applied to fungus disorders for almost two decades, ringworm is a much less severe problem to cure. In treating your cat, the veterinarian is likely to follow this course: Griseofulvin will be administered in tablet form (this will be up to you to do) for perhaps a month. Once a week the cat will be bathed (again, by you) in an antibacterial fungicide, perhaps captan, which the vet will prescribe. Because of the danger of secondary infection, a broad-spectrum antibiotic probably will be injected by hypodermic.

MANGE

There are two kinds of mange, both caused by parasitic mites. Sarcoptic mange, also called scabies, is the less serious form, but it is easily transmitted from cat to man. Demodectic mange, also called follicular mange or red mange, is a very dangerous skin disease, but there is some doubt that this type occurs in the cat.

Sarcoptic mange: This is caused by an eight-legged, round mite that lays its eggs in tunnels that the female burrows under the skin. The larvae hatch in the tunnels and feed there. The adult mite's burrowing and the feeding of the larvae cause an intense itchiness. The cat scratches and rubs constantly. The mange usually makes its appearance first on the head. The hair begins to fall out around the affected area, and the skin becomes dry, reddish, thickened, folded, and wrinkled. Crusts develop.

To diagnose scabies, the veterinarian must take a scraping of skin from the affected area. This may hurt the cat just a little, but it will help it in the long run.

Sarcoptic mange is not difficult to cure, although the treatment may have to be continued for a while before the cat is free of both the mange and the danger of reinfection. There is one problem, however, in treating mange in the cat; there is a widespread belief among veterinarians that cats are adversely affected by phenol (carbolic acid), and many acaricides—the medicines that kill mange mites—contain phenol in some form, usually quite diluted. Your veterinarian may want to prescribe lime and sulfur baths or sulfur ointments. The vet will also want to administer an antibiotic by injection to guard against secondary infection.

Demodectic mange: This is caused by a long, wormlike mite that has eight short legs in the adult phase. The mites invade the hair follicles and the sebaceous glands surrounding them. Again, the mange usually begins on the head, most often on the ears. It can spread over the entire body from there. The onset of the disease is marked by sores of varying sizes, some of them scaly, with redness, loss of hair, and slightly thickened, dry skin, others with considerable redness, blood and serum oozing out, along with pus.

Deep scrapings of skin are necessary to produce the infested follicles and glands for microscopic examination, which is essential to the diagnosis of either form of mange.

Until quite recently, demodectic mange was so difficult to cure that veterinarians almost always recommended that diseased animals be put to sleep. That is no longer necessary—if the animal's owner is prepared to do the work that will be required for a cure. The work requires patience and persistence. A veterinarian must direct the treatment of this condition.

This warning must be added: In both forms of mange, but especially in demodectic mange, the treatment, onerous as it may be, must be continued after the cat is apparently cured, for the mites may still survive deep in the follicles. Never stop the treatment until your vet has told you that it is no longer necessary.

ECZEMA

Any dermatitis whose nature and cause are not known is likely to be called eczema. In other words, there is, properly speaking, no such ailment as eczema—but there are many disorders that are lumped together under that name. Heredity, allergy, irritation, exposure to rays, and any number of other causes are possible. Both scaly (dry) and crusty (moist) eczemas occur in cats and cause great itchy discomfort.

Follow your veterinarian's instructions precisely in treating eczema and be patient with the vet if there seems to be little improvement over a number of treatments. It would be unfair to expect veterinary medicine to be more advanced than human medicine, and anyone who has suffered from a chronic dermatitis is aware of how little is known about human skin ailments. I know of a man whose skin disorder was not cured until he had been going to dermatologists for eleven years. Your cat's eczema will probably be cleared up rather quickly, even if the vet does have to go about it by trial and error, trying first one drug and then another until he finds one that will be effective in the particular case.

FELINE PANLEUKOPENIA

This terrible disease has various other names: feline distemper (although it is not related to canine distemper at all), feline infectious enteritis, cat fever, and—the most descriptive of all—cat plague.

Like the Black Death that swept across Europe centuries ago, feline distemper sometimes flashes through a neighborhood, leaving behind so many dying cats that it appears a poisoner has been at work. But the poisoner, in this case, is a virus that cannot be seen with the naked eye. Losses from this plague are high, especially in young cats. Between 60 and 90 percent of the diseased cats are likely to die.

Feline distemper cannot be transmitted to dogs. Nor can canine distemper infect cats.

Summer is the time of greatest danger, but the disease may occur whenever there are new susceptible cats in a neighborhood; the period of greatest susceptibility is between four and six months of age. All secretions and excretions of infected cats contain the highly contagious virus. How long this virus contaminates is questionable. If a kitten is brought into a house in which a cat has died of distemper, the newcomer should be protected by serum and vaccine.

Almost all the internal organs are affected. No part of the body is untouched; the lymph nodes are among the first to be affected and the bone marrow is among the last. The incubation period is four to ten days, and then the cat is in grave danger.

These are the symptoms for which the cat owner must watch: fever, loss of appetite, vomiting, depression, weakness, dehydration. The cat usually won't drink water, although it may linger close to its water dish.

In treating your cat, the veterinarian may resort to blood transfusions; injection of serum, fluids, salts, and dextrose; and a broad spectrum of antibiotics.

An effective vaccine is available. Every cat should have the protection of this vaccine.

FELINE VIRAL RHINOTRACHEITIS

This disease is usually abbreviated to FVR. It was not until 1958 that the offending virus was isolated. Before that, it had probably been lumped with pneumonitis. Even today it is difficult to distinguish between the two, for the symptoms are essentially the same: high temperature, running eyes and nose, sneezing and coughing, and loss of appetite. Most cats recover in about two weeks. In laboratory observations, about one of every four cats died. A cat which has had the illness once can get it again.

There is now a vaccine which offers good protection against this disease.

PNEUMONITIS

As highly infectious as feline distemper, pneumonitis is far less dangerous to cat life. It is a long-drawn-out disease, severe in its manifestations, but it kills in less than 30 percent of the cases if the cat is in good health generally and receives proper care. An airborne virus, sprayed into the air when the sick cat sneezes, causes the malady.

As the virus goes to work inside the cat, the eyes become inflamed and begin to water heavily. Inflammation spreads to the nasal passages and the cat's nose begins to run. Pneumonia develops. The spleen may be slightly enlarged.

The cat's owner is likely to realize that something is wrong when he sees the cat's eyes and nose running. But there will have been subtler symptoms before that: a slight rise in temperature and, in many cases, some degree of sensitivity to light, along with occasional sneezing. The most obvious symptoms—the running eyes and nose—appear six to ten days after exposure to the disease. These symptoms persist for a week or two. The loss in weight which began with the first symptoms continues for about a month.

The veterinarian's treatment probably will include injection of antibiotics and possibly an antihistamine.

TUBERCULOSIS

Tuberculosis does not occur in a feline form, but cats can acquire TB from some other mammals. The cat appears to be immune to human TB, but it can contract the kind of tuberculosis to which cows and birds fall victim. In those parts of the world where milk is usually still not pasteurized, bovine TB in cats ranges up to 12 percent of all cats autopsied. Where milk is pasteurized, bovine TB in the cat is rare. So is avian tuberculosis. Some veterinary research has suggested that Siamese cats may be slightly more susceptible to tuberculosis than other cats.

COCCIDIOSIS

Cats, like dogs, rabbits, cattle, sheep, and swine, are susceptible to coccidiosis, an intestinal disease which can be acute or chronic. It is most common among young cats. Coccidiosis, which is not usually fatal, causes diarrhea and loss of weight.

CRYPTOCOCCOSIS

An internal fungus is responsible for cryptococcosis, a disease which can make a cat's life miserable for years if it is not detected and treated. It causes localized outbreaks in the nose, lungs, and brain of the cat. If a cat has suffered for a long time with a discharge from its eyes and nose, has difficulty breathing, coughs, tends to run a fever, or develops blindness, cryptococcosis should be suspected. The disease often ends in death, especially if it spreads to the brain, spinal cord, or lungs.

TOXOPLASMOSIS

A parasitic protozoon causes toxoplasmosis, an infection that can strike most of the internal organs of the cat's body. Infected cats run high fevers, develop pneumonia, breathe rapidly and with difficulty, sound wheezy, and refuse food and water. The death rate is very high. If the disease is diagnosed early, the cat may be saved by treatment.

RABIES

Rabies is much less common in the cat than in the dog—and even in the dog it is relatively rare. In Missouri, for example, over a ten-year period there were 1,368 cases of rabies in dogs, compared with 324 in cats. In a fifteen-year period following World War II, there were only 138 cases of rabies in humans in the United States, and only 5 of them were traceable to cats. (Most rabies in man in this country today comes from the bites of wild animals, especially foxes and bats. But in 1961 it was established that rabies can be transmitted by air, without any biting at all, which casts a new light on this dread disease.)

There are two forms of rabies, the paralytic and the furious. In the former, the chewing muscles and the throat are paralyzed, and the animal, unable to swallow, drools profusely. It usually does not become vicious and does not try to bite. Death comes in a few hours.

The furious form is more common in cats. The cat becomes alert, nervous; its pupils are dilated. It has a tendency to swallow foreign objects. The cat may seem very playful, but it will bite even when it is being petted. In a few hours the cat becomes incredibly vicious; it will bite at any moving object, including the most beloved owner. Swallowing becomes difficult. The cat may suddenly go into convulsions.

There is no cure for rabies in man or in cat. Because of this, and because of the epizootic nature of the disease, especially among wild animals, restrictions have been raised in some places against the transportation of animals. Cats being taken into Michigan, for example, must be accompanied by a health certificate issued by a veterinarian. Hawaii has a 120-day quarantine on cats, even those which are certified as having been vaccinated. Puerto Rico requires that any cat more than eight weeks old entering that island be vaccinated and certified to be healthy. Great Britain has a six-month quarantine on cats.

Any cat which has bitten a human must be kept under observation for a period prescribed by public health agencies. If the cat which did the biting has died, a veterinarian should be asked to send its head to a state public health laboratory for examination; in most states this is required by law. If it is known that the cat was rabid, any unvaccinated cat bitten by it should be put to sleep. The reason for this drastic step is simple: The incubation period in cats ranges from less than twenty days to more than sixty days—it may even, in some cases, be several months. Therefore, an unvaccinated cat bitten by a rabid animal must be kept confined, under close observation, for six months, according to the World Health Organization. If the cat owner is willing to keep his cat strictly isolated for that period of time, it need not be put to sleep.

A cat which had been vaccinated before being bitten ought to be revaccinated and confined inside the house—or taken outside only on a leash—for thirty days after being bitten, if the vaccination occurred within the past year.

There are several kinds of vaccines available to your veterinarian. Some vaccine is derived from chemically killed virus. Live virus attenuated by development through chick embryos is the basis for other vaccines. The killed-virus vaccine confers protection for about a year; the live-virus, for about two years.

ANEMIA

"Cats perhaps suffer more often and more severely from anemia than any other species," Dr. C. E. DeCamp once wrote in *Veterinary Medicine*. The anemia may be caused by loss of blood (from a wound, or example), the breakdown of red blood cells (resulting from some infections), or a decrease in the production of red blood cells.

The symptoms of anemia include lethargy, weakness, lack of appetite, and occasionally vomiting. In advanced cases the cat may appear restless and its breathing may be labored.

There is also a form of the disease called feline infectious anemia which is caused by either of two parasitic microorganisms. Some cats carry the disease in a latent form. Infected cats show the usual symptoms of anemia; in the acute form, high temperatures, lack of appetite, depression, and rapid loss of weight, and in the chronic form, normal (or even subnormal) temperatures, weakness, depression, and a more gradual loss of weight.

Transfusions of whole blood or serum are used to combat anemia in the cat. Antibiotics and other drugs are usually given to fight active or possible infection.

CYSTITIS

One of the most common problems in the cat is cystitis, which means, properly speaking, an acute or chronic inflammation of the urinary bladder. It is caused by infection but is often complicated by stones—those somewhat mysterious accretions of mineral particles in the kidneys or elsewhere in the genito-urinary system. It has sometimes been suggested that cystitis is especially prevalent in neutered cats, but some researchers have pointed out that this may be just an illusion, caused by the fact that most pet cats which come to the attention of veterinarians have been altered.

A female cat suffering from cystitis will urinate frequently—at least it will try to urinate. But only a few drops, if any, will appear. Nevertheless, the cat keeps trying, over and over again, until it's spending a good part of its time in the litter box. It may also forget some of its house training, too, and you may see it trying to urinate elsewhere, for example, in the bathtub. The cat may not take good care of its appearance and the coat will look poor. Laziness and lack of appetite are also among the symptoms. As the illness progresses, the cat may have blood in its urine.

A variety of drugs are available to the veterinarian in treating this condition in the female and the male. But the problem is much more serious in the male because its urinary passages are smaller.

The symptoms in the male may be the same as in the female, or slightly different. The male may be depressed and weak. Vomiting may occur. The urine may be scant, and darker and thicker than usual. The cat may lick its penis in an attempt to ease the pain. It will spend a good part of its time crouching. Any pressure on its sides may make it cry out with pain.

Stones slipping into the urethral passages block them. The origin of the stones is unknown. Although the stones are composed of minerals, scientists have been unable to cause stones by feeding cats diets high in ash.

The veterinarian may be able to dissolve the stone chemically, or he may have to anesthetize the cat and remove the stone surgically. Once it has occurred, the condition is likely to recur, whether the cat is male or female. In the male, it may be necessary to bypass the urethra. This can be done by creating a new opening in front of the urethra. In some cases, the operating veterinarian may wish to substitute a plastic urethra, which is wider and less likely to become blocked. After this kind of radical surgery, the cat is still able to control its urination—with some discomfort. This procedure is so unpleasant, however, that it is generally inadvisable.

When cystitis is suspected in either a male or a female cat, no time should be lost in rushing it to the vet. Cats have died in as short a time as forty-eight hours after the onset of symptoms. Often the cat's owner is under the misapprehension that the cat is constipated; before he realizes his mistake, the cat is in great pain because of the retention of urine in its bladder.

DIABETES

Although diabetes occurs in dogs and rarely in other domestic animals, it does appear in cats occasionally. In fact, one of my own cats—a nineteen-year-old male of Siamese-Burmese ancestry—was found to be suffering from diabetes mellitus.

The symptoms of diabetes are subtle at first and are likely to be overlooked for some time. They include listlessness and a tendency to sleep much more than usual, occasional vomiting, increased thirst and urination, loss of weight, and the eating of abnormally large amounts of food at mealtime. In advanced cases there is a distinct acetone odor to the breath. If not caught in time, the disease may cause the cat to lapse into a coma.

Even then the cat can be saved, if its problem is diagnosed correctly and vigorous action is taken by the veterinarian. The cat will, however, have to be hospitalized until its condition is stabilized.

Eventually the cat can be returned to its home, but its owners must be prepared for a tough regimen. Every day at the same time the cat must be given an injection of insulin. The food must be weighed before being given to the animal, and what the cat leaves must be weighed, too, in order to determine how many ounces of food have been eaten at each serving. The urine must be tested at least once and preferably twice a day.

The cat's owner must be prepared for emergency treatment if the cat goes into a coma or into convulsions.

CANCER

Cancer in almost all its forms is found in the cat. Up to 6 percent of all cats may suffer from cancer of the skin, mammary glands, and bones, and as high as 10 percent from leukemia and other cancerous conditions in blood-forming tissues. Dr. Jean Holzworth, of Angell Memorial Animal Hospital in Boston, believes that leukemia and other blood cancers are "extraordinarily prevalent in the domestic cat," but often go undiagnosed.

As in man, cancer in the cat often can be cured if it is detected in time. Unfortunately, however, a cat that is suffering from cancer often will give no outward sign of pain—that is, it will not cry or moan. But it will give other signs of trouble, such as failure to keep its coat clean, lethargy, depression, loss of appetite, and the like. Any unusual growths or lumps on or under the skin warrant a visit to the veterinarian. Wounds that do not heal and symptoms that fit into the pattern of a known disease but do not respond to the treatment for that disease also may indicate cancer.

9. SEX, MATING, AND KITTENING

In every society which has known the cat, it has been a symbol of sex. Few other animals participate with such wholehearted enthusiasm in the process of reproducing their species. This uninhibited—to put it mildly—attitude toward sex is recognized in the vulgar use of the word *cat* to describe a house of prostitution or generally promiscuous behavior.

Sexual behavior in the cat begins before puberty, in play. Kittens as young as three months may mount each other and engage in other significant movements. In this prepuberal period even female kittens sometimes exhibit the male pattern of behavior. The reason for this, some experts believe, is that male sex hormones appear in the cat in infancy, but female hormones are not present until puberty.

Puberty occurs in the female at an earlier age than in the male. Sexual maturity and physical maturity, in the sense of complete bodily development, do not coincide in the cat (this is true of man, too, of course). The female begins to display true sexuality about the age of six months, when she may go into her first heat. The heat cycle, also called her "season" or, more scientifically, *estrus*, is discussed in another section later in this chapter. Males become sexually mature, on the average, at eleven months. These ages for puberty are highly variable. In the male, for example, puberty may occur anywhere between six and eighteen months.

NEUTERING

Neutering should not be done before eight months of age, to permit the cat to develop as normally as possible. When puberty occurs, in either female or male, most cat owners will find that they can no longer postpone a decision on the question of whether to have the cat altered or permit it to remain whole.

If the cat is not going to be used for breeding—and that means most pure-bred cats and virtually all other cats—it should be neutered. Here are some of the reasons:

The male: A whole male cannot be kept in the house after puberty because it forgets its toilet training and "sprays" around the rooms, and its urine has an unendurable stench. Many novice cat owners get rid of their pets at this time, sadly, because they are unaware that castration will remedy both of these objectionable conditions.

Whole tomcats insist on roaming and they are often in fights with other cats. Their unsexed brothers, on the other hand, are happy to be stay-at-homes and usually are much less belligerent.

A neutered cat is just as good a mouser as any whole cat and its health is at least as good, if not better. Those cat owners who wonder if cats should be mated for the sake of their health can be assured that there is nothing inherently health-promoting in copulation.

The female: Many of the same arguments apply to the female, with some additional ones. A spayed female loses the wanderlust that afflicts a whole queen. It doesn't attract tomcats who would otherwise come around the house, spraying the shrubbery (and killing it) and making the night sleepless with their caterwauling.

The neutered female is saved from the stress of kittening and its risks, small though they may be. And there are no unwanted kittens to be put to sleep. This is a major consideration, for the world is full of unwanted cats that die of cold, exposure, disease, or the attacks of hostile animals. It is a curious thing that some people, in a rather obvious example of anthropomorphism, regard the neutering of cats as immoral but are perfectly willing to let the cat produce litter after litter of kittens who must be killed.

To reassure those who fear that the neutering of animals is a form of birth control—and feel that birth control is not in keeping with moral law—Friends of Animals, an organization which assists low-income families to pay the cost of spaying their pets, solicited an opinion from the Roman Catholic Archdiocese of New York on this matter. The Reverend Timothy J. Flynn, Director of the Archdiocesan Bureau of Information, replied, "I think that you should notify your members through whatever means you have at your disposal that the Church has no objection to the spaying of animals."

For most owners of female cats, the question of spaying is resolved abruptly after several nerve-wracking nights spent listening to their pets "calling" for a mate.

The neutering of either male or female can be done at any time, even immediately before, during, or after the female's season. The veterinarian who will perform the operation may have a personal preference in this matter of timing, and you ought to consult him first.

It is easier, and less expensive, to have a male unsexed. The organs are external and accessible. The cat is anesthetized and then castrated. Most veterinarians leave the scrotal sac intact after removing the testes from within it, so that the cat still looks like a male. The cat can be taken home the same day.

The spaying of the female, on the other hand, requires an abdominal incision to permit the removal of the ovaries and related organs. It is a minor operation, but the abdominal wall has been breached, and usually the cat must be kept in the veterinarian's hospital for a few days to ensure confinement and hence proper rest while the incision heals. It follows, therefore, that the operation should be more expensive for the female. The fees for neutering either sex, however, are very reasonable.

After spaying, many cat owners fear that their pets will grow fat. There is no sound basis for this fear. It is probably predicated on the fact that chickens are unsexed to fatten them as capons, but they are castrated at a very early age, even before the secondary sex characteristics have been developed. If any animal is unsexed before puberty, it tends to grow fat; after puberty, that is not true. If a cat is neutered at any time after the age of eight months, it should develop normally except in its sexuality. There is no reason why a neutered cat, fed a correct diet, should be fat.

Sexual behavior usually ends in the female cat within twenty-four hours after spaying—that is, before it is ready to return home from the veterinary hospital. In the male cat, interest in sex usually will diminish rapidly, and within a couple of weeks the cat has lost all appetite for amorous conquests. However, in some cases—usually cats which have engaged in copulation at some time before castration—the cat may go on trying to mount other cats for months or even years. This can be somewhat disconcerting to the cat owner, who is certain that the vet botched the job. He didn't. In such cases, the male's interest in mounting other cats is not really very strong.

THE MALE CAT

In the rest of this chapter, we will be dealing with whole cats, with cats which have not been unsexed. It is assumed that an uncastrated male is intended to be used for breeding purposes, and that it is, therefore, probably pedigreed, an above-average example of its breed, and an animal notable for its physical and mental soundness.

If the cat is a cryptorchid (that is, both testicles are undescended) or a monorchid (one testicle has been retained within the abdomen), it should not be employed in a breeding program. Indeed, it is well-nigh a physical impossibility to breed a cryptorchid, for the heat inside the body will kill the spermatozoa, although cryptorchids have been bred on an experimental basis. A monorchid can reproduce itself, but it should not be permitted to do so because this abnormality is an inherited fault. There is a relatively high level of late cancer in cryptorchids and monorchids that have not been castrated.

A cat with any genetically transmitted abnormality ought not to be bred. These abnormalities include polydactylism (too many toes on a foot), posterior reduplication (two feet at the bottom of each hindleg), bent or kinky tail, and cleft palate.

A stud cat cannot be kept in the house, so it ought to have an enclosed outside run if it does not roam freely. Such a run ought to be at least ten feet long and preferably twenty. Any tomcat so confined ought to have human companionship for a period every day. This can sometimes be combined with the cat's daily brushing.

THE FEMALE CAT

The queen, as a brood cat is called, should not be bred before her second season. This may be a bit of a problem, however, if her cycle is abnormal, and estrus abnormalities are common. Some females come into heat every three weeks. I had one that came into season every ten days. I know of another cat that never really was out of season. A veterinarian should be consulted regarding such abnormality.

No queen should be asked to bear more than two litters of kittens in a year, and it is better to restrict it to one. The best time for kittens to be born is in the spring, summer, or early fall.

THE HEAT CYCLE

Unlike humans—but like dogs and many other mammals—the female cat can mate only when it is in season. The male cat can mate any time. Most female cats have more than two heats each year. Some scientists believe that a normal female cat never has a heat in winter.

For those cats which are in season almost constantly if they are not bred, a progesterone derivative is available to suppress estrus. This hormonal biochemical, medroxyprogesterone, is given to the cat in tablet form. Within twenty-four hours the cat is thoroughly quieted and refuses mating. The dosage is maintained for another two to four days. After an interval of two to four months, estrus returns. The drug has no effect on future pregnancies.

The female cat has the same reproductive system as a woman. The major difference is in ovulation.

The first stage of the heat cycle is called *proestrus*. The uterus and the vagina undergo changes to get ready for copulation and pregnancy. The vulva begin to swell, although the swelling is not noticeable at first. The cat becomes more affectionate than usual. It also becomes fussy and restless. Its appetite may increase.

The second stage is *estrus*, the period when mating can occur. This usually lasts about four to seven days. During this time the uterine development that began in proestrus continues. The vulvar swelling is obvious. The cat becomes extremely affectionate.

It rolls on the floor and calls almost insistently for a mate. It usually loses appetite.

If the cat is not mated, a third stage, *metestrus,* occurs. In this stage the reproductive organs gradually reduce their activities and enter a period of quiescence known as *anestrus* until the next cycle begins.

Ovulation does not occur unless there has been coition.

MATING

The calling of the queen, to announce that it is in the mood to receive suitors, is quite unnecessary; tomcats clearly know several days before that their opportunity is fast approaching. Perhaps the slight vaginal discharge that occasionally occurs tips them off by an odor imperceptible to the human nose and usually unnoticed by the queen's owner because the cat cleans itself so well.

An inexperienced cat should always be mated with an experienced cat, for an unfortunate incident during its first mating—an attack by its mate, for example—can limit a cat's future usefulness in a breeding program.

When the actual mating occurs, no human help is necessary. The best procedure is to let the two cats into a room together. But humans should be standing by in the room in case of trouble. At this tense moment, either cat may turn on the other in a passion that is certainly not love.

The usual mating is quite uneventful, however. The female crouches in front of the male, treading with her paws, moaning, and arching her back, so that her head is higher than the middle of her back and her hindquarters are higher than her head. The male utters a brief cry and then approaches the female from the side and rear. Grasping the scruff of her loose neck fur in his teeth, he leaps astride her back. She lifts her tail aside as he kneads her sides with his forepaws and engages in a treading movement with his hindpaws on either side of her hindquarters. There is a series of rapid pelvic thrusts, and then the male is motionless as ejaculation occurs. Then he suddenly withdraws his penis as the female cries out in pain.

The female's cry of pain is caused by the barbs on the cat's penis. These are not felt when the penis enters the vagina, but when it is withdrawn, the barbs rake the walls of the passage. It is believed that the scraping of the vagina by the barbs is an essential part of coition in the cat, a nervous stimulus causing ovulation to begin.

Necessary though it may be, the female doesn't like it, and she is perfectly capable of whipping around to attack the male. A wise male, at this point, leaps to some place of safety—the top of a chair, for example.

When the stud is out of reach, the female usually rolls on the floor wildly for several minutes. The purpose of this is not known, if, indeed, there is a purpose. Perhaps she does it because she's ecstatic. On the other hand, maybe she just hurts.

To guard against an unsuccessful service, it is customary to arrange a second mating a day later.

After coition the spermatozoa and the ova begin their journeys toward each other. The ova migrate from the two ovaries through the oviducts to the uterus. In the upper third of the oviduct fertilization takes place as the handful of ova are surrounded by millions of sperm cells; this is usually eighteen to twenty-seven hours after coition.

The fertilized ova do not stop in the uterus; they continue on into the two long, cylindrical chambers that open off the uterus. These are called the "horns" of the uterus. The ova attach themselves to the walls of the horns at equal distances from each other, there to grow until the time of birth.

It is a curious thing that many of the ova begin to grow in the uterine horns and then atrophy, apparently being resorbed into the bloodstream after a while. The usual litter of kittens contains four, and one research group reported that the largest litter produced under their supervision numbered eight—but a cat was opened fifteen days after coition and was found to have at least twelve fertilized ova in its horns. This is believed to be typical.

As soon as ovulation occurs, blood seals the follicles of the ovaries in which the eggs are produced. These blood plugs mark the beginning of the *corpus luteum,* a yellow cellular mass that forms over the follicles in the ovaries. It produces a hormone which ends the heat cycle.

The cat is now pregnant, or "in kitten," as we say.

PREGNANCY

The period of gestation—the time from coition to parturition—in the cat varies from fifty-six to seventy-one days. The
normal time is sixty-five days. Kittens born on or before the
sixty-first day have scarcely any chance for survival.

The kittens in any litter may have more than one father, although each kitten can have only one. Because of the length of
time between coition and fertilization, it is possible for two or
more tomcats to deposit their sperm inside the queen. Each
ovum will accept only one sperm, so a given kitten will have only
one father. But, because there are spermatozoa from two or
more cats in the oviduct at the time, the next ovum may be
fertilized by a spermatozoon from a different cat. Thus, a Russian Blue female that escapes briefly for a romantic escapade
may produce kittens in one litter that have been sired by a Siamese and by a longhair.

True superfetation, that is, intercourse and impregnation
after a previous pregnancy is already under way, also occurs in
the cat, but it is extremely rare. In one pregnant cat which was
studied post-mortem, one full-term, fully developed fetus was
discovered, along with five embryos. And even the embryos did
not appear to be all the same age.

Usually, however, the period of pregnancy is not a time for
erotic antics; it is a time of growth, when the cat will grow in-
creasingly quiet and careful of herself as her time nears.

About the twenty-first day the cat's nipples become slightly
pinker than usual. This is the first outward sign that the mating
was successful and the cat is pregnant. Before another week is
out the veterinarian will be able, by feeling the uterine horns, to
confirm the fact. At the same time, the nipples will have begun
to swell and grow even more pink.

The pregnant cat should be treated normally. Until the last
week of pregnancy, it can run and play as well as ever. In the last
week, the cat itself usually will begin to show a certain amount of
caution about jumping and other activities. A few cats lack the
good sense to do this, however; and the owner of such a cat must
simply try to restrain it from overactivity until after the kittening.

The pregnant queen should be fed a good, well-balanced diet.

It is advisable to add nonfat milk solids or other calcium to the diet from the beginning, for pregnancy causes a terrible drain on the cat's calcium reserves. In the fifth week the cat's consumption of food will increase gradually and additional snacks or small meals can be added; the cat itself ought to be permitted to set the pace unless its demands get out of hand. A vitamin-mineral supplement also will help to ensure a healthy, vigorous litter.

Some pregnant cats suffer from constipation toward the end of their time. White petroleum jelly which is not carbolated can be smeared on the cat's nose; licked off, it will encourage bowel movement.

When about two-thirds of the gestation period has passed, some cats will occasionally roll on the ground for no apparent reason. It has been theorized that the first movement of the unborn kittens within the body of the queen—this is called the "quickening" of the kittens—arouses the cat to this action.

During the last two weeks of her pregnancy, the cat may often appear restless, roaming back and forth throughout the house. She is looking for a place to bear her young. This, then, is the time to make a kittening box and introduce the cat to it.

An inexpensive and easy-to-make kittening box can be made from a big cardboard box obtained from the grocer. It should be quite large, about the size of a cereal carton. A door should be cut in the front of the box, but a sill should be left halfway up, to keep the kittens confined when they begin crawling about. The top should be left on the box so that it will be dark inside, but it can be cut on three sides, with the fourth side acting as a kind of hinge to permit lifting of the top, facilitating access to the kittens.

An even layer of newspapers an inch or two thick should be laid on the bottom of the box. The cat will want to dig at the papers with her claws as she makes a nest for kittening. As the papers are torn up, they should be replaced with fresh, even papers again. When the cat is ready to take up her residence in the box for parturition, a blanket should be laid over the newspapers to make the box warmer for the kittens. When the cat's time is due, a big towel can be laid on top of the blanket to protect it from the stains of the afterbirth and other discharged matter.

Failure to provide a kittening box that meets with the cat's approval can result in her giving birth in some place that doesn't meet with *your* approval—your own bed, for example.

Just before the first kitten is born, the cat's temperature drops below normal, that is, below 101.5 degrees Fahrenheit (38.6 degrees Celsius). It later rises to normal. If it goes above normal, something is probably wrong and the veterinarian should be called at once.

The kittens, which had been carried high up near the chest, have now dropped down and toward the rear.

The cat begins to pant. The "water" breaks. Soon it can be seen that her flanks are moving, reflecting the labor rhythms that are pulsing along her uterus.

The length of time involved in kittening varies with the size of the litter, the age and obstetrical experience of the cat, and her muscle tone and general health. Four kittens may be born in two hours, or they may take two or three times that long. An extremely long period between kittens indicates possible trouble and calls for a telephone consultation with the veterinarian.

Kittens are normally born head first. As the kitten emerges, the amniotic sac surrounding it can be seen, like a thin, transparent plastic cover. Most cats will remove the sac immediately with their teeth and tongue, but occasionally a cat fails to do this instantly. If the mother doesn't do it at once, the cat's owner must be prepared to tear the sac with his fingers and carefully wipe it away from the kitten with a towel. The kitten will suffocate if the sac isn't quickly removed.

The next problem is the umbilical cord. Normally the mother severs the cord with her teeth, separating the kitten from its placenta (afterbirth). If she doesn't do this, it must be done by the cat owner. Sterilized blunt scissors can be used, cutting the cord about an inch and a half from the kitten's abdomen. The cord should be pinched for a minute or two to cut off the loss of blood through the severed cord. If necessary, the cord can be tied near the end with sterilized string or thread. If blunt scissors are not available, the cord can be torn apart with the fingers, but extreme care must be taken not to exert any pull on the kitten's stomach, for this will cause an umbilical hernia. For safety's sake, the cord should be torn about two inches from the kitten's body, with the kitten and the cord close to it protected by the left hand against any pull.

After removing the sac and severing the cord, the cat licks the kitten all over very vigorously. Indeed, she may appear too rough in your eyes, but this vigor is intentional; it helps to start the kitten breathing. If the kitten doesn't begin to breathe quickly, it may be necessary for the cat owner to take a hand. This means rubbing the kitten with a towel and, in case it is choked with mucous, holding it upside down and shaking it to let the mucous drain out. Even if the kitten does begin breathing when the mother is licking it, it is well to wipe it afterward with a towel in order to dry it still more.

Then the kitten can be set aside in the little box with a hot-water bottle. Be sure that the bottle is not so hot as to burn the kitten and that the towel protects the kitten from direct contact with the bottle. Do not handle the kittens unless it is absolutely necessary, and in that event as little as possible.

If the kitten, while it is in the small box, cries, put it on one of the mother's nipples for a few moments. That will comfort the kitten and the act of nursing stimulates the cat's labor pains, encouraging the birth of the next kitten.

After the sac is removed, the cord severed, and the kitten licked clean, the mother usually will eat the afterbirth. This is somewhat disconcerting to many humans, but it is sound instinct on the part of the cat. Eating the placenta cleans the nest of material which would otherwise rot and form a health hazard to the mother and her kittens. In addition, the afterbirth provides her with nourishment which she needs during birthing. Any afterbirth that she doesn't eat should be removed by the owner, however.

Before the afterbirth is eaten or removed, be sure to note each one down on a piece of paper. When the kittening is over, you'll never be able to remember whether all the afterbirths—one for each kitten—emerged, unless you mark each one down. You must remove them all, for a retained afterbirth can cause serious infection inside the cat.

If the afterbirth doesn't emerge, it is sometimes possible to draw it out gently by drawing on the end of the umbilical cord which is not attached to the kitten's body.

During the kittening, clean, cool water should be close at hand in case the cat feels thirsty. Some cats want to drink between kittens, and there is even an occasional cat that may want a little snack of fresh chopped meat or a saucer of milk.

Throughout the entire kittening, remember, above all, to keep calm. Your cat may need you, and you can't help her unless you keep a cool head. And don't forget that she will sense your mood; if you are nervous, you'll make her nervous, too.

PROBLEMS

Delayed birth: This can have a variety of causes. The veterinarian should be consulted if a kitten has not been born two hours after the onset of severe labor.

Breech birth: This means that the kitten is born hind first. It is more difficult for the cat to bring forth in this position, and she may cry out and try to move about in circles. Try to keep her calm, pet her, and support the rear half of the kitten with your hand. When she begins to push in an effort to force the kitten out, you can try—very, very gently—to remove the kitten. But don't pull it or exert strong pressure. If the kitten is stuck very long the vet may have to remove it, but this isn't usually necessary.

Open eyes: Sometimes kittens are born with their eyes open. For some reason, these kittens almost always die.

Fading: Occasionally a kitten will be born, will begin to breathe, and then will fade away and die, for no apparent reason. There seems to be no way to keep these kittens alive, which may be just as well. If they lived, they might be sickly all their lives.

CAESAREAN SECTION

Sometimes a veterinarian will decide that the kittens cannot be born naturally. The operation for removal of the living kittens is called, as in the case of humans, a "Caesarean section." Most mother cats and kittens survive it with little difficulty. The decision regarding such a procedure should be left entirely to your vet.

UNSUCCESSFUL PREGNANCIES

Not all pregnancies terminate successfully in live litters. Some pregnancies end in miscarriages, some are false, and some suddenly go in reverse, disproving the old saying that there's no such thing as being a little bit pregnant.

Pregnancy-in-reverse, an odd and quite rare phenomenon, is resorption of the embryos. The queen is mated and in due course the embryonic kittens can be felt in the horns of the uterus. The embryos grow bigger and bigger and then, for no known reason, they begin to grow smaller and smaller and finally disappear altogether. Cats in which this process of pregnancy-in-reverse is taking place have been put to sleep and then autopsied, and it has been found that the embryos had become soft, spongy or gelatinous masses; it was clear that the embryos were being broken down into simpler life forms and resorbed into the bloodstream.

This condition, which is scarcely ever seen, is more likely to occur in old cats than in young queens. It is possible that the aging process in the reproductive system may be responsible for resorption of the embryos.

Miscarriages can occur spontaneously—that is, without apparent cause—or as a result of disease or mishap. Sometimes a cat will fail to observe due caution with regard to jumping while heavy with kittens, and may fall and injure herself, resulting in abortion. A cat which has miscarried should always be taken to a veterinarian for examination.

It isn't always easy to tell immediately that a cat has miscarried, for many queens will eat the expelled embryos. This usually upsets the cat's owner, but it is a perfectly natural reaction. Usually, however, there will be some bloodstains, even if the embryos have disappeared.

False pregnancy in animals is a rather startling concept to most people, but it frequently occurs. It differs from species to species, however. In the dog, for example, false pregnancy may follow any heat, even without mating. In the cat, on the other hand, false pregnancy occurs after coition. The intercourse has been unsuccessful, of course, but the cat's owner cannot tell, for the cat shows every sign of pregnancy. The nipples become flushed and enlarged, the flanks are distended, and the cat puts

KITTENING CHART

This shows on what date kittens may be born if the mating occurs on the date listed on the top line.

JANUARY

MATED	1	2	3	4	5	6	7	8	9	10	11	12	13	14	15	16	17	18	19	20	21	22	23	24	25	26	27	28	29	30	31
KITTENS	7	8	9	10	11	12	13	14	15	16	17	18	19	20	21	22	23	24	25	26	27	28	29	30	31	1	2	3	4	5	6

MARCH ... *APRIL*

FEBRUARY

MATED	1	2	3	4	5	6	7	8	9	10	11	12	13	14	15	16	17	18	19	20	21	22	23	24	25	26	27	28
KITTENS	7	8	9	10	11	12	13	14	15	16	17	18	19	20	21	22	23	24	25	26	27	28	29	30	1	2	3	4

APRIL ... *MAY*

MARCH

MATED	1	2	3	4	5	6	7	8	9	10	11	12	13	14	15	16	17	18	19	20	21	22	23	24	25	26	27	28	29	30	31
KITTENS	5	6	7	8	9	10	11	12	13	14	15	16	17	18	19	20	21	22	23	24	25	26	27	28	29	30	31	1	2	3	4

MAY ... *JUNE*

APRIL

MATED	1	2	3	4	5	6	7	8	9	10	11	12	13	14	15	16	17	18	19	20	21	22	23	24	25	26	27	28	29	30
KITTENS	5	6	7	8	9	10	11	12	13	14	15	16	17	18	19	20	21	22	23	24	25	26	27	28	29	30	1	2	3	4

JUNE ... *JULY*

MAY

MATED	1	2	3	4	5	6	7	8	9	10	11	12	13	14	15	16	17	18	19	20	21	22	23	24	25	26	27	28	29	30	31
KITTENS	5	6	7	8	9	10	11	12	13	14	15	16	17	18	19	20	21	22	23	24	25	26	27	28	29	30	31	1	2	3	4

JULY ... *AUGUST*

JUNE

MATED	1	2	3	4	5	6	7	8	9	10	11	12	13	14	15	16	17	18	19	20	21	22	23	24	25	26	27	28	29	30
KITTENS	5	6	7	8	9	10	11	12	13	14	15	16	17	18	19	20	21	22	23	24	25	26	27	28	29	30	1	2	3

AUGUST ... *SEPTEMBER*

MATED	JULY	1	2	3	4	5	6	7	8	9	10	11	12	13	14	15	16	17	18	19	20	21	22	23	24	25	26	27	28	29	30	31
KITTENS	SEPTEMBER / OCTOBER	4	5	6	7	8	9	10	11	12	13	14	15	16	17	18	19	20	21	22	23	24	25	26	27	28	29	30	1	2	3	4

MATED	AUGUST	1	2	3	4	5	6	7	8	9	10	11	12	13	14	15	16	17	18	19	20	21	22	23	24	25	26	27	28	29	30	31
KITTENS	OCTOBER / NOVEMBER	5	6	7	8	9	10	11	12	13	14	15	16	17	18	19	20	21	22	23	24	25	26	27	28	29	30	31	1	2	3	4

MATED	SEPTEMBER	1	2	3	4	5	6	7	8	9	10	11	12	13	14	15	16	17	18	19	20	21	22	23	24	25	26	27	28	29	30	
KITTENS	NOVEMBER / DECEMBER	5	6	7	8	9	10	11	12	13	14	15	16	17	18	19	20	21	22	23	24	25	26	27	28	29	30	1	2	3	4	

MATED	OCTOBER	1	2	3	4	5	6	7	8	9	10	11	12	13	14	15	16	17	18	19	20	21	22	23	24	25	26	27	28	29	30	31
KITTENS	DECEMBER / JANUARY	5	6	7	8	9	10	11	12	13	14	15	16	17	18	19	20	21	22	23	24	25	26	27	28	29	30	31	1	2	3	4

MATED	NOVEMBER	1	2	3	4	5	6	7	8	9	10	11	12	13	14	15	16	17	18	19	20	21	22	23	24	25	26	27	28	29	30	
KITTENS	JANUARY / FEBRUARY	5	6	7	8	9	10	11	12	13	14	15	16	17	18	19	20	21	22	23	24	25	26	27	28	29	30	31	1	2	3	

MATED	DECEMBER	1	2	3	4	5	6	7	8	9	10	11	12	13	14	15	16	17	18	19	20	21	22	23	24	25	26	27	28	29	30	31
KITTENS	FEBRUARY / MARCH	4	5	6	7	8	9	10	11	12	13	14	15	16	17	18	19	20	21	22	23	24	25	26	27	28	1	2	3	4	5	6

on a great act of motherhood in bloom. A veterinarian cannot feel embryos in the horns of the uterus, but many cat owners neglect to take their cats to the vet for examination, so this revealing examination is lost to them.

The burlesque comes to an end usually about the end of the seventh week after coition. The nipples lose their redness, the swelling subsides, and the flanks return to normal. There may be a slight vaginal discharge and the cat may even—in very rare cases—expel a sac which is empty except for the amniotic fluid. The cat will break the sac and eat it, just as she would have done if there had been a kitten inside it.

It is all part of the fascinating miracle of life reproduced, which must fill with awe and wonder anyone who watches the process of kittening.

10. THE OLD CAT

With good care and good luck, a cat can live quite a long time—more than twice as long as a dog. These later years can be years of health and happiness for the cat if a few simple rules are followed.

Overriding every other need of the cat at any age, but especially in the twilight years, is the cat's hunger for affection. The cat may make its presence less forcefully felt because of its more extended sleep and less energetic play, but it wants attention more than ever. It should be treated with gentleness, tenderness, and the dignity befitting its years.

These later years are not the time to introduce a second cat into the household. If there is more than one cat in your home already, that's splendid. But don't light the fires of jealousy in your old friend at this late age by bringing a young cat into its private preserve. The time to get a second cat is when your first cat is still fairly young.

Like an old man or woman dozing before a television set, the old cat sleeps a great deal of the time, even longer than it did when young, and all cats, as every owner knows, sleep a great deal of the time. The old cat needs its rest to counteract the erosive effects of time on its body.

Although the need for rest may be obvious, the need for play may be less apparent. Nevertheless, it is a very real and important need. As long as the cat lives, it will want to play, for play is exercise, the hunt, the world of imagination, all rolled up in one. A rolling ball will ever be a fleeing mouse. A dangling string will always be a treacherous viper. A cat no longer interested in playing is a cat that is losing interest in living. It is the task of the cat's owner to maintain that interest in play by taking the time every day to participate in the cat's games. And there's no better way of demonstrating your affection for your old friend.

DIET

A sound, well-balanced diet in the cat's earlier years is the best way to ensure good health and vigor in its later days. This kind of diet, described previously in this book, will provide the vitamins, minerals, proteins, fats, and carbohydrates that will prevent or delay the crippling degeneration of tissues in old age.

The later years may call for some changes in the diet. The old cat certainly ought to be given a vitamin-mineral supplement, possibly one of the daily multiple vitamin and mineral tablets sold for humans. B-complex vitamins are especially important in maintaining healthy mouths.

At no age should a cat be permitted to choose its own diet, and this is most emphatically true of the old cat. On the other hand, it may be necessary to ask the cat to accept rather strange diets to meet special health needs. For example, cats with chronic kidney disease, not uncommon in older cats, may have to eat low-protein diets like spaghetti with meat and tomato sauce, macaroni and cheese, or tunafish and noodle casserole.

Water is as important to the cat in old age as in youth. It should be clean, fresh, and cool, and available to the cat at all times.

HEALTH PROBLEMS

In all animals, old age is a time of gradual deterioration of tissues. The degenerative effects of aging cannot be altogether prevented, but they can be slowed or alleviated.

The eyes, the ears, and the mouth should be watched with special care in the older cat. A veterinarian should examine the animal not less than once a year, and preferably twice. The tartar on teeth must be scaled off. Loose or decayed teeth must be extracted.

Eczema is one of the common problems of older cats. Usually this is not a fungus skin disturbance but an allergic disorder.

Foods, seasonal factors, and even personal habits, such as sleeping on a TV set or under a radiator, may be the root of the trouble. In most cases the veterinarian can give considerable relief with chemical skin baths and injections of cortisone.

Constipation is another frequent complaint of the old cat. The usual remedies for this problem—mineral oil, Vaseline on a paw, or malt-flavored petroleum jelly, which is especially prepared for cats—will *ordinarily* stimulate a sluggish colon. Occasionally a cat will do well with a bulk-producing remedy for constipation used by humans, such as Metamucil or Mucilose. Brewer's yeast in tablet or powder form is advisable. For really stubborn cases, an infant suppository will work wonders; it can be employed two or three times a week.

In extreme cases of chronic impaction causing constipation, surgery may be recommended as a last resort. A strip of intestinal muscle is removed and the tube of the dilated intestine is decreased. This rare procedure often ends the constipation problem permanently.

When diarrhea occurs in the old cat, it may be traceable to one of the familiar causes discussed previously (see Chapter 8), or it may be a symptom of chronic pancreatic disease, which sometimes causes loss of weight in old cats even when they continue to eat well. The cat defecates more often and the stools are frequently light tan or grayish and sometimes contain undigested food particles. The veterinarian can counteract this condition with tablets containing pancreatic enzymes.

Chronic pancreatitis is only one of a host of chronic diseases which may afflict old cats, for in felines as in humans the process of aging renders the body vulnerable to prolonged illness. Chronic kidney disease is a frequent problem. In the early stages there is a gradual loss of weight and of appetite, and later the cat vomits, and is very thirsty, and urinates a great deal. Little can be done for this condition, except for changing the diet to lower the intake of protein.

Diabetes mellitus, a metabolic disease that may result from overactivity of the adrenal or pituitary glands or a pancreatic infection, is most common in very fat, old males. (It has been said that males of this description that have been castrated are more susceptible, but this may merely reflect the greater numbers of castrated males in veterinary practice. Relatively few whole males come under the care of a vet.) A diabetic cat is insatiably hungry but loses weight. It drinks a great deal of water and urinates very often. It has a wide-eyed expression. A cat with this condition can be maintained on insulin under a veterinarian's direction, unless the disease is complicated by involvement of the pancreas or the kidneys.

Teetotalers though they may be, cats can get cirrhosis of the liver and other chronic liver ailments. The disease is difficult to diagnose because the symptoms are those of many other feline afflictions: finicky appetite, vomiting, diarrhea, loss of weight, constipation, thirst, anemia, and so on. Dr. Jean Holzworth of Angell Memorial Hospital in Boston, a confirmed cat lover as well as a specialist in feline disorders, says regretfully that "by the time liver impairment can be recognized it is usually beyond treatment." So don't expect a miracle from your veterinarian.

Blood disorders of various kinds, including anemia and an abnormally low white-cell count, are not unusual in old cats. Sometimes leukemia is involved, but often a nonmalignant condition can be discovered as the source of the trouble.

Malignant tumors are all too common in old cats, and they may be located in any part of the body. It is unusual to discover genital tumors, however, and cats rarely suffer from lung cancer. Fortunately, surgery can permanently eliminate many cancerous growths in the cat. If a cat does not have a heart ailment and its general condition is good, surgery can be performed at quite an advanced age, even over twenty years old. In the professional journal *Small Animal Clinician* Dr. E. F. Thomas, of Sarasota, Florida, reported on a twenty-two-year-old Siamese female which was subjected to surgery. A tumor on a mammary gland and a cyst in the chest were removed. Less than three hours after the operation the cat was on its way home. The sutures were removed a week later and the cat was in top shape.

DEATH

The end of a dear friend can never be anything but a time of sorrow, and none of us likes to look ahead to that day. But endless processes of life and death cannot be denied, and it is better for death to find us prepared than for us to close our eyes and ears and minds to the inevitable fate that awaits us all. Our cats are mortal, and one day death must be their lot.

With many cats the terrible day finally comes when a cat's owner must decide whether his pet is to be put to sleep. This is a decision that can be made by no one but the cat owner himself. Occasionally that unhappy person will argue to himself that the cat doesn't really appear to be in pain, so there's no reason to destroy it. But the uncomplaining cat may be in silent agony from the depredations of an internal cancer; animals are stoic about chronic pain. A cat owner who keeps his animal alive because he "just can't bear to part with it" is guilty, although he refuses to face the fact, of as much cruelty to his animal as any sadist might inflict. Such a person is selfishly putting his own welfare above the cat's. He wants the cat with him, fears the pain of separation, and so permits his cat to suffer. For all too many of us, the last kindness we can offer to our pets is the gift of painless, merciful death, even though it leaves an aching void in our own hearts. It takes a kind of courage to make this hated decision, but it is courage that each of us must summon. It is our responsibility to the cats we love, which have gladdened our lives.

Having once decided to put the cat out of its pain, the owner should put the matter in the hands of his veterinarian. It is best to have the vet come to the house to do it, but vets are so busy these days that such a visit may be out of the question. In that case, take the cat to the vet. *But do not leave the cat there!* There are two reasons for this injunction:

If you remain with your cat while it is being put to sleep, it will be less frightened. And surely the last act of love is to make the death of your cat as free of terror as possible.

It has happened—rarely, thank God!—that an unethical veterinarian here or there has been given a cat to be put to sleep and instead, secretly and without any authorization from the owner, has kept the cat alive and used it for experimental purposes. As rare as this sort of thing is, it has happened. A sure way to prevent its happening to your pet is to be present when it is put to sleep.

Many cat owners fear that the sight of the cat in its death throes will be more than they can bear. But if you are present when your cat is put to sleep, you'll find that there are *no* death throes. It is a death as peaceful and merciful as anyone could wish. Indeed, you may think it a pity that such a death will be impossible for you when your time comes.

The cat is held in its owner's arms. A hypodermic needle is slipped into the vein so skillfully that the cat is usually unaware of it. The fatal dose—an overdose of a sedative or anesthetic—is injected. The cat closes its eyes and falls asleep, as quietly as it would in your lap before the fireplace on a cold winter night. Its sleep is deeper and deeper and then, so subtly that you will not notice it at first, the chest will stop moving as breathing ends. It is all over, a very few minutes after you arrived.

POST-MORTEM EXAMINATION

Occasionally a veterinarian will ask a client to authorize an autopsy of a cat. A few owners find the thought of such an examination distressing. There is no rational reason for this attitude. The cat is dead and lives only in the minds and hearts of those who loved it. It cannot suffer pain or indignity now; it has peace at last. All that remains is a fleshly shell that no longer even looks like the cat its owner knew so well.

By permitting a post-mortem examination, which can determine the cause of death and any other factors that may have been involved, the cat's owner is giving other cats a better chance at life and health. From the examination of dead animals come advances in the treatment of living animals. Your cat, itself, lived a healthier life because other cats were examined post-mortem. It is now your duty to repay that obligation, if your veterinarian so requests, by permitting an examination of your own cat.

AFTER DEATH

Occasionally, especially in the suburbs or the country, a cat will be simply buried near the house after death. This is unwise, unless the grave is quite deep and rocks are piled on it, for wild animals may dig up the body or workmen, building in future years, may unearth the skeleton.

The better course is to handle this matter through your veterinarian. Three avenues are open to the cat owner:

The body can be left with the vet for disposal. This is routine.

Through the vet, arrangements can be made to have the body cremated. The ashes can then be scattered over the cat's favorite outdoor places or buried. Crematoria charge very little for their services.

A plot can be purchased in a pet cemetery in many parts of the country. Usually your vet will be familiar with the pet cemeteries, if there are any, in your vicinity. In the New York City metropolitan area, for example, there are at least two such cemeteries, one operated by Bide-A-Wee in Wantagh, Long Island, the other the Hartsdale Canine Cemetery (which also accepts cats, despite its name) in Westchester County. These cemeteries have headstones and monuments and for an annual fee flowers are planted on a grave every year. Cats, dogs, trained bears, goats, pet birds, even turtles, are buried in these cemeteries. The sentiments on the monuments reflect the anguish and loss we all feel when a beloved and faithful friend has gone.

11. CAT SHOWS

The many breeds of cat, discussed in Chapter 2, could not exist without stud-book organizations, which help to maintain the integrity of breeding programs by establishing the pedigrees of the cats registered with them. Moreover, the cat shows held under the auspices of those seven organizations, by identifying the superior cats in each breed, serve to maintain and improve the quality of the cats being bred.

The stud-book organizations—that is, those cat fanciers' associations which certify the pedigrees of cats—are listed in Appendix B. The cat shows they sponsor are listed each month in the "Show Calendar" pages of *Cats Magazine* (information about which can also be found in Appendix B). Anyone interested in pure-bred cats should make it a point to subscribe to the magazine and to attend at least one or two cat shows. The shows will be a memorable experience.

The cat shows are sponsored by local clubs affiliated with the national organizations. If your interest in showing and breeding cats is serious, you will want to join a club in your vicinity.

When you buy a cat for showing or for breeding purposes, it is essential that you get the cat's "papers," as most people refer to them. These consist of (1) a certificate of registration issued by one of the national organizations and (2) a pedigree covering at least two generations. The registration certificate will give the date of birth of the cat, a description of it, the name and address of its owner, the name of the breeder, the name of the sire and the dam and their registration numbers, and, of course, the formal name of the cat in question, and its registration number. I say *formal* name, because few show cats are called by their registered names around the house. Many an elegant creature with a five- or six-word appellation is simply "Nutsy," or a similarly familiar name, around the house. (Incidentally, the first part of the cat's formal name—the part which ends with an apostrophe—signifies the cattery where the cat was bred; for example, "Zsa-Zsa's Peter Pan of Alpha-Omega" tells us that the cat was bred at the [fictitious] Zsa-Zsa Cattery. In like manner, the end of the name, that part which follows the preposition *of*, usually designates the cattery to which the cat now belongs, in this instance, the Alpha-Omega Cattery.)

In order to enter a cat show, you must write for an entry form about two months before the event. The person to whom you should write is listed in the announcement of the show in *Cats Magazine*. The cost of entry is small, generally under five dollars. Some associations require that you join in order to participate. The fee for joining is nominal.

The entry form must be returned to the show-giving club about a month before the event. When you received the entry form, you should also have been sent information about the place where the show is being held, the size of cages, and other pertinent matters.

To be eligible for showing, a kitten must be at least four months old. *Championship* classes are barred to kittens under eight months old. Of course, the cat must be entered under its formal name.

At most cat shows, litter boxes and litter are provided to exhibitors. So are food dishes. Some clubs even make cat food available.

These are the things you will want to take with you to the show (in addition to your probably reluctant feline entry, of course): a soft mat of some kind, for the bottom of the cage, so the cat will be comfortable; materials for cleaning up in case the cat throws up or otherwise embarrasses itself; food and water dishes, in case none are provided; dry food; some cloth—curtain material, or something of the sort—to drape around the cage, so the cat won't get too excited by the proximity of other cats; something (clothespins, perhaps) to hold the drapery up around the cage; cotton to swab the cat's eyes, if necessary; a bottle of water, so your small friend won't have to try getting adjusted to the scent and taste of strange water (and the water in some cities is really strange these days, even to human senses); show cleaner material, any number of products which can be used to clean the cat's coat without the use of water; thin wire or pipe cleaners, for fastening things; and a suitcase to carry all of this. Of course, you must also take your entry papers, registration papers, and pedigree. Grooming materials are an obvious need. Less apparent is the need for a pen or pencil and a note pad, but you'll find lots of use for writing materials. And, if you're like most exhibitors, you'll need your checkbook, not only to pay for hotel accommodations if you stay overnight, but also to buy some of the fascinating items offered for sale at many shows.

Before entering the hall where the show will be held, the cat must be examined by a veterinarian, who is always in attendance just outside. The vet checks the cat for symptoms of contagious disease and for the absence of claws (declawed cats are barred from championship competition).

Inside the show hall, the exhibitors and their friends usually devote the first few minutes to examining the show book, a catalog which lists all the cats entered in the show, the classes in which they have been entered, the exhibitors, and the judges. The judging schedule often can be found in the show book, too.

At this point it should be noted that there are two kinds of cat shows: the Specialty show and the All-Breed show. In the Specialty, entries are limited to a breed or a larger category—Longhair, say, or Shorthair. The All-Breed show allows for numerous breeds, which are divided into classes.

At a typical show there are at least four judges, and each cat will be judged by each of the judges. The judge has a table and about ten cages; the judge's area is called a "ring." The cats he or she judges are identified only by catalog number. In order to prevent attempts at influencing the judging, the rules forbid exhibitors and spectators to speak to a judge while the judging is in progress.

These are the major classes:

Novice: for unaltered cats which have not won a first-place ribbon in a previous show held under the auspices of that national organization.

Open: for unaltered cats which have not yet won their championship in the sponsoring national organization.

Champion: for unaltered cats which have already earned the title of Champion. The requirements for this title vary from one national organization to another. For example, the Cat Fanciers' Association says that, to become a Champion, a cat must have won six winner's ribbons under at least four different judges, but the Cat Fanciers' Federation requires only four winner's ribbons under at least three different judges. (In Hawaii, two winner's ribbons under two different judges are sufficient.)

Grand Champion: for unaltered cats which have already earned the title of Grand Champion. This title is awarded to cats which have already earned the title of Champion and then have gone on to win first or second place in other shows, amassing a certain number of points for their total wins. The number of points needed, and the basis on which points are awarded, vary from one national organization to another.

Although the main reason for holding any kind of breed show—dog show, cattle show, and so on—is to improve the breeding of the animals, the cat fancy includes competition among *altered* cats in its shows. Obviously, the selection of superior animals which have been neutered cannot help to produce better cats, but there it is. Man, and woman, does not, after all, live by logic alone. So do not worry about the logic of it; just accept the fact that altered cats have their own competition at cat shows. They do not, however, compete against unaltered cats. The classes for competition of altered cats is the same as for unaltered animals—Novice, Open, Champion, and Grand Champion (although some national organizations call an altered Champion a "Premier," and an altered Grand Champion a "Grand Premier").

There are also other nonchampionship classes at cat shows. These may include:

Any Other Variety: for any cat or kitten which is registered and eligible by ancestry to compete, but which does not meet the breed standard in some disqualifying way.

Experimental (or Provisional) Breed: for unaltered cats and kittens of a breed not yet recognized by the national organization, but for which judging standards have been approved.

Household Pet: for cats and kittens which are not pure-bred or which are pure-bred but suffer from a fault which would disqualify them from championship competition. (This is the class, of course, which is the most touching for those who can empathize with the pride of the competing cat lovers.)

Kitten: for all kittens (that is, cats under eight months) except those entered in the other nonchampionship classes.

In all classes, for championship competition or not, the color of the ribbons indicates the placement: first, blue; second, red; third, yellow; fourth, green. The colors for ribbons and rosettes awarded for various achievements—Winners, Best of Color Class, Best of Breed, and the like—are not uniform but depend instead on the rules of the governing organization.

With this explanation, you should now be able to enjoy a visit to a cat show. If your only previous exposure to animal judging has been a dog show, you'll find some similarities (the fundamentals of judging are the same) but some startling differences. The most striking difference is the quiet. Where a dog show is a bedlam of barking, howling, whining animals, a cat show is almost like a library in its hush. There may be a few mild meows and even an occasional screech or two from an indignant feline which has just been inspected unceremoniously, but a cat show is, nevertheless, a very quiet and relaxing place to spend a weekend.

If you don't want to appear foolish, be restrained in your comments to the exhibitors you will meet. For example, many people who have never bred animals are likely to express their conviction that pure-bred animals, more often than not, are "too highly bred." On the face of it, that criticism is totally meaningless. What does "highly bred" mean? An animal is well bred or badly bred, never highly bred or lowly bred. There is good breeding and bad breeding, but there cannot be high breeding or low breeding. The basis for that critical phrase—"too highly bred"—is the unspoken belief on the part of many persons that a pure-bred animal is likely to be weaker, less healthy, and not as intelligent as a mixed breed. That belief, which is wrong (many experiments have shown that pure-bred animals, by and large, are stronger, healthier, and brighter than mixed breeds, barring some exceptional specimens, of course), probably gains its strength from the fact that most humans are of mixed ancestry and are therefore prejudiced in favor of mixed breeds.

Another error made by people who are unfamiliar with practical genetics has to do with what theologians call the degrees of consanguinity—how closely the generations are related. Let an outsider hear that a cat is inbred, and he or she recoils with horror. Again, this reaction is wrong. It is an attempt to impose the human taboo against incest on animals. In fact, inbreeding is one of several options in any breeding program:

Inbreeding: the breeding of closely related animals. The closest inbreeding is of brother and sister; next, father and daughter, or mother and son. Inbreeding can improve good qualities but it can also deepen faults, so it is employed with great caution.

Line Breeding: breeding within a blood line, but not with close relatives. The breeding of cousins, or of even more distantly related cats, is line breeding.

Outbreeding: the breeding of one cat to another of a completely different ancestry. However, both cats must be of the same breed.

With these fundamentals in mind, you should be prepared to go to your first cat show. You'll enjoy it. For a cat show not only displays the best of a wonderful species of animal, it is also a social function, where cat lovers and exhibitors gather to talk, exchange notes, and compare experiences, surrounded by cats. What more could one ask for?

12. THE EXOTIC CATS

Although jaguarundis, pumas, bobcats, and cheetahs occasionally are kept as pets in this country, the most common jungle cats found in our cities are the ocelot and the margay. In the strictest sense, these are not wild cats, for the dictionary defines the wild cat as an *undomesticated* species of cat, and these cats, which are kept as pets, obviously have been domesticated. This is an important distinction, for some cities have ordinances against the keeping of wild animals. A good lawyer, however, can usually defend your right to keep an ocelot or a margay.

The ocelot is the most common jungle cat in the Americas, and its range actually includes part of the United States; like the margay and the jaguarundi, it is sometimes found in the southwestern border states. It has been mistaken for a small leopard, which probably explains its scientific name, *Felis pardalis*. The ground color of its beautiful coat is a pearly light buff. There are horizontal black stripes on its face, head, and neck. On the legs and tail are black spots, and the body is covered with black rings and dots. The tail is nearly half the length of the body.

There may be more than one variety of ocelot, for the numerous specimens in captivity, as pets or in zoos, show a wide range of differences, especially in size. Most ocelots weigh about forty pounds, but it's not unusual for this cat to weigh over sixty pounds.

The margay looks like a small ocelot with a long tail. Its markings are so similar to the ocelot's that it is nearly impossible to distinguish between kittens of the two species. But the margay grows to weigh only about ten pounds, roughly the size of a domestic cat. Its tail, however—a long, thick, expressive appendage—is outsized, being perhaps 75 percent as long as the body.

Among margays, too, there may be several varieties; or there may be several similar species that include the margay. It is known that there are a number of small South American jungle cats that differ only slightly from each other. One of them is even smaller than the margay usually kept as a pet in the United States.

The ocelot and the margay are both nocturnal, arboreal, and carnivorous. They are extremely intelligent and are fearless fighters. One ocelot was found with a seven-foot boa constrictor that it had killed and partly eaten.

Most of the exotic cats offered for sale in the United States used to be jungle-born, but in recent years the passage of laws designed to protect endangered species has put an end to that. Now most of the ocelots, margays, and other cats available in this country were bred here by fanciers, and even those cats can only be sold under very restricted conditions. (The laws are changing so rapidly that there is no point to my trying to inform you about the legal position now. For current information contact Ken Hatfield, president of the Long Island Ocelot Club, 1991 Southwest 136th Avenue, Davie, Florida.)

These cats make excellent pets—but not for most people. If you do not have the proper temperament to handle a jungle cat, which is not the same thing at all as handling a domestic cat, you'd better think twice about acquiring an ocelot or a margay. Meg Merrill, a New Yorker whose margay, Monte, was featured in national magazines, has said, "You must have the patience of Job, the forgiving heart of a saint, the energy of a bolt of lightning, and a deep love of felines (it also helps if you are fleet of foot)."

In this chapter we shall present some basic information about the care of these animals, for those who insist on keeping jungle cats as pets, and for cat lovers who are simply curious about the exotic cats.

KITTENS

Ocelots and margays—and all the other jungle cats—ought to be acquired as kittens, from breeder-fanciers in this country. Like all kittens, these babies are likely to be easily frightened. They must be treated with extreme kindness and understanding and patience.

Occasionally a classified ad offering an ocelot or a margay for sale will appear in a newspaper. Usually this is a cat that has not proved satisfactory to its owner. By the time the ad appears, the cat is usually close to a year old, and its lifelong habits have been set. There is very little prospect of changing it for the better. For that reason, it is usually not advisable to buy a jungle cat under those circumstances.

Treated with compassion and love, however, the jungle cat will grow up to be a loving pet. Despite the gloomy writings of some "experts," people who invariably lack personal experience with these animals, an ocelot or a margay, properly raised, will *not* revert to the wild when it matures. It will simply become more treasured than before.

Some people think that a wild animal must have more stamina than a domesticated creature. These are the people who also believe that an alley cat must be hardier than a pedigreed cat, or a mongrel dog sturdier than a purebred. This misconception comes from an oversimplification of the perfectly sound theory of the survival of the fittest. While the most fit among a wild species may survive in the majority of cases, they are not necessarily more fit—or even as fit—as animals which have been raised in civilization. The wild animal's diet often is not as good. It may be infested with parasites which would have been eliminated from a domestic animal. It lacks the protection of vaccines, antibiotics, and all the other medical advances of civilization.

In buying a kitten, one should always find out from the seller whether the cat has received any shots and, if so, for what disease (enteritis, probably). Were the shots serum or vaccine? When were the shots given? Remember that jungle cats have an unusually high susceptibility to the diseases of domestic cats.

An explicit agreement should be made with the seller that approval by the buyer's veterinarian is a condition of the sale. The veterinarian should be asked to examine the cat for general health, ringworm, external parasites, worms, and physiological defects.

Most kittens reach their buyers at about the age of two months. Many of them are suffering from malnutrition and sometimes this has caused, or is about to cause, rickets. The cat needs vitamin-mineral supplements that will provide a high calcium intake. Ground lean beef, with just a bit of fat in it, makes a good diet to begin with. Then, perhaps a week later, diced meat can be fed, and the size of the chunks can be gradually increased as the cat grows bigger. Raw meat is best for the cat, including both muscle and organ meat. Pork should not be fed to the cat. Liver, kidneys, and canned foods usually won't work out because they cause diarrhea, as does milk. Sometimes a jungle cat will accept boneless fish. Celery or lettuce leaves may interest some cats. (They may go after your house plants, too.)

The feeding schedule is roughly the same as that given on page 126 for domestic cats.

At about five months, teething begins. The baby teeth give way to the permanent teeth. Sometimes a permanent tooth will grow into place beside a baby tooth instead of displacing it, and then a veterinarian may have to remove the baby tooth.

As the kitten grows older, it may not be quite the size you expected. It may be bigger than the margay you ordered, or smaller than the ocelot you wanted. This is regrettable, but it's not really the fault of the person who sold you the cat. It is very difficult to differentiate between the two species when they are very young kittens.

Both ocelots and margays can be raised in the same way as domestic kittens as far as sleeping accommodations and other problems are concerned. But the jungle cat should be protected even more from any startling incident that may upset its feeling of security. The panic of a jungle cat can be so great that a fatal heart attack can occur.

TOILET TRAINING

Ocelots and margays are not housebroken as easily as domestic cats. It may take months to train a jungle cat to use a sanitary pan. Some of these cats, without any training by their owners, eventually decide to use a toilet seat instead. The method used in housebreaking a jungle cat is the same as that described on page 95 for domestic cats. However, before it is toilet-trained, the jungle cat may use anything that can contain water—including the bathtub, the sink, or large pots and pans.

Sometimes it's a good idea to have several litter boxes, one for

each place that the cat seems to favor. You may end up with a litter box in every room. The box should be higher on the sides
than an ordinary domestic cat's box, for the jungle cat usually
urinates while standing up.

CLAWS AND TEETH

The same arguments pro and con removal of a domestic cat's
front claws are relevant in the case of jungle cats. There is the
difference, of course, that the claws of an ocelot or a margay are
much more formidable than those of a house cat. On the other
hand, a jungle cat may slip outside the house, especially if you're
keeping it in the country on your vacation. Then it may need its
claws for protection. But certainly there are sound arguments
for removing the front claws.

If the claws are to be removed, the operation ought to be performed only by a veterinarian who is experienced in dealing with
these animals, or one who has been in touch with such vets. For
the names of vets with this experience (as for other helpful information dealing with ocelots, margays, and other exotic cats),
contact Catherine Cisin, of Amagansett, Long Island, New York,
who is the founder of the Long Island Ocelot Club. Mrs. Cisin is
the author of a book entitled *Especially Ocelots,* which can be ordered by writing to her. (Another helpful booklet is *The Margay:
An Exotic Pet,* which can be obtained from the author, Meg Merrill,
2 Horatio Street, New York, New York. Please enclose a stamped,
self-addressed envelope.)

Some owners of jungle cats have the canine teeth removed or
filed down. This requires careful surgery to prevent a fractured
jaw. When it is over, the shape of the cat's face will be slightly altered, but the animal will have no trouble eating. On the other
hand, it is a permanent solution to the problem of the jungle cat
that uses its teeth too roughly in play.

NEUTERING

Both males and females ought to be unsexed, for the same reasons as domestic cats. The surgery should be performed when
the cat is ten or twelve months old.

PLAY

Jungle cats are extremely playful. They are also nocturnal animals, which means that your cat may make your nights sleepless
by dashing back and forth across your bed. Some owners manage this problem by fixing the cat's bed in a cage and closing it in
at night.

Nevertheless, the cat will need a great deal of play. All ordinary cat toys are fun for jungle cats. The toy should not be capable of being torn and swallowed, nor should it have any sharp
objects on or inside it.

Jungle cats, being arboreal, love to climb. A six-foot stepladder
will make such a cat ecstatic; the cat will climb up and down, nap
on a top step, leap on and off the ladder.

Margays sometimes will lurk in playful ambush on top of a
door, then take great glee in leaping onto the shoulders of the
first person who passes through the door. This can be an un-
nerving experience until the owner becomes accustomed to it.
But it's all in fun, and there's no meanness in it.

WATER

Unlike most domestic cats, ocelots and margays often like water.
A tubful of water may delight them and lead to all manner of
games. Sometimes the cat will even go for a swim.

COEXISTENCE

Given the proper, cautious introductions, a jungle cat will get
along well with domestic cats. Mrs. Merrill, for example, had a
margay named Monte (for Montezuma) and two long-haired
cats. One of the longhairs didn't like Monte and made that clear
at the beginning; Monte gave that cat a wide berth. But the other
longhair, a blue, was fond of Monte, and Monte was utterly
devoted to the blue. They slept together, cuddled into one inex-
tricable mass, and Monte was extremely protective of his pal.

Children and jungle cats get along well together, too, but it's
generally inadvisable to bring an ocelot or a margay into a
household in which there are children under ten. These cats are

strong, energetic, and fast-moving, and they can barrel into a child and knock it over without intending any harm. A child should be big enough to cope with a jungle cat before it is exposed to one.

THE LONG ISLAND OCELOT CLUB

Many owners of exotic cats belong to the Long Island Ocelot Club (LIOC), which must be one of the most misleadingly named organizations anywhere. The club is not limited to owners of ocelots; its members include people who own margays, pumas, cheetahs, bobcats, and jaguarundis, too. Even the geographical designation in the name is deceptive, for the club is an international organization with branches all over North America.

The club's newsletter is full of stories of the members' exotic cats and their antics, adventures, and tribulations. Club meetings are a delight for anyone who has ever wanted to know jungle cats better, and there is an annual national convention of the LIOC.

Anyone who has an interest in exotic cats would do well to contact Catherine Cisin (see page 220) for additional information.

THE EXOTIC CATS AS PETS

Given the proper care, an ocelot or a margay will develop into an unusual, spectacular, beautiful, and above all affectionate pet that could warm the heart of a statue. To see one of these cats, born in the jungle in a state of wildness, pressing itself close to the cheek of its master or mistress, is to feel a wonder at the great world of nature and the mysterious power that such an intangible thing as love can exert in its creatures.

13. A COMPANION TO MAN

The cat was the last animal to be domesticated by man. "Millennia passed between the earliest evidence of keeping cats in captivity and domestication," the German zoologist Dr. Bernard Grzimek has pointed out; "it took longer to domesticate the African wild cat than any other animal. The reason for this is probably that of all domesticated animals, the cat is the only solitary one, that is, the only one that does not live in social groups."

It is usually theorized that the cat was first domesticated in Egypt, but this may not be correct. Since we know that ocelots and margays are easily tamed, and that this is true, perhaps to a lesser extent, of bobcats, there is no logical reason to rule out the possibility that the cat also was domesticated in other parts of the world at an early age, including pre-Columbian America. It is true that the early discoverers and explorers made no mention of domesticated cats in the New World. But there is some evidence that indicates that the cat could have been a part of Amerindian life. For example, Frederick J. Dockstader, director of the Museum of the American Indian, has reproduced in his *Indian Art in America* a cat effigy carved by the key dwellers of Florida in the period from A.D. 1000 to 1600. This carving does not look like the sort of thing one would expect of a people who viewed the cat only as a predator to be feared or hunted. It is a rather anthropomorphic representation with a distinctly familiar air to it.

There are other indications that the domestication of various small cats may have occurred in many parts of the world many millennia ago. Sanskrit writings three thousand years old refer to the cat; as a domesticated beast, it could have been carried from Egypt to India by then, but that seems highly unlikely, especially because the Egyptians, until nearly the Christian era, did their best to prevent the exportation of cats. Although recent discoveries proved that cats were kept in Jericho around 7000 B.C., the assumption is that these were domesticated wild cats, and isolated examples, at that. The same assumption must be made about the cats which were kept by the Lake Dwellers of Switzerland about 2000 B.C.

On the other hand, statuettes from the sixth century B.C. have been found in Hacilar, Turkey, showing women playing with cats, and they appear to be domestic cats as we know the animal. In China, Confucius watched his cat catch a mouse about 500 B.C., according to an ancient tradition. In the fourth century B.C. people in what is now Jordan were drawing cats on the face of cliffs. A hundred years later there were domesticated cats in the area that is now Iraq.

That the cat was domesticated in ancient Egypt we know beyond any doubt. The process of domestication undoubtedly was a long-drawn-out affair. It seems safe to assume that it began with the finding of a litter of kittens whose dam had been slain. These would, of course, grow up as tame cats. Their progeny, in turn, would be tame. In time, the cat might become the totem of the tribe, a representation of deity in the tribal animism, especially as its usefulness in keeping down vermin became apparent. Throughout the Nile Valley the cat spread, preceded by its fame, entrusted with the guarding of granaries and homes against rodent pests.

Feline creatures that could be domestic cats—we can't be sure; they might be lions—appear on a stylized carving from Abydos which goes back to the First Dynasty in Egypt, at least five thousand years ago. By the second millennium before Jesus, the cat was a well-established domestic animal in Egypt. In *The Book of the Dead,* a collection of hymns and religious texts, there is a vignette of the cat, symbolizing the sun, decapitating a serpent that represents darkness. The same collection bears other references to the cat, including the statement that "the male cat is Ra himself, and he is called 'Mau' by reason for the speech of the god Sa, who said concerning him: 'He is like unto that which he hath made'; thus his name became 'Mau.' " This is possibly the first pun in history: the Egyptian word for "cat" was *mau* and *mau* was also the word for "like." (The naming of the cat has always fascinated felinophiles, as T. S. Eliot shows in his light-hearted poem "The Naming of Cats" in his book *Old Possum's Book of Practical Cats.*)

The cat was deified by the Egyptians. The cat goddess was Bast (other versions of this name were Pasht, Ubastet, and Bubastis), one of the major figures in the Egyptian pantheon. She was the goddess of moonlight, linked with the great sun god Ra, who was himself often referred to as the Great Cat. The connection between the Egyptians' night-loving pet and moonlight will be obvious to anyone who has heard a back-fence conversation between a couple of cats at midnight. And everyone who has ever owned a cat will understand why Bast was also the goddess of fertility. Other aspects of this deity involved wisdom, with which the species is well endowed, and hunting, an activity for which it is admirably equipped.

An important city, Bubastis, one of the six major cities of Lower Egypt, was named for the goddess and dedicated to her worship. It is now represented by high mounds designated on modern maps as Tel Basta. It was east of the Nile Delta, not far from one branch of the great river. Bubastis appears in the Bible under the name Pi-beseth; the prophet Ezekiel (30:13, 17) says, "Thus saith the Lord God, I will also destroy the idols, and I will cause their images to cease out of Noph. . . . The young men of Aven and of Pi-beseth shall fall by the sword: and these cities shall go into captivity."

The worship of Bast was not restricted to Bubastis. There were temples to the goddess elsewhere, including a famous edifice at Thebes in Upper Egypt.

The Greek observer Herodotus was interested in the Egyptian reverence for the cat. "When a man has killed one of the sacred animals, if he did it with malice aforethought," he wrote, "he is punished with death; if unwittingly, he has to pay such a fine as the priests choose to impose." When a cat died, a wise Egyptian tried to be somewhere else so that he couldn't be accused of its murder.

"The number of domestic animals in Egypt is very great," Herodotus recorded, "and would be still greater were it not for what befalls the cats. As the females, when they have kittened, no longer seek the company of the males, these last, to obtain once more their companionship, practice a curious artifice. They seize the kittens, carry them off, and kill them, but do not eat them afterwards. Upon this the females, being deprived of their young, and longing to supply their place, seek the males once more, since they are particularly fond of their offspring.

"On every occasion of a fire in Egypt the strangest prodigy occurs with the cats. The inhabitants allow the fire to rage as it pleases, while they stand about at intervals and watch these animals, which, slipping by the men or else leaping over them, rush headlong into the flames. When this happens, the Egyptians are in deep affliction.

"If a cat dies in a private house by a natural death, all the inmates of the house shave their eyebrows. . . . The cats on their decease are taken to the city of Bubastis, where they are embalmed, after which they are buried in certain sacred repositories."

The English scholar W. M. Conway has discussed this matter of mummification, which was carried out with the rich and with cats, but not with the poor in Egypt. "A rich man's cat was elaborately mummied, wound 'round and 'round with stuff and cunningly plaited with linen ribbons dyed two different colors," according to Conway. "His head was encased in a rough kind of papier-mâché, and that was covered with linen and painted, even gilt sometimes, the ears always carefully pricked up. The mummy might be enclosed in a bronze box with a bronze . . . statue of the cat seated on the top. Even finer burial might await a particularly grand cat. . . . A poor man's cat was rolled up in a simple lump, but the rolling was carefully and respectfully done."

It is painful to record that in the latter part of the nineteenth century vast numbers of the mummified cats were dug up at Tel Basta and pulverized and spread on the land as manure. Large quantities were also pulverized and shipped to Europe as a cheap fertilizer. No one protested until zoologists and archeologists realized, too late, that the cat cemeteries were exhausted. In 1951 there was one cat mummy in the British Museum in London and there were a few in the Metropolitan Museum in New York and in one or two other museums, and that was all.

In 1952, however, a crate that had been brought back from Egypt shortly after the turn of the century was discovered in the vaults of the British Museum. It had never been opened. Inside it were 192 mummified cats, seven mongooses, three dogs, and a fox, all from Gizeh. They were believed to have lived in the period from 600 to 200 B.C.

Four of the cats were jungle cats (*Felis chaus*), but all the others appeared to be very much like the domestic cats we know, but not identical to them. Indeed, they seemed like an intermediate stage between the Kaffir cat (*Felis lybica*) and our domestic cat. The cat skulls, to mention one characteristic, were substantially larger than the skulls of today's cats.

Inevitably, despite official attempts by the ancient Egyptians to prevent the exporting of cats, the cat began to be distributed throughout the world. We know that those restless, far-roving traders, the Phoenicians, carried cats with them from Egyptian ports, and since the Phoenicians had colonies as far west as Marseilles and made voyages of trade even along the Atlantic coasts, we can assume that they spread the cat's fame widely. Whether the other lands bordering on the Mediterranean already had domesticated their own varieties of cat is something we shall probably never know. Certainly we can theorize that the Egyptian cats were bred to the native cats in those other lands, deliberately or by accident, whether the native cats were wild or domesticated.

Only in the Holy Land, sandwiched between Egypt and Phoenicia, does the cat appear to have been ignored. The Jews must have known the cat, as the quotation from Ezekiel would indicate—after all, the Jews probably made its acquaintance during their bondage in Egypt. But there is no reference to the cat in the canon of the Bible, although dogs, leopards, and other animals are frequently mentioned. In the Apocrypha there is one reference to the cat, in the Book of Baruch (6:22): "Upon their bodies and heads sit bats, swallows, and birds, and the cats also."

The first known appearance of the domestic cat in the British Isles followed the Roman invasion. The Romans had taken to the cat with enthusiasm. This clean, orderly, pest-hating little animal was obviously just the thing for the Romans, a people who loved cleanliness and order and hated vermin. The cat was the only animal admitted to the temples of Rome, and even the cult of the cat may have spread from Egypt to Italy. The excavations at Pompeii exposed the skeleton of a woman with the skeleton of a cat clasped in her arms. She apparently had died trying to save her frightened pet. In Britain the paw prints of cats have been found on tiles from the Roman towns of Silchester and Uriconium, and the skeleton of a cat was uncovered in the ruins of a Roman villa that was destroyed by fire at Lullingstone about A.D. 200.

The collapse of civilization into the Dark Ages also brought the period of respect for the cat to an end. The cat was still useful for controlling the population of rodents. Its past association with the pagan deities lingered in the minds of men, for the cat began to be viewed as a part of the nether world of black magic. After all, witchcraft was called "the old religion," and there is some reason to believe that those who practiced witchcraft believed they were remaining true to the religion that Christianity had displaced. As a part of the world of witchcraft, the cat was doomed to share the fate of other witches.

The long, horrible history of man's incredible cruelty to the cat began. It has not ended yet.

The cat became the most common witch's familiar, that is, a spirit that acted as an intimate servant. (John Van Druten recalled this in his play *Bell, Book, and Candle,* about a twentieth-century witch and her familiar, a Siamese cat named Pyewacket—the most common name for a feline witch's familiar in medieval times.) The cat was tried with its master or mistress before the ecclesiastical court on a charge of witchcraft, suffered the tortures prescribed for sorcerers, and then was burned alive.

A typical case was that of Elizabeth Francis, tried and condemned as a witch at Chelmsford, England, in 1556. She had, according to the evidence at the trial held after she had been tortured, learned the art of witchcraft from her grandmother, whose name was Eve. When Eve taught this evil worship to Elizabeth, the chronicles said, "she counselled her to renounce God and His Word and to give of her blood to Satan, as she termed it, which she delivered her in the likeness of a white spotted cat, and taught her to feed the said cat with bread and milk, and she did so; also she taught her to call it by the name of Satan and to keep it in a basket." It was said that Satan would do whatever

Elizabeth required—kill a neighbor's swine, for example—and in return the cat demanded a whole chicken to eat and one drop of Elizabeth's blood. And then he'd go back to sleep in his basket. Not an unreasonable fee for such services as he performed.

The hideousness of the treatment that the poor cat often suffered is sickening. One unpleasant custom was to toss a condemned criminal into the water to drown in a closed cloth sack full of cats, which would claw him in their own terror and misery. Public celebrations were often climaxed by the burning of live cats, to add to the gaiety; when Elizabeth I was crowned Queen of England, a wicker likeness of the Pope, filled with cats, was burned, and it is recorded that the wretched animals "squalled in a most hideous manner as soon as they felt the fire." Cat-burning was especially popular on religious feast days, including the Feast of St. John, Shrove Tuesday, the first Sunday in Lent, and Easter. Instead of being burned, the cats were sometimes suspended over a fire so that they roasted alive, the theory being that the greater pain the cat—the embodiment of the Devil—endured, the greater the merit to the torturer.

To ensure good luck, cats were often sealed alive into the walls of houses, convents, and public buildings, to die of suffocation.

No torment was too vile to inflict upon the poor beast. For sport, bowmen would hang a cat tied in a leather bag to a branch of a tree as a target for their arrows. An alternative of this unspeakable sport was to swing a cat by the tail in great circles while the archers tried to hit it. The phrase "to fight like Kilkenny cats" comes from the game of the Hessian troops who occupied rebellious Ireland in 1798; to amuse themselves, the soldiers tied two cats together by the tails and threw them across a clothesline to fight each other.

Cats were killed for their fur, which was used to trim cloaks. Sometimes their flesh was eaten. The cat is still used as a substitute for rabbit in stews in some rural areas of France. In China, cat and lizard were the main ingredients of a dish called "the tiger and the dragon." (It must be said that, although the cat has been used for food in the Eastern world, it has not generally been viewed there as an object of loathing, as in the West.)

There is some evidence that nature gave the cat revenge for the wrongs inflicted upon it, in the form of the plagues that have swept across the world, decimating the human populations. Between the sixth century and the fourteenth, the bubonic plague—the Black Death—was dormant. During this period cats were despised in Christendom, but many persons kept them as pets and as vermin exterminators, and they were not subjected to an all-out war of extermination. And so, in the nature of cat fecundity, they proliferated.

But in the fourteenth century the witch hunts began and the wholesale destruction of the "evil" cats got under way. Almost immediately the plague began to rage across Europe like a forest fire, spread by the rats that the cats had hitherto kept under control. In the fourteenth century alone, twenty-five million persons perished of the plague. In all, one-fourth of the population was wiped out. And the loss of life in subsequent plagues was equally great.

What part did the butchery of the cats play in this? We cannot speak with certainty. But we know that cats were killed by the thousands before the plagues began. And we know that cats kill rats, and rats spread the plague.

Lieutenant Colonel A. Buchanan, a British medical officer stationed in India at the turn of the century, had an opportunity to study this question firsthand, in an area still afflicted with plagues and epidemics. His observations made him certain that cats played a major role. In 1908 he published his report in *The British Medical Journal* under the title "Cats as Plague Preventers." He asserted that there was a correlation between the number of cats and the incidence of plague. Villages with large cat populations had little plague, but those with few cats were devastated. In one village, for example, there were thirty-six cats and forty houses—nearly a cat per house—and not a single case of plague. But in another village there had been thirty-eight cases of plague, twenty-one of them ending in death. The plague had struck twenty-one homes, and only one of those homes had a cat (and that one cat was a mere kitten, not old enough for ratting).

Perhaps He who marks the sparrow's fall also keeps His eye on the cat.

The Eastern world—the non-Christian peoples—never subjected the cat to the persecution that it suffered in Europe. In the Koran the cat is not mentioned (although the dog is "unclean" in Mohammed's eyes), but Islamic tradition is friendly to the cat. There is a story which has been repeated by Moslem writers since the days of the Prophet, of how Mohammed was called away while his beloved cat was sleeping against his arm. To avoid disturbing the cat, the Prophet cut off the sleeve of his robe in order to leave.

This story is similar to those told about Albert Schweitzer, the great medical missionary and a great admirer of animals. Visitors to his clinic at Lambarene have reported seeing Dr. Schweitzer writing prescriptions with his right hand while his left arm went to sleep—because Sizi, his cat, had cuddled up against that arm and was not to be disturbed.

Cats were not always objects of hatred in ancient Europe. Before the cat-hating began in earnest, a number of leaders demonstrated their appreciation of the cat's virtues. Howel the Good, a Welsh prince, for example, promulgated a code in A.D. 936 that established a fixed value for cats. The code read: "The worth of a cat that is killed or stolen: its head to be put downwards upon a clean, even floor, with its tail lifted upwards, and thus suspended, whilst wheat is poured about it, until the tip of its tail be covered; and that is to be its worth; if the corn cannot be had, a milch sheep, with her lamb and her wool, is its value; if it be a cat which guards the king's barn.

"The worth of a common cat is four legal pence.

"Whoever shall sell a cat is to answer for her not going a caterwauling every moon; and that she devour not her kittens; and that she have ears, eyes, teeth, and nails; and be a good mouser."

In southeast Wales this code was changed slightly. In the version that was law there, "there are three animals whose tails, eyes, and lives are of the same worth: a calf; a filly for common worth; and a cat; excepting the cat that shall watch the king's barn."

In the fourteenth century the Italian painter Baroccio executed his *Madonna of the Cat,* which now hangs in London's National Gallery. Many other painters inserted cats into their art works. The cat was intimately associated with a number of holy folk, including St. Ives and St. Gertrude, both thirteenth and fourteenth century. Petrarch loved cats, and so did Cardinal Richelieu and Dr. Samuel Johnson and thousands of others, famous and obscure.

Nevertheless, it is accurate to say that the cat remained an object of general hatred in the Western world until the last century or so. Then, in the burst of creative thinking that followed the French Revolution and the Enlightenment, artists of all kinds—novelists like Victor Hugo, poets like Paul Verlaine, painters like James McNeill Whistler, composers like Alexander Borodin—discovered the esthetic delights in the cat: its grace, agility, beauty, charm, as well as its keen mind and humorous idiosyncrasies, of course.

This process is still taking place. The cat is becoming more chic. It is losing much of the aura of evil, although we still depict a black cat with a witch on a broom in symbolizing Halloween. It is now respectable to like cats and to keep them.

Nevertheless, ailurophobia, the abnormal fear of cats, remains with us. Dr. Peter J. Steincrohn, who conducted a syndicated health column in newspapers, printed this letter from a reader:

"My friends have just about convinced me that I have gone off my rocker and need a head-shrinker. They laugh at my fear of cats. Even my sister says I can overcome it if I try. It isn't funny. I break out into a cold sweat and turn sick in the stomach over a little cat. What can I do about it except stay away from my cat-owning friends? I really feel stupid when I act that way. I know people who are afraid of dogs, bugs, mice, snakes, etc. Yet they think I'm being silly about cats."

Cases of ailurophobia like this are cropping up in psychiatric journals with increasing frequency. A cat hater who once would have been honored for his piety is now pitied for his neurosis.

There are others who delight in their pathological hatred of cats. In the October 1961 issue of a magazine called *Shooting Times,* an article appeared under the byline of Bruce Allen entitled "Common Cat—Pest or Pet?" It recommended that cats be hunted down like any other small game, pointing out that only fourteen of the fifty states protect cats from hunters. The editors claimed "an overwhelming endorsement of the article" in the letters they subsequently received. Six letters on each side of the controversy were published. The hunters who favored deliberate slaughter of cats appeared to consider these animals "evil"—"house pets of Satan," one writer called them.

Few people are wishy-washy about the cat. The dog has fervent admirers and some equally ardent enemies, but there are a large number of people who can take the dog or leave it, who simply do not feel strongly about it one way or the other. This is not the case with the cat. There is little neutral ground in regard to these little animals. In general, a person either loves cats with a passion or hates them with an equal fervor. Very few people are able to take a middle-of-the-road approach.

The reason for this polarity of feeling is certainly not obvious. It has long been a theory of mine, however, that the cat—although we may not realize it consciously—figures largely in our minds as a sexual symbol. Dr. Theodor Reik, the eminent psychoanalyst, has told me that he is certain that this is true, that the clue to the extreme feelings of love and hate toward the cat lies in the individual attitude toward sex and life. The cat is the freest of all domestic animals in its sexuality. It is for that reason that Bast was also a goddess of fertility. In the bleak centuries of witch-burning, the cat was often described as an incubus or a succubus, an evil spirit who had sexual intercourse with a human. There are and always have been many sexual beliefs associated with the cat. On March 5, 1654, for example, Jean Simpson of Rothiemay, in Scotland, went before the presbytery at Botarie. The poor girl was convinced she had "cats in her bellie" because a male cat had jumped over the table and the food while she was eating. The presbytery found that she was full with child, not with cats. Whether this was good or bad news for the unfortunate girl is not recorded.

There is reason to believe that dislike of cats is instilled by conditioning. Some years ago a study was made among more than five thousand Kansas schoolchildren. It was found that most children under ten liked cats very much. The peak of cat popularity among boys was reached when the boys were between nine and ten years old; 35 percent of the boys favored cats then. Among girls, the peak age was between eight and nine, when 42 percent liked cats best of any animal.

Surely some conclusions can be drawn from this study. It seems apparent that the children began liking cats naturally. Then, as the children grew bigger, they were exposed to an increasing amount of propaganda against the cat, in the form of cat-hating statements or superstitions, for example, that it is bad luck to let a black cat cross your path. The study showed that cats never lost as much ground with the girls as with the boys, undoubtedly reflecting the absurd but general belief that there is something rather effeminate about the cat, even if it is a battle-scarred tom.

The world is full of false beliefs about the cat. But the worst victim of these beliefs is not the durable cat, which has survived man's persecution for two thousand years. Rather, it is the cat hater himself, who is deprived of the pleasure, the comfort, the thrill, the stimulation, the amusement, and the sheer delight that a cat can give.

APPENDICES
INDEX

Appendix A. A NOTE ON BREEDING

Males are extremely rare among three varieties of cats: the Tortoise-shell, the Tortoiseshell-and-White (Calico), and the Blue-Cream. They occur perhaps once in a million births (the ratio is pure guess, and probably conservative). When males are produced, they are almost always sterile. It is true that one or two male Tortoiseshell and Calico cats have actually grown up to sire kittens. However, I know of no Blue-Cream male which has ever grown beyond kittenhood.

For those readers who may be wondering what conceivable (no pun intended) connection there can be between the Tortoiseshell and the Blue-Cream, it is worth mentioning here that geneticists describe the blue-cream of cats as the dilution of black and red, a dilution being the reduction of color caused by a scarcity of pigment granules. It has been said that the genetic phenomenon seen in these three breeds is the only known example of sex-linkage in mammals except for the sex-linked defects in man, such as hemophilia and baldness.

Because of this sex-linkage, it follows that Tortoiseshells and Calicoes with the proper size and distribution of patterns cannot be bred to order as other breeds can be; they happen. And so there are relatively few of them that measure up to the standard for the breeds.

These cats happen, theoretically, when cats of the three colors indicated are bred together. In practice, this does not always work out, because so many other genetic factors are at work at the same time. But carry out this breeding plan consistently, and Tortoiseshells should result. Carry it one step further, and a Calico should be produced.

Here is one Tortoiseshell breeding plan:*

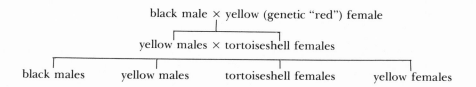

black male × yellow (genetic "red") female

yellow males × tortoiseshell females

black males   yellow males   tortoiseshell females   yellow females

---

*This chart is based on material in A. C. Jude's invaluable book, *Cat Genetics* (All-Pets Books, Inc., Fond du Lac, Wisconsin, 1955), to which cat fanciers interested in breeding problems should refer.

Reverse the beginning of the breeding plan, however, and this is the result:

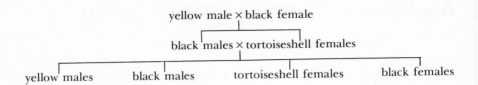

yellow male × black female

black males × tortoiseshell females

yellow males   black males   tortoiseshell females   black females

The following breeding patterns in Blue-Creams may be of interest:

Blue females bred with blue males produce blue females and blue males.

Blue females × cream males = blue-cream females and blue males.

Blue-cream females × blue males = blue females, blue-cream females, blue males, and cream males.

Blue-cream females × cream males = blue-cream females, cream females, blue males, and cream males.

Cream females × blue males = blue-cream females and cream males.

Cream females × cream males = cream females and cream males.

If all of this seems bewilderingly complex, it is. But a rudimentary knowledge of these unusual breeding problems is essential to anyone who wants to learn about cats.

Appendix B. PUBLICATIONS AND ORGANIZATIONS

The organized cat fancy—that is, the world of pure-bred cat breeding and exhibition—has been treated briefly in Chapter 11. Extended treatment of the fancy is, of course, impossible in a book like this, which is intended for the ordinary cat owner. Everyone who loves cats should, however, try to get to a cat show at least once in order to enjoy the tremendous variety of cats, compare them with his or her own, and decide whether it would be fun to take part in this avocation.

The best way to find out about cat shows is to read the pet column or cat column in your local newspaper. There are also two magazines which carry news and information about cat breeding and showing:

Cats Magazine
P.O. Box 4106
Pittsburgh, Pennsylvania 15202
(monthly—$7.95 a year)

Cat Fancy
11760 Sorrento Valley Road
San Diego, California 92121
(bi-monthly—$4 a year)

There are eight stud-book organizations in the cat fancy in the United States, and one in Canada. These are the organizations which sanction cat shows—in other words, they establish the rules and conditions under which the shows are held. Information about cat shows, show rules, breed standards, and other matters can be obtained directly from these organizations, which are always happy to welcome a newcomer into the cat fancy:

American Cat Association, Inc.
Secretary: Althea A. Frahm
302B South Brand Boulevard
Glendale, California 91204

American Cat Fanciers' Association
Secretary: Mrs. Cora Swan
Box 203
Point Lookout, Missouri 65726

Cat Fanciers' Association, Inc.
P.O. Box 430
Red Bank, New Jersey 07701

Cat Fanciers' Federation, Inc.
Corresponding Secretary:
Mrs. Grace M. Clute
2013 Elizabeth Street
Schenectady, New York 12303

Crown Cat Fanciers' Federation
Secretary:
Mrs. Martha Rose Underwood
1379 Tyler Park Drive
Louisville, Kentucky 40204

Independent Cat Federation
Secretary: Mrs. Carolyn Alig
3512 East Milton Street
Pasadena, California 91107

National Cat Fanciers' Association,
   Inc.
Secretary-Recorder:
Mrs. Frances Kosierowski
1450 North Burkhart Road
Howell, Michigan 48843

United Cat Federation, Inc.
Secretary-Recorder: Jean Ford
6616 East Hereford Drive
Los Angeles, California 90022

Canadian Cat Association
Secretary-Registrar:
Mrs. Dorothy Lamb
Suite 5
14 Nelson Street West
Brampton, Ontario

These organizations have member clubs in various parts of the United States and Canada which put on cat shows. Write to each organization and ask for information about its member clubs in your own vicinity.

Because cats, more than any other animal, are subjected to cruel treatment by sadistic, callous, or thoughtless persons, many cat lovers extend financial support to humane organizations and often participate actively in the work of these groups, which are always in need of additional volunteers. It is impossible to list all the local humane organizations in America, of course. Here we can only list the national organizations and a few New York City groups which are typical of local agencies elsewhere:

NATIONAL

Pet Pride
15113 Sunset Boulevard
Pacific Palisades, California 90272

Animal Welfare Institute
P.O. Box 3650
Washington, D.C. 20007

The Humane Society of the United
   States
2100 L Street Northwest
Washington, D.C. 20037

World Wildlife Fund
1319 18th Street Northwest
Washington, D.C. 20036

The Fund for Animals
140 West 57th Street
New York, New York 10019

Friends of Animals, Inc.
11 West 60th Street
New York, New York 10023

Bide-A-Wee Home Association, Inc.   The Humane Society of New York
410 East 38th Street   313 East 58th Street
New York, New York 10016   New York, New York 10022

The above list excludes national organizations which are relatively ineffectual and local organizations whose policies are such as to lay them open to severe criticism by humanitarians.

Although the author is not in sympathy with the anti-vivisectionist point of view, the strong sentiments of many cat lovers on this subject make some mention of this issue unavoidable. I believe that the most effective and well-operated anti-vivisectionist organization is the Vivisection Investigation League, 41 East 58th Street, New York, New York 10022.

Appendix C. BOOKS AND ARTICLES

Rare, out-of-print, and hard-to-get books often can be purchased from the Cat Book Center, Box 112, Wykagyl Station, New Rochelle, New York 10804. Its catalog of cat books is available in answer to a letter of inquiry.

An admirable bibliography of cat books appears in *The Tiger in the House,* one of the books listed below. It is highly recommended to anyone who wishes to delve deeply into cat lore. *The Tiger in the House* is itself one of the most charming works ever published on the cat, and an indispensable volume on the shelf of any cat lover.

The following list is not intended to be a complete bibliography, but rather an enumeration of books which may prove helpful or interesting:

Aberconway, Lady Christabel (ed.), *A Dictionary of Cat Lovers,* London, 1949. Interesting vignettes and quotations.

Adamson, Joy, *Born Free,* New York, 1960. The now famous story of a wild lioness that grew up as a pet.

————, *Living Free,* New York, 1961. A sequel about the lioness and her cubs.

Blair, W. Frank, et al., *Vertebrates of the United States,* New York, 1957. A scientific survey.

Brown, Beth (ed.), *The Wonderful World of Cats,* New York, 1961. Stories, mostly for younger readers, by Lafcadio Hearn, Lewis Carroll, Rudyard Kipling, and others.

Burden, Jean, *The Classic Cats,* New York, 1975. A guide to the most popular pure-breds: sound and sensible.

Carr, Samuel (ed.), *The Poetry of Cats,* New York, 1975. Verse about the tiger on the hearth by poets ancient and modern.

Cisin, Catherine, *Especially Ocelots,* Amagansett, New York, 1961. A valuable pamphlet by the founder of the Long Island Ocelot Club.

Clarke, Frances E. (ed.), *Of Cats and Men,* New York, 1961. Essays and short stories about the cat by famous writers.

Colbert, Edwin H., *Evolution of the Vertebrates,* New York, 1955. A superb scientific survey.

Cole, William, and Tomi Ungerer, *A Cat-Hater's Handbook,* New York, 1963. Humor.

Corbett, Jim, *Man-Eaters of Kumaon,* New York, 1946. An exciting and oddly compassionate firsthand account of the tigers and leopards of India.

Darlington, Philip J., Jr., *Zoogeography,* New York, 1957. An analysis of the geographical distribution of animals.

Drimmer, Frederick (ed.), *The Animal Kingdom,* New York, 1954. A three-volume survey, written for laymen, of the world's fauna.

Dukes, H. H., *The Physiology of Domestic Animals,* Ithaca, New York, 1955. A veterinary text.

Eddy, Frederick B., "The Panther of the Hearth," *The National Geographic Magazine,* November 1938.

Edey, Maitland, *The Cats of Africa,* New York, 1968. A readable account of some splendid great and lesser cats.

Fisher, James, Noel Simon, and Jack Vincent, *Wildlife in Danger,* New York, 1969. A comprehensive and authoritative account of the animals, birds, and plants of the world which are threatened with extinction.

Froman, Robert, *The Nerve of Some Animals,* Philadelphia, 1961. True stories about wild animals, including pumas and jaguars, in their encounters with man.

Gay, Margaret Cooper, *How to Live with a Cat,* New York, 1953. A light-hearted handbook.

Grey, Zane, *Roping Lions in the Grand Canyon,* New York, 1924. A true account of puma hunts by the famous author of Western novels.

Groder, Morris L., *Tricks and Training for Cats,* Fond du Lac, Wisconsin, 1959.

Grzimek, Dr. Bernard (ed.), *Grzimek's Animal Life Encyclopedia,* New York, 1975. Authoritative, very detailed, and truly encyclopedic.

Hagan, William Arthur, and Dorsey William Bruner, *The Infectious Diseases of Domestic Animals,* Ithaca, New York, 1957. A veterinary text.

Hazen, Barbara Shook, *The Dell Encyclopedia of Cats,* New York, 1974. Brief, but well done.

Howey, M. Oldfield, *The Cat in the Mysteries of Religion and Magic,* New York, 1956. An invaluable study, from the ancient Egyptians to the present day.

Johnson, Bruce, *American Cat-alogue,* New York, 1976. The cat in American folk art.

Joy, Charles R., *The Animal World of Albert Schweitzer,* Boston, 1959. The great philosopher's doctrine of reverence for life set forth in his charming and unusual anecdotes about animals.

Jude, A. C., *Cat Genetics,* Fond du Lac, Wisconsin, 1955. Indispensable to the serious breeder and exhibitor.

Kirk, Robert W., D.V.M., *Current Veterinary Therapy V: Small Animal Practice,* Philadelphia, 1974. A veterinary text.

Krutch, Joseph Wood, *The World of Animals,* New York, 1961. A magnificent collection, subtitled: "A treasury of lore, legend, and literature by great writers and naturalists from the 5th century B.C. to the present."

Lessing, Doris, *Particularly Cats,* New York, 1967. A great novelist's nonfiction expression of her life with cats. Charming.

Lockridge, Frances and Richard, *Cats and People,* Philadelphia, 1950. Facts and opinions about the cat by a mystery-writing couple.

McGinnis, Terri, D.V.M., *The Well Cat Book,* New York and Berkeley, 1975. A first-rate handbook.

Mellen, Ida M., *A Practical Cat Book,* New York, 1939. A manual of care.

———, *The Science and the Mystery of the Cat,* New York, 1949. Cat lore.

Merck Veterinary Manual, 4th ed., Rahway, New Jersey, 1961. A veterinary handbook of diagnosis and treatment.

Merrill, Meg, *The Margay: An Exotic Pet,* New York, 1961. An authoritative booklet.

Mery, Fernand, *The Life, History, and Magic of the Cat,* New York, 1967. A big, beautiful, profusely illustrated translation of a French work.

Millard, Adele, *Cats in Fact and Legend,* New York, 1976. A pot-pourri.

Morris, Mark L., *Nutrition and Diet in Small Animal Medicine,* Denver, 1960. A veterinary text.

Pommery, Jean, D.V.M., *What to Do till the Veterinarian Comes,* Radnor, Pennsylvania, 1976. Translation of a French work.

Pond, Grace, *Complete Cat Guide,* London and New York, 1968. The cat fancy from a British point of view.

———, *The Observer's Book of Cats,* London, 1959. An early work by a top British writer on cats.

——— (ed.), *The Complete Cat Encyclopedia,* New York, 1972. A superb work for the serious cat fancier, authoritative and comprehensive.

Proceedings of the National Conference on the Ecology of the Surplus Dog and Cat Problem, Chicago, 1974.

Red Data Book, Morges, Switzerland, 1973. The internationally accepted authority on threatened and endangered species, published by the International Union for Conservation of Nature and Natural Resources.

Repplier, Agnes (ed.), *The Cat,* New York, 1912. "Being a record of the endearments and invectives lavished by many writers upon an animal much loved and much abhorred."

Sanderson, Ivan T., *Living Mammals of the World,* New York, n.d. One of the best surveys of mammals, especially good on the cat family.

Schneck, Stephen, with Nigel Norris, D.V.M., *The Complete Home Medical Guide for Cats,* New York, 1976. A useful handbook.

Scott, John Paul, *Animal Behavior,* Chicago, 1958. A report on scientific observations.

Scott, W. S. (ed.), *A Clowder of Cats,* London, 1946. An anthology of writings about the cat.

Simpson, George Gaylord, *Principles of Animal Taxonomy,* New York, 1961. An outline of zoological classifications.

Sinnott, Edmund W., et al., *Principles of Genetics,* New York, 1958. A scientific text on inheritance.

Soderberg, P. M., *The Care of Your Cat,* New York, 1957. A manual by a British expert.

————, *Pedigree Cats,* London, 1957. An excellent text on the breeding and exhibition of pure-bred cats.

Spies, Joseph R., *The Compleat Cat,* Englewood Cliffs, New Jersey, 1966. A general guide.

Stanek, V. J., *Introducing the Cat Family,* London, n.d. Contains many photographs of rare wild cats.

Suehsdorf, Adolph, "The Cats in Our Lives," *The National Geographic Magazine,* April 1964.

Unkelbach, Kurt, *Catnip,* Englewood Cliffs, New Jersey, 1970. A terse, highly readable guide to the selection and training of a cat by a first-rate writer.

Van Vechten, Carl, *The Tiger in the House,* New York, 1960. The greatest book ever written on the lore of the cat.

Vesey-Fitzgerald, Brian, *Cats,* London, 1957. A superb paperback by the old master of animal writers.

Weideger, Paula, and Geraldine Thorsten, *Travel with Your Pet,* New York, 1973. A useful handbook.

Wilson, Meredith D., *Cat Breeding and Showing,* New York, 1972. A good introduction for the novice.

Worden, Alastair N., and W. Lane-Petter (eds.), *The UFAW Handbook on the Care and Management of Laboratory Animals,* London, 1959. An enormous (951-page) manual, prepared by the Universities Federation for Animal Welfare, which contains some excellent material on the cat.

Young, Stanley P., *The Bobcat of North America,* Harrisburg, Pennsylvania, and Washington, D.C., 1958. A fascinating, comprehensive work by the foremost expert on these animals.

————, and Edward A. Goldman, *The Puma: Mysterious American Cat,* New York, 1964. The most thorough (and compassionate) study of the biggest cat in North America.

Index